A HISTORY OF
ARAGON AND CATALONIA

A HISTORY OF
ARAGON AND CATALONIA

BY

H. J. CHAYTOR

WITH EIGHT MAPS

AMS PRESS
NEW YORK

Reprinted from the edition of 1933, London
First AMS EDITION published 1969
Manufactured in the United States of America

Library of Congress Catalogue Card Number: 73-92610

AMS PRESS, INC.
New York, N. Y. 10003

PREFACE

VISITORS to Eastern Spain and students of Spanish have on several occasions asked me to recommend a book from which they could learn the facts of Aragonese history without the trouble of extracting them from some general history of the Spanish peninsula. Except for the admirable outline study given in R. B. Merriman's *Rise of the Spanish Empire* (New York and London, 1918), there appears to be no separate history of Aragon and Catalonia in English and this book is an attempt to fill the gap. It is, of course, impossible to deal with the history of Aragon without continual reference to that of other Spanish provinces or kingdoms, and it may be argued that the history of such a country as medieval Spain ought not to be treated sectionally. On the other hand, there is a contrast between Aragonese and Castilian history in medieval times which is not always sufficiently emphasized by general histories of Spain. While Castile and Leon were occupied with domestic quarrels and with the task of reconquering their country from the Moors, Aragon and Catalonia were able to extend their dominions overseas, thanks to the energy and ability of a succession of rulers who can compare favourably with the representatives of any other royal house in Western Europe during medieval times. While Castilian history is too often a dreary waste of selfish intrigue and incompetency, Aragonese history is a record of expansion and adventure. This fact is of much importance for the later history of the united kingdoms by reason of its effects upon Spanish thought and literature. It was from the Aragonese side that French and Italian influences entered Spain in greater volume and with greater force than at any other point of ingress. In this respect, the history of Aragon can be treated as a unity in itself.

In the case of geographical names I have used the Spanish

v

forms in preference to English or Catalan forms. In the
case of proper names I have used the forms most likely to be
familiar to English readers and much inconsistency has been
the result ; it seems pedantic to write " Jaime " or " Jacme "
instead of James ; on the other hand, I have retained
" Pedro," as this form is widely accepted in English works.
The Catalan " Pere," though more logically applied to a
Catalan sovereign, strikes the English reader as unfamiliar,
and " Peter the Great " is too strongly suggestive of Russia.
I can only hope that these inconsistencies will not make
identification difficult. The bibliography has no pretensions
to completeness ; I have mentioned only the works which I
have found most useful ; I am particularly indebted to
the various writings of Sr. R. Menéndez Pidal and to the
histories of Zurita, Schmidt, Balaguer, Bofarull and Altamira.

I have to thank Professor W. J. Entwistle, of Oxford, for
many valuable corrections and suggestions, and also Professor
E. Allison Peers, of Liverpool, for much useful advice. Mr.
F. A. Kirkpatrick, Reader in Spanish in this University, and
Dr. J. W. Barker have kindly read the proofs, and with
them I have to thank Mr. A. R. Clack of this College for
the Index.

H. J. C.

St. Catharine's College,
   Cambridge,
      June, 1933.

CONTENTS

A *   vii

CONTENTS

CONTENTS ix

CHAPTER XI PAGE

ALFONSO IV **161**

His Castilian policy. Moorish invasion. War with Sardinia and Genoa. Domestic troubles. His death.

CHAPTER XII

PEDRO IV **166**

His character. He exiles his stepmother. Alliance with Castile against the Moors. Quarrel with James of Mallorca. Capture of the island. Quarrel with the nobles. Civil war. Victory of the Crown. Pedro's reprisals. Revolt of Sardinia. War with Castile. Henry of Trastamara. Invasion of Aragon. Peace concluded and broken. The battle of Nájera. War with Henry of Trastamara. Claims to Sicily. Pedro's death.

CHAPTER XIII

JUAN I AND MARTIN **194**

Character of Juan. Dissatisfaction of the nobles. French invasion. Alliances by marriage. Anti-Semitic riots. The problems of Sardinia and Sicily. Martin in Sicily. Death of Juan. Foundation of the Consistori de la Gaya Sciensa. Bernat Metge. Martin accepts the crown. The Great Schism. Pedro de Luna as Benedict XIII. Operations in Sicily and Sardinia. Death of Martin.

CHAPTER XIV

THE "COMPROMISE" OF CASP **204**

Six claimants to the throne. Electors choose Ferdinand of Castile. He secures the crown. Attempts to end the Great Schism. Quarrels concerning finance. Premature death of Ferdinand.

CHAPTER XV

ALFONSO V **212**

Attempts to conclude the Great Schism. Expedition to Sardinia and Sicily. Attack on Corsica. Affairs in Naples. Alliance with Juana II. Alfonso at war with Juana. Returns to Aragon. War with Castile. Álvaro de Luna. Five years' armistice. Juana captures Naples. Alfonso returns to Italy. Alliances with Northern cities. Death of Juana. Claimants to the kingdom of Naples. Alfonso defeated by the Genoese. Alliance with Milan. René of Anjou in possession of Naples. Alfonso captures the town. Discontent in Aragon. Intrigues of the King of Navarre. Defeat of Aragon at Olmedo. Alfonso in possession of Naples. Carlos de Viana. Death of Alfonso.

LIST OF MAPS

PROLOGUE

THE visitor from France who enters Spain on the eastern side at Port-Bou and travels by train to Barcelona, will be able to observe some, at any rate, of the characteristic features of Catalonia, at one time the most important part of the medieval kingdom of Aragon. Modern Catalonia includes the provinces of Gerona, Lérida, Barcelona and Tarragona, but the linguistic boundary is more widely extended and covers Roussillon on the north side of the Pyrenees, the little state of Andorra, some districts in the east of Aragon, the northern part of Valencia and the Balearic Islands. The Iberian mountains and the valley of the Ebro isolate Catalonia from the central Castilian plateau ; its climate and history have been strongly influenced by the Mediterranean which it faces. The mountain-ranges on the north and west, the long coast-line and the fact that one of the few low Pyrenean passes allows easy communication with France, are considerations which will partially explain the political and commercial development of the country and the formation of the Catalan nationality.

Catalonia is a country of varied geographical character ; the Pyrenean districts are a region of forest and pasture land, through which streams run down from the mountains to meet the sea or to join the Ebro ; the most important of these, the Noguera Ribagorzana, forms the frontier between Catalonia and Aragon. Then follows a series of plateaux continuing to the Sierra de Montsech, after which begin the undulating plain of Lérida and the Llanos de Urgel ; the fertility of these is in strong contrast with that arid character of the plateaux which is sufficiently expressed in the name Mont-Sech (dry mountain). The coastal district is also mountainous, but is green and fertile ; within it such depressions as the Gulf of Rosas, and the plains of Gerona and of the Llobregat near Barcelona, produce a variety of trees and fruits found only in warm climates, date palms, orange trees, agaves and cacti. Catalonia is thus a rugged and mountainous region, the scenery of which is not remarkably picturesque, though certain summits, such as the famous Montserrat, the Montagut and the Montsant, attract attention by their isolated positions.

Catalonia has been inhabited by Iberians, Phœnicians, Greeks, Carthaginian-Phœnicians, Romans, Gauls, Goths and Arabs. From this mixture of races emerges the modern Catalan, an energetic and business-like character, anxious to be up and doing ; not content, as other Spaniards often are, to enjoy or tolerate things as he finds them, he is convinced that the present can be improved and is possessed by an activity impatient to achieve that object. It seems that the restlessness which carried him to Sicily, Greece and the Levant in medieval times finds expression at the present day not merely in industrial and commercial enterprise, but also in republican and socialist tendencies which have made him notorious as the chief exponent of syndicalism in Spain. In any case, the fact that Catalonia can produce almost every agricultural product in sufficient quantity, with the exception of corn, to supply her own needs, is due rather to the steady labour of the inhabitants than to any special fertility of the soil ; wine, oil, rice, almonds, nuts and vegetables are good and abundant ; the northern districts send down much serviceable timber ; stock-breeding, sheep and poultry-farming flourish. More than this, Catalonia is the most important industrial area in the peninsula ; recent developments in hydraulic and electrical engineering have greatly accelerated industrial progress. Textile industries absorb more labour than any other branch, but hardware, paper, soap and leather production also flourishes under the protection of tariffs. Barcelona is the best equipped port in Spain and about a third of the total of Spanish imports enter the peninsula at this point. Much of these are in the form of raw material for Catalan industries. Apart from wine, the export trade is not large ; most of the manufactured product is consumed by the home market. Barcelona is thus a collecting and distributing point for the numerous smaller industrial centres scattered throughout the province ; it is the most cosmopolitan city in Spain and,

in the eyes of its inhabitants, the most beautiful. An
antagonism to Castilian government has become traditional
among Catalan patriots ; there is a belief that their country
has always paid more than its due share to the central
government ; an embittered recollection of the centralizing
policy which strove to suppress their language and privileges ;
the possession of this language, which, unlike the Basque,
has an important literature as old as that of Spain ; proximity
to France and a long connection with that country ; the
influences of climate and environment, added to the consciousness of these grievances and capacities, will help to
explain the long continuance of a separatist or regionalist
agitation. But the typical Catalan is not to be regarded as
either a sinister political intriguer nor as absorbed in the task
of getting rich ; he and his compatriots are a cheerful, kindly
folk, with a feeling for art and music in every class of their
society ; to visit some local fiesta and to watch the dancing
of the Sardana is to reach the real character of the people :

La Sardana és la dansa més bella
de totes les danses que es fan i es desfan ;
és la mòbil magnífica anella
que amb pausa i amb vida va lenta oscil.lant.
Ja es decanta a l'esquerra i vacil.la ;
ja volta altra volta a la dreta dubtant,
i s'en torna i retorna intranquil.la,
com mal orientada l'agulla d'imant.
Fixa's un punt i es detura com ella.
Del contra punt arrecant-se novella
de nou va voltant.
La Sardana és la dansa més bella
de totes les danses que es fan i es desfan.

Very different in character is the old kingdom of Aragon,
as may be observed even in the course of the railway journey
from Barcelona to Zaragoza. The luxuriant vegetation of
the Catalan sea-board, the prosperous harbours and the
busy energy of commerce are exchanged for dry and thirsty
uplands, thinly populated, where towns and hamlets dependent upon a scanty water-supply are often isolated by distance from their neighbours, and wrest a living from the
soil in poverty and exclusiveness. Once again, geographical
conditions have influenced local character. Aragon descends
gradually from the Pyrenees, the highest points of which

form her northern frontier, to the basin of the Ebro ; in prehistoric times, this district was a great salt lake, confined by the coastal mountains and the central Spanish plateau, until the waters found a way to the sea near Tortosa. This coastal range also screens the country from the moist eastern winds of the Mediterranean and increases the aridity of the soil. Where the salts have been washed out of the ground by the more important streams and rivers, vegetation flourishes, and almonds, olives, figs and vines are successfully cultivated ; elsewhere is heath and waste land, for lack of irrigation. Aragon was less affected than Catalonia by infiltrations of foreign blood and influence, and the Aragonese is more native to the soil than the Catalan. The inaccessible mountain district of Sobrarbe in the north of the kingdom claims for Aragon, as can the Asturias for Castile, the honour of being a starting-point from which the repulse of the Muslim invaders was begun. The tenacity by which that process was accomplished is apparent in the Aragonese of modern times, who appears as a hard-working, obstinate character, not always easy to lead and difficult to drive. " El aragonés clava un clavo con la cabeza," says the proverb suggested by these national characteristics, and never were they more apparent than when questions of personal liberty or of local privilege were at stake. Yet the people were not absorbed in these matters to the exclusion of all else ; Aragon developed a dialect of its own which is represented in literature, and the national dance-song, the Jota Aragonesa, has become known far beyond the frontiers of Spain. Such are some of the impressions which a traveller in these countries may receive. We proceed to consider the succession of historical events which may, in part, account for them.

A HISTORY OF
ARAGON AND CATALONIA

A HISTORY OF ARAGON AND CATALONIA

CHAPTER I

ROMANS AND GOTHS

Early inhabitants. The Carthaginians. The Roman occupation. Its influence. Christianity. The Barbarian invasions The Visigothic occupation. Its culture. Church influence. Legal codes. Causes of Visigothic weakness and collapse.

THE medieval chroniclers retrace the history of Spain to the great-grandson of Noah ; a modern historian can find no definite starting-point before Phœnician times. Who the Iberians were and what kind of fusion with the Celts produced the so-called Celtiberian race ; who precisely were the Ilergetes, the Sedetani, the Cosetani and a number of other peoples whose tribal names appear within the limits of Catalonia and Aragon ; these are problems rather for the ethnologist and the folklorist than for the historian. The Phœnicians are said to have entered Spain in the eleventh century B.C. and were followed by the Greeks in 630 B.C., Phocæans and Rhodians, if Herodotus can be trusted ; the Greeks settled on the east coast, where the towns of Rosas and Ampurias retain their Greek names and provide the earliest known specimens of Spanish coinage ; the famous Saguntum, afterward Murviedro, situated further south, was also a Greek colony. The Greeks are said to have improved the agricultural wealth of the peninsula by introducing the vine and the olive. Then came the Carthaginians who were invited by their Phœnician relatives about the end of the fifth century to support them in a quarrel with the native Spaniards. The Carthaginians settled in the country

1

and gradually subdued the Tyrian colonists. These were all commercial enterprises, the promoters of which clung to the coast-line, made little attempt to penetrate into the interior and avoided collision as far as possible with the native populations.

Hamilcar Barca began a new policy after the close of the First Punic War, which had ended in 242 B.C. with the Roman conquest of Sicily. He considered that Spain might be made a counterpoise to the Italian peninsula and become a suitable base of operations from which to attack Rome and restore Carthaginian supremacy in the Mediterranean, a policy continued by his son-in-law Hasdrubal and his son Hannibal. The main centre of Carthaginian occupation was naturally in the south ; as soon as the question of a land route to Southern Gaul and Italy came under consideration, the Carthaginians attempted to secure a foothold in the north-eastern district of the peninsula. Hamilcar is said to have defeated the Ilergetes and to have founded a second Carthage somewhere south of the Ebro ; the site has been variously identified with those of the modern Villafranca del Panadés, Tortosa, Cantavieja and other places. He pushed northward towards the Pyrenees, attracted not only by strategical considerations, but also by the gold and silver mines which were worked by the colonists of Ampurias ; the vigorous resistance which he encountered from the native tribes obliged him to secure a definite base of operations which he found on the site of the modern Barcelona, to which he gave his own name, Barcino. It is not likely that so commodious a harbour or so convenient a site would have been overlooked by earlier settlers and there was probably a Phocæan colony already in occupation. These attempts to consolidate the Carthaginian power were continued by Hasdrubal and Hannibal ; they attacked such tribes and settlements as were in alliance with Rome, and Hannibal's siege and capture of Saguntum became the occasion of the Second Punic War in 218 B.C. Scipio Africanus entered Spain in 209 B.C. and completely defeated the Carthaginians. The Roman occupation of Spain then began.

The Catalan district was the first part of Spain to come under Roman occupation, and Tarragona became its administrative centre. The native populations were inclined to support Rome in her struggle with Carthage ; Rome professed readiness to leave them in the enjoyment of their own laws and customs, as far as was compatible with her task of maintaining peace ; Carthage regarded them rather as a source of wealth for exploitation. Rome suggested liberty, Carthage denoted subjection ; and the conciliatory policy of Scipio secured for the moment the support of all who regarded the Carthaginian power as dangerous to themselves. The Greek and Carthaginian settlements along the eastern coast were also prepared to accept the Roman rule, for the reason that they were incompetent to protect themselves from the natives of the interior who eventually became a source of continual trouble to Rome. The Iberian tribes had developed a civilization with a character of its own, though little is known of it in detail. Polybius speaks in high terms of the condition of agriculture and cattle-breeding in Spain ; the Turdetani in the region of Seville, who appear to have been the most civilized of the native tribes, are said to have possessed a written legal code and to have employed mercenaries to carry on their wars. Herodotus describes them as enjoying a civilised rule under a king, Arganthonius, who welcomed Phocæan colonists in the fifth century B.C. To some extent, therefore, the ground had been prepared for the reception of Roman culture, which was readily adopted by the southern and eastern districts, and the process of latinization proceeded more rapidly in the larger Spanish towns than in any other of the Roman possessions overseas. Roman money, for instance, was in circulation in Spain at an earlier date than in any other Roman province, and Spanish native coinage, struck in imitation of the Roman, appeared about 195 B.C. The territory which Rome gained from the Carthaginians was divided into Further and Hither Spain, Hispania Ulterior and Citerior, the former including the modern provinces of Andalusia and Granada, with a coast-line from Huelva to Port Aguilas, while the latter was composed of the province of the Ebro, the modern Aragon and Catalonia, Murcia and Valencia, which had been the headquarters of the army in Spain during the Second Punic War. In 205 B.C. these provinces were under separate governors with proconsular power ; the fixed boundary between them appears in 197 B.C. Its existence was due to military necessities : at this time the provinces were strips of coast-line so easily cut as to make two self-contained organizations necessary.

Spain produced large quantities of wheat, olives and wine in which the valley of the Baetis (Guadalquivir) was especially abundant ; but the Romans were particularly attracted by the mineral wealth of the peninsula, which was to them as Peru and Mexico were regarded by sixteenth-century Spaniards. The copper mines on the Rio Tinto are among the oldest in Europe ; gold and silver was found in the Sierra Morena and also in the mountains of the north. In the early days of the Roman occupation, Further Spain was much the more productive province of the two, and it was the reckless and ruthless exploitation of it which drove even the unwarlike Turditanians into revolt in 197 and brought the consul Marcus Porcius Cato to the pacification of the province. To this cause were also ultimately due the Lusitanian and Celtiberian wars in which the Romans were frequently defeated and were obliged to supplement their military incapacity with the weapons of perfidy and assassination. When Scipio, the conqueror of Carthage, had pacified Spain in 133, the process of exploitation proceeded apace. Many mining properties passed into private hands and the State seems to have retained the gold mines only. Slave labour was used and Polybius states that there were forty thousand slaves employed in the mines of New Carthage alone. These may not have been all of them Iberians, but the probability is that many of them were. Tributes were exacted by extortionate methods and the moneylenders were no less rapacious than the officials. It was not until the Augustan age that any improvement took place ; it was then also that the Roman power was extended over the west and north. Here the native populations knew little of civilization and were continually engaged in intertribal warfare. When the Romans attempted their pacification, they found them to be formidable opponents, and the short two-edged sword with which the Roman infantry was subsequently armed, was a weapon first introduced to their notice by the Spaniards. These tribes were unable to combine either for military or political purposes for any length of time, and were more competent to conduct a guerrilla than a war ; hence, while there was no serious menace to the Roman power, there was rarely any definite state of peace ; the Spaniard, as Cæsar afterwards put the case, was neither quiet in peace nor strenuous in war. The only method of pacifying such a country was a comprehensive scheme of colonization, and Rome was neither able nor willing to embark upon such an undertaking in 200 B.C., nor indeed long afterwards. Thus when a Viriathus, a Sertorius, or any leader able to impose his will upon the native populations arose to lead them against Rome, he found ample material ready for his purpose. It was left to Augustus Cæsar to consolidate the Roman power and definitely to pacify the country, and such names as Astorga (Asturica Augusta), Zaragoza (Cæsarea Augusta), Badajoz (Pax Augusta) still commemorate his achievement.

The history of these events is one rather of the colonial policy of Rome than of Spain, and contains, as has been said, some of the least creditable chapters in that narrative. The important point for us is the fact that Rome found it necessary to maintain a standing garrison of four legions in Spain, in contradiction of her usual policy of sending out troops only as and when they were required. The result for the eastern province was a permanent military occupation and the thorough romanization of such towns as Tarragona, the capital of the northern province, a fact which had its influence upon the later history of Aragon and Catalonia. Rome was forced to remain in occupation of the peninsula, for the reason that there was no native central power to whom authority could be delegated. It was possible to deal with the Numidian kingdom of Libya or with the Massiliot republic in Gaul under the forms of alliance and diplomacy ; it was not possible so to deal with half a hundred petty chiefs, and to retire from Spain would have been to leave the country open to any adventurer with capacity enough to combine its divided forces. This is one of the reasons for the rapidity with which Spain absorbed Roman civilization. The depth of this influence is apparent in Spanish laws, institutions and architecture, but especially and most permanently in language ; as an instance may be noted the fact that between the years 80–73 B.C. Sertorius wished to educate young Spaniards of good birth upon Roman methods and chose as a centre for that purpose the town of Huesca situated a little to the north of Zaragoza. The name itself, Osca, suggests a foundation from Southern Italy; the coinage in which Spanish tribute was paid at a later date was often known as argentum Oscense, money of Osca, so that the town must have had an important mint; and in this region of Spain Menéndez Pidal finds certain dialectical peculiarities (e.g. the reduction of *nd* to *n*, as *quano* for *cuando*) which also belong to the Osco-umbrian district of Southern Italy, though H. F. Muller regards the suggested connexion as very doubtful. In some respects, modern Spanish is nearer to Latin even than modern Italian, and the complete romanization of the country which produced this and other results was the work of the four centuries which followed the reign of Augustus Cæsar. Spain became one of the most important provinces of the Roman Empire ; Spanish corn became as indispensable to Rome as Egyptian ; Spanish soldiers were as highly esteemed as were Spanish poets or rhetoricians ; Cicero himself could find nothing more derogatory to say of the poets of Córdoba than that their Latinity displayed " pingue quiddam atque peregrinum " ; Ovid, Maecenas and Augustus himself owed something to the teaching of Marcus Porcius Latro, a native of Córdoba. In later centuries Spain produced administrators, rulers and literary men of the highest rank ; the emperors Trajan, Hadrian and Marcus Aurelius were Spaniards and to their days belong the high roads, the bridges and aqueducts which still arouse the admiration of the traveller. The two Senecas and Lucan, the nephew of the younger, belonged to Córdoba; Pomponius Mela, the geographer, was from Algeciras ; Columella, the agriculturist, from Cádiz ; Martial was born near Calatayud and returned to die there ; Quintilian's home was at Calahorra.

The condition of the north-eastern part of the country during this period calls for no special comment. The government was that of the rest of the country as regarded local and municipal administration. In the time of Hadrian, the great province of Tarraconensis was divided into three districts, Gallæcia, Tarragona and Carthagena ; Tarragona was as productive as it now is ; olives and vines were widely cultivated and Tarragona wines were appreciated in Rome ; the local flax produced the finest linen to be found within the Empire. Tarragona itself, as the centre of administration, and the residence at different times of consuls, prætors,

Scipios, Augustus, Galba and Hadrian, was one of the most important towns in the peninsula. It enjoyed all the privileges of Rome, and contained a capitol, numerous temples, a forum, palace and circus, public baths and the famous aqueduct which still rivals that of Segovia. To judge from the remains that have been discovered, Barcelona, Zaragoza, Ampurias and other places may have been equally rich in public buildings of this kind. Communication was secured by the system of high roads, the maintenance of which was always a principle of Roman administration.

Christianity gained a footing in the Spanish peninsula at an early date ; St. Paul in his Epistle to the Romans asserted his intention of visiting Spain, but Spanish tradition on this question has always pointed to St. James the Greater, Santiago, the patron saint of the peninsula, whose bones rest at Compostela after their miraculous transportation from Jerusalem, and to doubt this story was, in former times, to proclaim oneself no Spaniard. There are those who assert that he visited Spain in person and Catalonia first of all in order to preach the gospel. It is not antecedently impossible that the north-east province would be the first to receive Christianity, in view of its continual commercial relations with Rome by land and even more by sea ; the Claudian expulsion of the Jews probably carried Christians to Spain ; and the assertion of some chroniclers that St. Paul founded the Spanish Church at Tarragona in A.D. 60 with the help of his disciple Thekla is a likely conjecture, if it is nothing more. The early history of the Church in Spain is one of persecutions and martyrdoms, complicated by the medieval tendency to embroider the life of a martyr with the miraculous and, in later times, by the desire of any town of importance to find some patron saint or martyr as the central figure of the annual *fiesta*. There is no evidence to show that the Spanish Church was subjected to any general and systematic persecution before the time of Diocletian ; the most celebrated name in the north-east is that of Fructuosus, who suffered death with some of his deacons at Tarragona under Gallienus. Gerona, Barcelona, Vich and other places have also a number of martyrdoms to proclaim. According to Prudentius, the first of Christian poets, the darkest hour came before the dawn ; Diocletian's edict was executed in Spain by one Dacian, the

Governor of Aquitaine, who undertook to deal with the
religious question in Tarraconensis, and among his victims at
Zaragoza and Valencia, the most illustrious were St.Vincent and
St. Lawrence. A year or two later, in 306, the edict of Constantine brought persecution to an end and a dozen years later
Christianity became the religion of the Empire. About this
time was held the first Christian council of which we have any
record, at Iliberis, whether in the north-eastern town of that
name or at the Iliberis in Bætica is uncertain. The most distinguished figure was Hosius, Bishop of Córdoba ; Tarragona and
Barcelona appear to have been represented in this council
and also at the Council of Arles which followed it. Tarragona
was the birthplace of Orosius, the opponent of Priscillianism,
whose defence of Christianity against paganism was famous
in the Middle Ages. Marcus Aurelius Prudentius, the greatest
poet of the early Christian Church, was born at Calahorra,
on the borders of Navarre ; but he held an official post at
Tarragona before he went to the Emperor's court at Milan.
A patriotic Roman citizen, and a convinced Christian, he
had also a love of art and a spirit of toleration which enabled
him to see that paganism had produced some achievements
worthy of preservation ; he reveals to us something of the
manners and customs of his age, of the feelings and practice
of early Christianity, and the lyrical fervour of his thought
has secured him a place in every collection of early Latin
poetry.

In 406 the crumbling defences of the Roman Empire were
broken down by successive waves of invading barbarians
from the north of Europe, and Spain underwent two invasions
of this kind. In 409 the Suevians, Vandals and Alans overran
the greater part of Galicia, Lusitania and Baetica ; in 414 the
Visigoths conquered part of Catalonia ; the name is said to
represent Goth-Alaunia. The Visigoths then entered into
alliance with the Roman Empire, and fought to expel the
other barbarians from Spain, with intervals of fighting on their
own account and for their own benefit. The downfall of the
Western Empire in 476 left the Visigoths in independent
occupation of the country ; they had already annihilated
the Alans and had driven the other barbarians into Africa ;
in 585 they destroyed the Suevian kingdom of Galicia.
In 554 they had called in a number of auxiliary troops from

the Byzantine Empire, who occupied a considerable portion of the coastlands for nearly a century until they were expelled by King Suintila at the outset of the seventh century ; to this incident may be retraced in part the Byzantine element in early Spanish art.

Spain, which had given endless trouble to Rome at the height of her power, thus offered no greater resistance to the barbarian invaders than she showed at a later date to the Muslim attack. There were two reasons for this apparent pusillanimity. The real fighting power of the country had disappeared. Spain had given her best soldiers for years to the Roman legions and Rome had scattered them over the face of Europe. From the furthest limit of Northern Britain, where Spanish legions kept the Roman wall against the Picts, to the Danube provinces, whither Latin was carried by Spanish troops, the Spanish soldier had fought and died. His own country had seen no fighting for four centuries, and the garrison that sufficed for the preservation of order in this, the most peaceable of the Roman provinces, was not composed of Spaniards, but of degenerate provincials who could not be trusted in posts of danger upon the outskirts of the Empire. Further, there was little or no sense of nationalism in the country ; slaves and paupers formed too large a part of the population of Spain. *Latifundia perdidere Italiam*, said Pliny, and the explanation is applicable, in part, at least, to Spain. The growth of large estates worked by slave labour, the expropriation of the small landholder and the demoralizing effect of slavery in the towns had ruined the manhood of the nation. Those, moreover, who had anything to lose had groaned for years under an iniquitous and oppressive system of taxation : of what use to be Roman citizens, if they had to pay dues as such in addition to their taxes as provincials ? If they had in any case to support a horde of rapacious officials, no change could matter much and any change might be for the better. The native Spaniard had little for which to fight and less inclination to fight for it.

The Visigothic rule is usually stated to have extended from 415 to 711, during which period thirty-five kings are named. Thirteen of these died violent deaths and the fact that ten of these deaths took place before 555 is sufficient to show the unsettled nature of the early Visigothic period, when Franks,

Alans, Suevians, Vandals and Huns were attempting to
secure dominion in various parts of the old Roman Empire.
Generally speaking, the Visigoths accepted the Roman culture
which they found in Spain and which they had already
experienced elsewhere. The impression which they made
upon Spain in general and upon the north-east part of it in
particular was not very profound. But two points should
be noted. In the first place, the early Visigothic kingdom
regarded Spain as a part of a wider dominion ; Spain could
be ruled from Toulouse by Theodored or from Arles by
Euric. The notion that political frontiers should be determined by geographical boundaries is weakened, and henceforward we find the Aragonese and Catalan districts constantly conjoined with Septimania in subordination or in
predominance, as political changes might determine. This
fact implied continual traffic across the Pyrenees by one
or other of the three passes at the east of the range and its
effect upon the civilization of North-East Spain should not
be left out of consideration.

The second point of importance is the growth of Church
influence and wealth which is one of the outstanding features
of the Gothic period. The conversion of Reccared in 587 put
an end to dissension upon the Arian question ; it was a
conversion due rather to political necessity than to religious
conviction. By the end of the sixth century Gothic
nationalism had been profoundly modified by Roman
civilization, which was gradually welding the diverse elements
of Spanish society into something more homogeneous ;
intermarriage between Roman and Visigoth was forbidden
by law until 652, when it was authorized by Reccaswinth,
but there is no doubt that it was frequent before that date
and that his authorization merely recognized what could no
longer be prevented nor ignored. It was clear that Arianism
was not likely to survive the changes that were passing over
society in general. There were more definite political reasons
for orthodoxy ; the Gothic monarchy was elective, the
elector nobles were inclined to regard their nominee rather
as their agent than their ruler, and had become wealthy,
turbulent and disloyal. It was not possible for the King to
solve the problem as Isabella afterwards did, by turning to the
towns for popular support ; the small farmer class had almost

disappeared and the lower classes were generally in a state of serfdom. The one power that could be used to check the aggression of the nobles was the Church, and when the Church had been given an official position by this public abjuration of Arianism, she was able to absorb much of the political power and influence that the nobles had hitherto monopolized. In 633 the Fourth General Council of Toledo assumed the right of confirming the King's election to the throne and claimed to assert that right in the case of his successors ; the Church was also ready to use the weapon of excommunication against recalcitrant rulers ; she was now able to take part in the royal councils, and the chief ecclesiastics were consulted upon questions of policy and legislation. From the fourth century the Church had continued to acquire the privileges and the wealth which afterwards made it a power in the land, and its progress was now accelerated. Whereas in early Christian times bishops were elected by the people, from the seventh century the right to elect was exercised by the King or, in his absence, by the metropolitan bishop of Toledo, who became the head of the Spanish Church, after the removal of the capital from Seville ; the number of episcopal sees amounted to some eighty ; in the province of Tarraconensis there were bishops of Tarragona, Barcelona, Gerona, Lérida, Tortosa, Vich, Urgel, Ampurias, Tarrasa, Zaragoza, Tarazona, Huesca, Pamplona and Calahorra. The diocese in those days was rather in the nature of one large parish and tithes were paid directly to the bishop. Thus, when the Church became the King's counterpoise to the nobles, the influence which might be exerted by such bishops as Leander of Seville and his younger and more famous brother, Isidore, was almost unbounded. The first mention of monastic life occurs in a canon of the Council of Zaragoza, in 380, forbidding clerics to become monks ; early foundations of monasteries are said to have been made in Gerona, Barcelona, Tarragona and Montserrat under regulations resembling the Benedictine rule, though some authorities deny that this rule was known in Spain until after the Visigothic period. Provincial Church councils were not infrequent ; eight were held in Tarraconensis between 464 and 615, which seem to have been attended by most of the bishops in the province. Much of their energies were spent

in reforming the manners of the clergy; the Council of
Lérida, held in 546, ordains penalties for clergy who commit
homicide, even upon their enemies, or who quarrel with one
another, imposes celibacy upon them, requires obedience to
canonical law, and forbids them to take part in the dances
held at Christian marriages, though they may share in the
marriage feast with the decency becoming to Christians;
runaway slaves are to have the right of asylum in churches,
and intercourse with heretics and the unbaptized is forbidden.

The unifying policy denoted by the introduction of ecclesiastical uniformity was also carried out as regarded law. The
Visigoths had as much respect for law as the Romans themselves and some of their kings were energetic legislators.
The Breviarium of Alaric II, prepared shortly before his
death in 506, became the nucleus of additions made by
successive rulers until Chindaswinth established a code
which attempted to reconcile the differences between Gothic
and Roman law; this was revised by his son, Reccaswinth,
and promulgated as the Lex Visigothorum; known as the
Fuero Juzgo, it remained in force throughout the greater
part of Spain, even after the downfall of the Visigothic rule.
To the desire for uniformity may also be ascribed the persecutions of the Jews which began after Reccared's conversion.
Numbers of them escaped across the Pyrenees and settled
in the south of France, where their co-religionists were both
numerous and prosperous. To this movement may be due
the strength of the Jewish population in Aragon at a later
date; some fugitives found a temporary refuge near the
Pyrenees, across which they could escape, if conditions became
too severe; others drifted back from France, when the storm
of persecution had blown over.

The Gothic kingdom collapsed before the Muslim attack
even more rapidly than the Roman power had fallen before
the barbarians. Similar causes were at work in both cases.
The Visigoths had been regarded by the Spanish population
as friends rather than as foes, as deliverers rather than as
conquerors; they were the most civilized of all the barbarian
invaders, they had entered Spain as the nominal allies of
Rome and their eventual assumption of power was rather a
change of government than a conquest. Great had been their
opportunities. For nearly three centuries the peninsula

had been undisturbed by invasion ; internal convulsions had been few ; the civil wars, the family disputes, the divisions and revolutions of the Frankish kingdoms were unknown in Spain. Under the inestimable advantage of political unity, the Visigoths governed one of the richest countries in Europe, inhabited by a hardy and frugal race ; yet they were swept aside in a moment by a handful of African marauders. Once again, there was no sense of nationalism in the country nor was the Gothic system of government calculated to produce any such feeling. The legal codes were primarily directed to secure the maintenance and preservation of privilege obtained by the accident of birth ; the Fuero Juzgo divided society into *Nobiles*, subdivided as *primates* and *seniores*, all of whom were Goths ; the Hispano-Roman population were *Viliores*, divided into *Ingenui* or free-born, *Liberi* or freedmen, and *Servi* who were *boni* or *viles*. Inter-marriage had helped some of the *Ingenui* to improve their condition and status ; but for the lower classes there was no prospect. Immediately below the state of freedom came that of patronage ; the patron professed certain responsibilities towards the client, securing him in the possession of his land in return for half the produce of it, and protecting his family in the event of the client's death. A slave who obtained freedom was obliged to enter the state of patronage and was unable to change his patron, as the freeman could do. His evidence was not accepted against that of a freeman, nor might he marry without his patron's permission ; the Fuero Juzgo strongly prohibited any kind of marriage that tended to break down class distinctions. Slaves existed by birth, though reduction to slavery as a punishment was not uncommon ; their condition was little better than that of cattle ; they could accumulate no property, for all that they had belonged to their masters, who could dispose even of their children as they pleased ; the Fuero Juzgo certainly forbade the use of mutilation as a punishment for slaves, but short of this, any other form of cruelty was permissible.

The Church was incompetent to produce any improvement of these conditions. Bishops were themselves landholders and therefore slaveowners ; their influence upon the kings was either disastrous or negligible. If they censured the members of a faction which sought to depose the reigning monarch, so soon as the revolution had been accomplished, they were equally ready with fulminations against future disturbers of the new occupant of the throne. In peaceful times, the principle of election to the throne greatly diminished the power of the kings. If in early days the King had been elected by the free Visigoths only, in the later period the Council had secured the right of approving such election, and the Crown lost the independence that the hereditary principle might have secured for it. The councils had no national authority behind them; they were assemblies of churchmen and of a few court officials and landed nobles, allowed by the weakness of successive kings to assume political and legislative powers which they exerted with little sense of responsibility. Apart from a few men of learning and piety, the majority of the Church appear to have been as ignorant as they were bigoted; the Fuero Juzgo condemns those who use incantations to bring hail upon the crops of their enemies or who invoke the devil and his satellites with charms and sacrifices; the prevalence of such superstitions is no good testimonial to the efficiency of Church teaching. The vigour of municipal life had been weakened during the Roman administration, which saw in city independence a menace to the power of the central authority; the Visigoths did nothing to strengthen it and continued the system which they found in existence. The towns were left in the hands of the nobles, who administered their affairs through officials nominated by themselves, and a clause in the Fuero Juzgo suggest that they were inclined to tax the towns for their own profit to a ruinous extent.

The rank and file of the army was chiefly composed of slaves. In the reign of Wamba legislation had been passed, determining in what order and to what extent the several classes of the nation should serve. But the arrival of contingents was dependent upon the will of the nobles, who preferred a semi-independent existence upon their own estates with their own bands of retainers; if they were disaffected or indolent, the system broke down. Such was the case when the hour of trial arrived, and the army that Roderic led to the banks of Lake Janda was beaten before it set out, composed as it was of men who had nothing to gain by victory and who felt that a change of masters consequent upon defeat might be rather a gain than a loss. The Visigoths had been tried and found wanting ; with the exception of their legal codes, they had no contribution to make to Spanish history ; their influence upon the language or the art of the country was negligible ; they were caretakers who had not even maintained the house in repair ; unable to improve or even to continue the Roman civilization which had absorbed them, it was time that they should make way for a new order, and if centuries of confusion followed their disappearance, yet from these birth-pangs came forth the Spanish nation of to-day.

CHAPTER II

THE MUSLIM CONQUEST

Its importance. The invasions of Spain and Southern France. The settlement. Charlemagne's expedition. Frankish influence. Formation of the Spanish mark. Social conditions under Muslim rule.

THE Muslim conquest, which may be considered as the commencement in Spanish history of the period known as the Middle Ages, was an event of vast importance not only to Spain but to Western Europe at large. Preceding centuries had seen the collapse of the Roman Empire under the pressure of migratory movements from the north ; the rapid spread of Islam transformed conditions in the east and south. The Mediterranean ceased to be the medium for the interchange of Roman and Hellenic culture ; this once Roman sea became a frontier-line in dispute between two civilizations. From Toledo to the Taurus an Asiatic culture was advancing upon Europe at a time when the old union imposed by imperial Christianity had broken down ; the separation between Eastern and Western Churches had been accompanied by an inevitable difference between political ideals ; the East continued to regard the Christian Church as subordinate, even in matters of dogma, to the imperial authority ; the West was beginning to regard pope and emperor as allied and co-ordinate forces ; the Hellenic and the Germanic empires were thus pursuing divergent paths. Islam, however, admirably fitted as it was for a conquering creed, proved in the event incompetent to maintain its ground. The fanaticism which had united a number of obscure Arab tribes, previously divided by local feuds and distinguished by the practice of degraded forms of Judaism and Christianity, was conjoined with a spirit of toleration for the religions of conquered peoples, at any rate in the form preached by Mahomet. In no other way could Islam have maintained its

16

dominion over peoples so diverse and beliefs so divergent as those entertained by Zoroastians, Berbers, Brahmins and Christians. The belief that a Muslim conquest implied the extermination of the conquered infidels is a mistake. But this toleration which allowed subject-races to practise their own religions, was also a cause of internal dissension ; the liberty with which the founder's tenets were interpreted and the comparison of them with systems of thought encountered in alien civilizations, were activities which did not make for unity of creed, and Spanish Islam was doctrinally no less fissiparous than European Protestantism at a later date. Moreover, the political structure of the Empire was incoherent and a change of dynasty or even of policy at Bagdad was not necessarily followed by the obedience or agreement of distant emirs and walis. There was the further tendency to degeneration under settled conditions of life ; Islam was most vigorous as a militant power ; of its instability in peace, Spain can provide examples enough. On the other hand there were certain powerful bonds of union. Mecca was universally venerated as the religious centre of the faith, and the obligation of pilgrimage to it stimulated the interchange of ideas and produced effects upon the Muslim world analogous to those of the crusades upon Latin Christianity. The sacred text of the Koran, continually studied with meticulous devotion, established one language as the official means of communication. The avidity with which the Arabs assimilated the cultural achievements and the intellectual discoveries of other nations was no less remarkable than the rapidity and completeness with which new ideas were disseminated from end to end of their empire, and this process was facilitated by the possession of a common official language. The intellectual life of Bagdad was thus reproduced at Córdoba and Hellenic thought returned to Europe in the process. Spain was the point where two civilizations thus came into conflict and fusion ; hence the importance of the Muslim invasion transcended the limits of the Spanish peninsula.

The beginnings of the Muslim conquest have been surrounded with legend. So catastrophic an overthrow was unaccountable to later generations, and the new nation formed by adversity among the mountainous regions of the

2

North ascribed the collapse of the Visigoths as much to Roderic's disregard of tradition and prophecy as to the treachery of Count Julian. That this Count, the Governor of Ceuta, conspired with the disaffected Bishop of Seville and with the sons of Witiza whom Roderic had deprived of the succession to the throne, is a proceeding characteristic of the times nor is the invitation to a common enemy out of key with the rest of the picture. But the royal amour with the fair La Cava, the enchanted tower and its guardians and other similar details, are more in the style of Amadís de Gaula than of sober history. The fact is undoubted that in 709 an Arab chieftain, Tarif, whether invited by Count Julian or not, crossed from Africa with some five hundred marauders, landed at the spot where the town of Tarifa preserves his name, conducted a successful foray and returned to Africa with news of the defenceless condition and wealth of the country. In 711, one Musa, the Vali or Governor of Mauretania Tingitana, gave his consent to another expedition, which was led by Tarik, whose name survives in Gibraltar, Gebel Tarik, the hill of Tarik ; he made the crossing twice, the second time in 712 to bring reinforcements. After scattering, the enemy, he marched northward in three columns, captured Toledo and was censured for his precipitation by Musa, who had hurried over from Africa in his anxiety to be there before the booty was exhausted ; most of his compatriots felt the same anxiety, and successive waves of invaders crossed the straits in any ⸪ ·aft that would hold them. The following years were a period of confusion and disorder ; marauding troops scoured the country, while Musa and his lieutenants continued their northward advance. In no quarter did they meet with any serious opposition, except Mérida, which resisted for two years. If cities closed their gates, they did so merely with the hope of securing favourable terms of surrender ; the governing classes fled and the lower classes were indifferent, slaves and criminals were freed, Jews no longer feared their persecutors. To speak of the invasion as a conquest is to misrepresent the course of events ; for the conquered, it was a social revolution ; for the conquerors, it was a gigantic freebooting expedition crowned with surprising success ; religion in the first instance was not the motive impelling the invaders ; they came for loot.

Musa and Tarik had proclaimed the sovereignty of the
Caliph as they advanced and that potentate cut short their
victorious careers when they had advanced nearly to the
Pyrenees ; they had apparently quarrelled upon the division
of the spoil and were summoned to Damascus to give an
account of their actions. Musa's son, Abdelaziz, was left
in command ; he had had fighting enough, settled in Córdoba,
and is said to have married the widow of Roderic, thus
repeating the story of the Goth Ataulf and the fair Placidia.
Musa found no welcome at Damascus ; he was disgraced and
punished ; nor did Abdelaziz long maintain his court at
Córdoba ; suspected of aiming at independence of the caliph,
he was assassinated. His successor, Al-Horr, was ordered to
organize the conquered territory and to continue the war—in
other words, to provide adequate rewards for his followers
and to send more booty to Damascus. Such parts of Spain
as the Muslims had occupied had been already stripped of
plunder ; but the north-eastern part of the peninsula had
not been seriously ravaged and the Muslim hordes had not
yet crossed the Pyrenees ; fugitives from Southern Spain
had also carried some wealth into those districts. Al-Horr,
therefore, crossed the mountain barrier and invaded Septimania in 719. This expedition was the beginning of a series of
campaigns into Southern France led by successive emirs, who
met with a stronger resistance than they had encountered anywhere in Spain. Al-Sama, the successor of Al-Horr, attacked
Toulouse in 721, but was defeated and killed by Duke Eudon,
who succeeded in raising the siege of the town with an army
from Aquitaine. Other emirs attempted to secure a footing
in the South of France, and in spite of the great defeat
inflicted upon the Muslims by Charles Martel at Poitiers in
732, they retained possession of Septimania, until their
domestic quarrels forced them to relax their hold about 740,
when the Berber immigrants who had entered Spain in such
numbers as to form the majority of the Muslim population,
revolted against the domination of the Arabs properly so-
called. But it was not until 759 that Pippin the Short, who
had succeeded Charles Martel as King of the Franks, was
able to drive the Muslims out of Septimania.

Al-Horr and his successors could represent themselves as the
emissaries of an organized government, that of the Caliph

at Damascus, the link between them being the government in Africa ; as a matter of fact, the political connection between Africa and Damascus was loose and that between Africa and Spain was not much closer. The several Muslim tribes and nations were often at variance among themselves, and though they admitted a nominal suzerainty on the part of Damascus, the only real bond of union was their religious faith and their belief in the brotherhood of all true believers. This faith, as has been said, was not the motive cause for their invasion of Spain. Tarik's expedition was a marauding raid which had succeeded beyond the wildest expectation, and the settlement in Spain was constantly disturbed by rivalries and factions fostered in Africa and often stimulated by the Berber priests. Berbers, Syrians, Egyptians and Arabs all required satisfaction, which was eventually secured to some extent by settling the various tribes in the districts which most nearly resembled their native environment ; the Egyptians received Murcia, where they might practise the art of agriculture ; mountainous districts and pastures were found for the men of Palestine and the hill tribes of Morocco ; the Yemenite tribes were settled in the Seville district, and the ruling Syrians of Damascus occupied Granada. In the hands of these latter the government remained ; but it was not until the tenth century that the civilization vaguely known as Moorish was firmly established and that its cultural achievements became possible.

Under the new government the subject-population was well treated and was certainly better off than it had been under the nobles who had fled for refuge to the mountains of the north. Apart from some sporadic outbreaks of persecution, provoked in part by the Christians themselves, the religion, the rights and even the property of the Spanish population were respected ; Christians retained their churches and were able to celebrate daily mass under the eyes of the Muslim authorities ; living among Muslims, they were known as Mozárabes or Mozarabs, and the Mozarabic ritual which they continued from Gothic times was not replaced by the Roman ritual until 1071, and is still continued in chapels of the cathedrals of Toledo and Salamanca ; the only burden upon them was a small annual poll-tax. The slave who professed the Muslim faith secured his freedom, but the new government showed no anxiety to proselytize. Such Christians as accepted Muhammedanism formed the class known as renegados or muladíes. The Jews, who had perhaps suggested and had certainly welcomed the invasion, were not only tolerated but were distinguished by the special consideration of the new rulers. These took one-fifth of the land for themselves and distributed the rest among their adherents ; the government holding was allotted to Spanish cultivators who paid rent on the metayer system : the large estates were thus broken up and agriculture was improved in consequence.

For the first forty years after the Muslim invasion, some twenty emirs held the power in Spain with varying success, under the Ommeyad dynasty of caliphs at Damascus. This dynasty was overthrown in 750 by the Abbassids and the capital was removed to Bagdad, where it remained until the Muhammedan Empire was broken up by the Mongols in 1258. The repercussion of these disturbances was felt among the outlying provinces of the Muslim Empire, and North Africa either refused to recognize the Abbassids or declared itself independent. Abd ar-Rahman (755–788), a member of the Ommeyad family, escaped from the general overthrow of the dynasty, and made his way to North Africa, where he attempted to establish an independent state. When he found his difficulties insurmountable, like Hannibal or Sertorius, he turned to Spain, gained sufficient help to fit out a small expedition, and landed at the mouth of the Guadalquivir in 755. Dissensions among the emirs of the peninsula provided his opportunity, and by 758 he was able to declare himself independent of the Abbassid Caliph. He reigned at Córdoba for thirty-two years, during which time he laid the foundations of the Moorish Empire in Spain. While he was consolidating his power, the Franks were able to make some advance in the north-east, and one Suleiman, the Governor of Gerona and Barcelona, was obliged to offer his submission to Pippin, who was, however, prevented by other calls upon his energies from pushing his advantage further in this region.

The general situation in the old province of Tarraconensis at this period is not clear. While Al-Horr and his successors were invading Septimania, it is obvious that they must have had possession of the modern Catalonia, through which their passage lay. After the victory of Charles Martel, no doubt incursions were made by the Frankish forces. While civil war was being waged in Andalucía between the Muslim leaders, Zaragoza became the centre of gravity in the north-east. Yusuf, who was elected Governor of Spain in 747, entrusted the governorship of the town to Sumail, a chieftain who had risen to eminence as the leader of several petty tribes in opposition to the Yemenites and whose influence was greater than his own. Sumail was aware that Yusuf wished to get rid of him, but the importance of the post and the opportunity which it afforded for harassing the Yemenites who occupied the district induced him to accept it in 750. Three years later he was besieged by a coalition of his enemies, but the arrival in Spain of Abd er-Rahman and his rise to power put an end to civil war in this region and transferred it to the south. Abd er-Rahman's success in establishing himself as the independent caliph of Córdoba by no means brought peace to Spain. Not only was he harassed by chieftains holding commissions from the Abbassid caliph, who refused to recognize an Ommeyad ruler of Spain, but the ruthless treachery and the vindictive cruelty of his career stirred up continual conspiracies and confederacies among his own subjects.

One of these became the occasion of Charlemagne's famous expedition in 778, the disastrous retreat from which provided the subject-matter for the Chanson de Roland, Three malcontent chiefs, Al-Arabi, Governor of Barcelona, Yusuf's son-in-law, Abd er-Rahman ibn Habib, and Yusuf's son, Abu 'l-Aswad, were inspired with such animosity against the Caliph of Córdoba that they were prepared to accept the help of a Christian king to secure his overthrow. They visited Charlemagne at Paderborn where he was holding the Diet, and proposed an alliance with him against the Emir of Córdoba. The immediate problem before the Emperor was the attitude of the Saxons ; they had recently submitted to his dominion and were prepared to accept Christianity ; their most formidable leader, Wittekind, had been driven into exile. Feeling therefore that his hands were free, Charlemagne undertook to co-operate. It was agreed that he should cross the Pyrenees with an army, while Al-Arabi would raise the country north of the Ebro and acknowledge Charlemagne's sovereignty. The other two were to distract the attention of Abd er-Rahman by raising the Abbassid standard and advancing from the south. If this ingenious strategy was ever proposed, which some historians deny, it miscarried hopelessly ; the movements were not synchronized, the leaders quarrelled among themselves, and when Charlemagne entered Spain, the only allies upon whom he could count were Al-Arabi and his associates in the north, such as Abu Thaur, the Governor of Huesca, and Galindo, the Christian Count of the Cerdagne. Charlemagne advanced as far as Zaragoza, when he was recalled by tidings of a Saxon revolt of the most serious kind ; Wittekind had returned, and the absence of the Frankish army had enabled him to ravage the country as far as Cologne. Charlemagne marched by the valley of Roncevalles, where the Basques, the enemies of the Franks, lay in ambush ; they allowed the main body to pass, but attacked and defeated the rear-guard, plundered the baggage train and dispersed ; Roland, one of the commanders of the rear-guard, perished with his troops. Abd er-Rahman was then able in 780 to conquer Zaragoza, to defeat the Basques and to reduce the Count of the Cerdagne to subjection, thanks to the energy of a Saxon chieftain of whose name he had never heard. The Chanson de Roland is wholly inspired by the crusading spirit of the eleventh and twelfth centuries, and does not reflect either the historical facts or the prevailing temper of the eighth century. That Charlemagne, who is represented as the champion of Christianity, was in league with the unbelievers, as were Galiano and other Christians, are inconvenient facts which are not mentioned in the poem and were probably unknown to the composer of it. The Reconquista, the process of driving the Arab invaders out of Spain, was not in its early stages a religious crusade ; the early struggles were political in character, waged by nobles and ecclesiastics for self-preservation, for the recovery of territory or of prestige. Hence, as will be seen, Muslim and Christian are found acting in alliance upon occasion and intermarriage is not uncommon.

Charlemagne's expedition impressed the Arab governors of the north-eastern towns with the idea that the Frankish monarch was a power to whom they could turn, should they happen to be at variance with their own authorities. Thus, in the course of the next few years, Barcelona, Gerona and Huesca appear to have acknowledged and rejected Frankish supremacy. The Franks in course of time came to regard this part of Spain as a Frankish mark, the maintenance of which was important for the security of the Empire. Louis, Charlemagne's son, is said to have spent some time in the district, when he assumed the government of Aquitania and Septimania and received an Arab embassy at Toulouse in 790. The peace then concluded was broken in the following year by the successor of Abd er-Rahman, Hisham or Hixem, a fanatic who proclaimed a religious war against the Christians, and the frontier at both ends of the Pyrenees was continually disturbed. Charlemagne was occupied with the Saxons and Louis was engaged in supporting his brother in Italy ; the Muslims seized the opportunity of devastating Catalonia and in 793 a marauding raid was pushed up to the walls of Narbonne and Carcassonne, and Gerona was lost to the Franks. Hisham's successor, Al-Hakam, was hampered at the outset of his reign by the necessity of suppressing conspiracies against his rule ; the conspirators applied to the Franks for help, who thus obtained an opportunity of recovering the lost ground. An expedition was sent in 797 and Gerona was regained, while the Arab governors of Barcelona, Huesca and Lérida submitted to Louis. Al-Hakam drove out the Franks and re-established his supremacy as far as the Pyrenees, but Louis returned with a larger force, captured Barcelona in 801, and placed Count Bera or Bara in it as governor. In the next year he captured Tarragona and ravaged the country to the walls of Tortosa. Some years of warfare followed with varying success to either side ; in 812 Al-Hakam made peace and about the time of Charlemagne's death the Franks were in occupation of the coast-line as far as Tortosa and of the plain as far as Huesca ; they also held the southern slope of the Pyrenees. Here various Visigothic nobles were able to establish themselves in independence of the Arabs under the protection of the Frankish Empire which attached increasing importance to the security of the Spanish mark. When Louis divided his empire among his sons in 817, Septimania was separated from Aquitaine and the Duchy of Toulouse and entrusted to Lothair with the Spanish mark, which included the Basque frontier, as well as the counties of Jaca and Ribagorza and the Mediterranean sea-front. This arrangement continued until 865 when Charles the Bald divided the mark into Septimania proper with Narbonne as its capital, and the County of Barcelona which became independent about 877 under Count Wifred or Wilfred the Hairy.

During this period, the Beni-Kasim, a renegade Visigothic family, had succeeded in establishing themselves in Zaragoza and in founding a kingdom entirely independent of the Emir of Córdoba. Huesca and Tudela formed part of this kingdom which dominated most of the north-east plain. Its most able ruler, Musa II, maintained his independence against both Franks and Arabs. Independence apart, the Beni-Kasim had no definite policy ; they fought against the Count of Barcelona, against the Christians of Castile and the Arabs of Córdoba, and their alliances were as varied as their hostilities ; they lent support to the renegades of Toledo, Muslim subjects of Visigothic origin, who forced the Emir of Córdoba to recognize their independence in 873, under payment of an annual tribute. Musa styled himself " the third King of Spain," and was respected or feared by all his neighbours : Charles the Bald was willing to send him presents. On his death in 862, the Emir of Córdoba overpowered this kingdom, but was soon driven out by the Beni-Kasim in alliance with Alfonso III of Leon, who had even entrusted them with the education of his son Ordoño. This was not the only movement of the kind. In Andalusia and Extremadura malcontent leaders had succeeded in establishing governments independent of Córdoba, where political and religious dissension had seriously weakened the central power. These separatist tendencies were checked by Abd er-Rahman III, who came to the throne in 912.

Conditions in such parts of north-eastern Spain as came under Muslim rule did not differ materially from those which prevailed in the south or west, except for the fact that population was more scattered and migration more frequent. Catalonia especially was a land of passage for those who fled to Southern France before the Muslim invaders or returned in the wake of Frankish armies. Those inhabitants who remained in continuous occupation were probably better off than they had been under Visigothic rule. The invaders were not generally concerned with the conversion of the inhabitants to Muhammedanism, although the fanaticism of individual leaders might vary upon this point. The principle was that those who did not accept Islam had to pay a special tax to the conquerors, in addition to the tribute imposed upon their district. Conversion thus meant pecuniary loss to the conqueror and this and other military reasons guaranteed a large measure of religious toleration to the Christian subjects, the Mozárabes, who retained possession of their churches or were allowed to build new ones. Cases occurred when Muslims and Christians used the same edifice for religious purposes. Christian bishops were maintained, church councils were held, though the Caliph claimed the right of nominating bishops and convoking councils, and visits to and from foreign prelates were perfectly possible. Moreover, the attention of Muslim theologians and religious leaders was distracted from the Christians by their own quarrels and disputations upon dogmatic questions; separatist schools of religious thought often assumed the importance of sects, while the ruling classes and especially the Arabs were indifferent or frankly sceptical. Nor was the process of conquest necessarily cruel or sanguinary; the campaign against the north-eastern districts in 714 is said to have been one of devastation and terror, but such a case was exceptional. Tribute and taxation could be paid in produce; the conquerors took one-fifth of the land as State property, this was let out to native Gothic cultivators who paid one-third of the annual produce; the land of such nobles as submitted without resistance was left to them on payment of an annual tribute. Land was provided for Muslim leaders and soldiers by confiscating the property of the Gothic owners who resisted or fled. Their serfs continued to work on the land and paid one-third or one-fifth of the produce to the new owners; thus the serfs were better off than they had been under Gothic rule and the latifundia were broken up and brought under cultivation. Slaves also were better treated, and could obtain liberation by conversion to Muhammedanism. The Jews, in particular, gained many advantages from the change of rulers; they were no longer exposed to the risk of persecution and found many opportunities for developing their capacity for finance and administration.

Intermarriage between Muslims and the conquered inhabitants was frequent in all classes of society ; though Muslim law did not require the conversion of a Christian wife, voluntary conversions were not infrequent. Almanzor married a daughter of Sancho II of Navarre, and the lady is said to have embraced Muhammedanism with the approval of her family. Christians could and did hold positions of trust in Muslim courts with no compulsion to become renegades ; Christian troops appeared in Muslim armies ; Christian kings formed alliance with Muslim emirs. In short, during the early stages of the Muslim occupation, hostilities were due to economic and political, not to religious causes, a fact which was obscured by later chroniclers who regarded such toleration as disgraceful infidelity and were anxious to invest the Reconquest with the character of a crusade at the earliest possible date. This continual intercourse naturally had its effect upon both the Christian and Muslim elements in the population ; nor must it be forgotten that the Muslim· population was itself of a heterogeneous character. Even among the Arab nucleus, the aristocrats among the invaders, tribal differences were often a disruptive force ; for them and the Berbers, Egyptians, Yemenites and other races in Spain there was no common language ; by degrees a lingua franca came into use, which differed considerably from pure Arabic, the official language of the conquerors, and included numerous Latin terms borrowed from the native population. The general effect of Muslim influence upon Spanish civilization was not apparent until a later date ; in any case, that influence was comparatively weak in the north-east part of Spain. Zaragoza was certainly a Muslim centre, but the chief Muslim architectural achievement, the palace or *aljaferia*, was built in the period of Muslim decadence and the botanists and philosophers who flourished there were overshadowed by the greater names in the southern centres. Aragon and Catalonia were never out of touch with Southern France and its more congenial civilization, while such districts as might have been directly affected by Muslim influence were but thinly populated.

CHAPTER III

THE RECONQUEST

Formation of Christian states in the north, Navarre and Aragon. Sancho the Great. The Cid. Muslim rule in the north-east. Its culture. The Crusade of 1064. The Cid's early campaigns. His exile. Barcelona, its growth and importance. The Cid in Zaragoza. Affairs in Valencia. The invasion of the Almorávides. The Cid's operations in the East. Conquest of Valencia and alliance with Aragon. Consolidation of the conquered district. Death of the Cid.

VISIGOTHIC Spain had maintained the character of a united kingdom, secured by the existence of a king and court and a general similarity of administrative methods. It was, however, a unity more apparent than real, and when the Muslim invasion had separated one district from another, such regions as remained in Christian occupation began to develop upon individual lines. In the north-west, the kingdom of the Asturias and Galicia continued the Visigothic traditions, customs and laws ; but the states which began to emerge in the north-east, Navarre, Aragon, Barcelona and smaller duchies, were under Frankish influence or predominance, and possibly contained racial elements peculiar to themselves : hence these states gradually developed institutions and methods of government which diverged considerably from the course of development followed in the west.

The original nuclei of these states consisted of bodies of refugees who retreated to the southern slopes of the Pyrenees and joined such populations as were already settled there. Some of these were already known to the Gothic kings as troublesome neighbours ; the Basque tribes had been a perpetual menace to the peace of such towns as Pamplona ; when they had taken Christian fugitives under their protection, raids which had been criminal in Visigothic days became meritorious when the Muslim was in power.

Peaceful tribes were stirred to aggression by the fear of invasion or the hope of booty, and thus the Reconquista was begun, primarily with the object of recovering lost territory, influenced occasionally in later days by religious motives or foreign encouragement, but in its beginnings individualist in character and utilitarian in intention. Thus arose, to enumerate them in order from west to east, Navarre, Aragon, Sobrarbe, Ribagorza, Pallars, Urgel, Cerdaña, and the component *condados* of Barcelona. The majority of these were soon absorbed by Aragon or Barcelona, but some consideration must be given to their early history, which has been obscured by the piety or patriotism of later chroniclers. These writers conceived that the Reconquista was begun by a few men banded together to defend the Christian religion against Mahomet and to recover possession of their country ; such men must have had a leader and a rallying-point, and when these were not known by tradition, they were invented, and excessive improbabilities were explained by reference to the miraculous. In consequence, the rise of the Spanish kingdoms remains one of the most obscure and difficult subjects with which historians of Spain have to deal.

The provinces of the Spanish mark formed part of the Carolingian Empire and appear to have accepted, in general, the institutions of that Empire. They formed part of the province of Septimania and were under the general authority of the Count of the province. The relationship of the social elements which composed the population was entirely feudal in character. The freeman could not stand alone and " commended " himself to an overlord, whose protection was given in return for service. He might hold land temporarily granted *in beneficio*, or as allodial property : in either case, he could not afford to stand outside the feudal system and if his holding was considerable he might himself become an overlord. Land recovered from the Moors was the property of the Crown, which made grants of it to particular subjects or to ecclesiastical corporations. Frontier landholders were excused certain taxation in return for the increased liability to military service which their position involved ; they might attach themselves to an overlord or make grants to vassals of their own, as circumstances required. Their aspirations were naturally towards independence and titles became by degrees hereditary. By inheritance and intermarriage, several feudal hierarchies might become united ; such a power was then able to attract other feudatories ; distance from the central authority favoured any movement towards independence and in this way arose a number of counties of which Barcelona became the strongest.

The region afterwards known as the Kingdom of Navarre was occupied from very early times by Basque peoples, who were always intolerant of authority and as ready to fight with Frankish lords in the north as with Muslims in the south. The latter overran the level parts of the province, seized Pamplona and drove the native inhabitants into the mountains where they maintained their freedom by a series of struggles against the Muslims as well as against the Carolingian rulers. In 824 they succeeded in driving out the Franks with the help of the renegade Beni-Kasim, after which they were free to turn upon the Muslims. About this time appears the name of one Íñigo Arista, who is said to have come from Bigorre and to have been Count of Navarre or of a part of it.

Legend relates that Sobrarbe owed its foundation to Voto and Felix, two nobles of Zaragoza, who became anchorites in a hermit's cave which Voto had discovered in Mount Pano, near Jaca : numerous fugitives gathered round them and were eventually organized as an army under the influence of the two holy men. One Garci-Ximenes was elected leader and, after his first victory over the Moors, acclaimed as king : a resemblance to the story of Pelayo and Covadonga is obvious. To this event is also ascribed the formula said to have been pronounced by the Justicia of Aragon at the coronation ceremony, when the oath was administered to the new King : " nos que valemos tanto como vos os facemos nuestro rey y señor con tal que nos guardéis nuestros fueros y libertades, y si no, no." This version is apparently due to Antonio Pérez, the secretary of Philip II, who improved upon the formula as given by Francesco Hotman in his *Franco Galia*, published in 1573 : neither of these writers can be regarded as reliable historians. Garci-Ximenes is said to have been succeeded by his son Garci-Íñiguez, who styled himself King of Pamplona and created the condado de Aragon with Aznar, a local chieftain, as count. The third

King of Sobrarbe was Fortun Garcés I. Between Sobrarbe and Navarre lay Aragon, a small and unimportant county to the west of the river from which it takes its name. These provinces of the Spanish mark were more or less subject to the Dukes of Toulouse until the weakening of the Muslim Empire gave them opportunity to expand, and the period is filled with the names of dukes and kings whose chronology is uncertain and whose achievements are shadowy. Sancho García in the first quarter of the tenth century is an authentic figure ; he repelled the Franks with the co-operation of the Moors and then turned upon the latter in conjunction with the Christians of the Asturias. He was known as Sancho Abarca, from the fact that he provided his troops with leather-soled shoes to increase their mobility ; his daughter married the famous Fernán González, the kingmaker of medieval Spain. Sancho's son entered into alliance with Ordoño II of Leon and attacked the Moors, but was beaten by them at Val de Junquera, though he eventually drove the enemy out of his country. His son, the grandson of Sancho Abarca, was Sancho the Great (1000–1035), who became the most powerful of the Christian rulers in Spain ; he was lord of Aragon, besides ruling over Navarre and Sobrarbe, and marriage connections had made him the uncle of Alfonso V, the King of Leon. The Count of Castile stood in the same relationship to Alfonso, and the three rulers made a combined attack upon the forces of Almanzor, who was then hampered by civil wars in Córdoba ; they thus gained an extension of their respective territories on the south. Alfonso's son, Bermudo III, who succeeded in 927, married a sister of García, the Count of Castile, who was also related to Sancho, as has been said. A quarrel which ended with the assassination of García, broke up this family compact and Sancho proceeded to occupy Castile and to dispute with Bermudo concerning the delimitation of the frontier. The Church negotiated a peace and Bermudo married his sister Sancha to Sancho's son, Fernando, who assumed the title of King of Castile in 1037. War broke out again ; Castile and Navarre attacked Leon and Bermudo was driven out of his kingdom into Galicia. Sancho thus ruled over Northern Spain from the frontiers of Galicia to those of Barcelona, and assumed the title of Rey de las Españas, which suggests that he and his contemporaries did not regard his kingdom as a unity. Before his death in 1035, he divided his possessions among his sons ; García received Navarre and the Basque provinces, Fernando took Castile, Ramiro took Aragon, and Gonzalo obtained Sobrarbe and Ribagorza. Thus was broken up the first combination which seemed to promise a union of Christian Spain.

The modern reader inevitably regards this and subsequent divisions as acts of singularly short-sighted policy, retarding

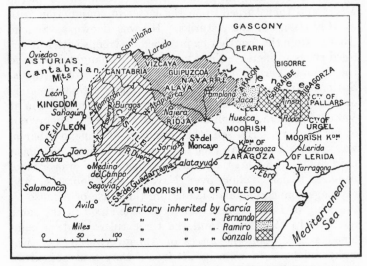

MAP 1. DIVISION OF THE ESTATES OF SANCHO THE GREAT

that organized co-operation against the Moors which alone was likely to recover Spain for Spaniards. The Germanic laws of succession still held good in Spain and the Roman principle of primogeniture was only tardily adopted. The Crown might be regarded as symbolizing the power of the nation which was one and indivisible ; such was the Roman, the ecclesiastical and the Visigothic conception of monarchy, a tradition continued in the Kingdom of Leon. There was another view, that of Teutonic feudalism, which regarded the realm as a piece of personal property and therefore divisible among heirs ; Navarre, with its Teutonic mode of coronation by elevation upon a shield as opposed to ecclesiastical coronation and unction upon a throne, was under the influence of this latter theory, which was also held by the Merovingian and early Carolingian kings of France. Sancho's action is among the first of similar acts of partition. Menéndez Pidal has suggested that the disintegrating influence apparent in the Carolingian Empire at the close of the ninth century had spread to Spain and will account for the rise of several petty kingdoms and duchies upon the model of the great feudal states in France. In any case, the division is indicative of the fact that national union was not an ideal in any degree present to the minds of Spanish rulers at this period of their history.

The Kingdom of Aragon was brought into existence by the will of Sancho the Great, who bequeathed the former county to Ramiro as a kingdom, Fernando obtaining Castile with the same title. Ramiro attempted to secure the Kingdom of Navarre from his brother García, but was defeated and driven out of the country; however, the death of his brother Gonzalo put him in possession of the counties of Ribagorza and Sobrarbe and thus turned his attention to the eastern side of his possessions. His war with Navarre had been undertaken with the object of gaining some outlet for expansion on the south and west; Aragon itself was confined to the upper part of the river of that name and its tributaries, and was cut off by the frontier of Navarre from its natural outlet towards Huesca. Ribagorza offered other possibilities, and Ramiro and his successors attacked the Moors with the purpose of extending his frontiers upon that side. In the ensuing wars Rodrigo Díaz de Vivar, the Cid, made his appearance on the side of the Moors of Zaragoza who were helped by Castile, a state of affairs which requires some explanation.

The great Al-Manzor had gained his successes with the help of Berber troops imported from Africa in place of the former Arab militia; he also employed so-called Slavs, troops of European origin who might be of Gallic, Germanic or Spanish as well as of Slavonic extraction; many of these held high offices in the Muslim state. In the troubled years which followed the death of Al-Manzor in 1002, we find the Berbers taking possession of the southern districts from Granada to Cádiz; the Slavs occupied the east coast from Almería to Tortosa; the former Muslim nobility held various cities

3

and districts in the interior, forming petty states of little importance (*taifas*), while the Caliph's power did not extend far beyond the gates of his palace in Córdoba. Hixem (Hisham) III, the last Caliph, died in 1030, at which time Valencia was held by Abd al-Aziz Al-Manzor, a grandson of the great Al-Manzor, while various Slav dependents of this ruler held petty states in the vicinity. Tortosa and the Balearic Islands were in the hands of Slav rulers. Further north, the previous organization for the defence of the Muslim frontiers was maintained by governors of Arab extraction ; thus the Beni-Hud held Lérida, Tudela and Zaragoza from 1039. Only two kingdoms among these petty principalities showed any capacity for expansion ; Seville, with which we are not concerned, was one ; Zaragoza was the other. The Beni-Hud had overpowered Tortosa in 1061 and Denia in 1076; members of the family also claimed to rule in Valencia. Thus the eastern side of the Spanish peninsula is composed of a number of petty states, both Christian and Moorish ; the western side, in comparison, shows much greater homogeneity. The east was consequently the natural area for adventurers and freebooters, whose inclinations were to be further stimulated by the rise of the crusading spirit, of which the exploits of the Cid are typical. The Cid cannot be regarded as a crusader, but he came to rely upon the Mozárabic or Christian elements among the Moors, and found that the Muslim populations were the strongest supporters of his enemies. Thus, in consequence of the Cid's career, the Reconquista began to assume a more accentuated political and religious colouring.

Relations between Christian and Moorish states during the eleventh century were marked by certain changes, symptomatic of which was the system of parias, monetary payments made by Moorish to Christian states in return for help or protection against enemies. Such a system of semi-vassalage was made possible by the fact that the process of nationalization among the Moors had advanced considerably : the Roman and Gothic strain had assimilated the Asiatic or African element, and the breach between the Christian civilization of the north and the Muslim culture in the south had considerably diminished. Moors and Christians were able to live side by side, no longer so abruptly divided as before by racial and religious differences. This equilibrium, such as it was, was eventually upset by the Almoravid invasions of 1086 to 1092, after which occupation of territory rather than the imposition of tribute became once more the Christian ideal. While the first half of the eleventh century was marked by the political weakness and instability of the Moorish states, it was a period of vigorous intellectual and artistic life, developed for the most part in the south. Córdoba and Seville were the chief centres of culture. Valencia and Zaragoza were the only centres of learning within the limits of the later Aragonese state. In the latter town, Moctádir and Mutamin, two Moorish kings with whom the Cid was on terms of friendship, were also philosophers and mathematicians of repute. The Moors in general admired learning ; few of the petty princes did not possess a library and many of them were anxious to attract scholars to their courts. Poetry and music were their special delights and were regarded as no less indispensable than wine at the Moorish banquets. The culture of the Christian courts was meagre in comparison with the achievements of the Moors ; the library of the famous monastery of Ripoll contained less than two hundred volumes in 1046 ; most of these consisted of patristic writings or of classical literature, until the Cluniac reform in the eleventh century banished the profanities of Virgil, Cicero and Ovid from monastic and, as far as possible, from secular life. The Moors despised the Northern Christians as uncultured barbarians ; but their own culture, however brilliant, was built upon no such social foundation as Christianity provided for the Northern states. The Moorish rulers were individualists ; the Christians had a common hope and purpose, often interrupted and obscured by political selfishness, but none the less real and steadfast.

It must not be supposed that the parts of Spain under Muslim domination at this time were in any sense permeated by Arab influence. The majority of the Muslim families constantly intermarried with persons of Gothic, Hispano-Roman or European extraction ; there was a large population of Mozárabes, Spaniards who had retained their religion and their church organization, living in their own quarters of the towns and paying tribute to the Moors ; there were also independent Christian lords, who for various reasons had been able to secure treaties of peace with the conquerors.

The population was, for the most part bilingual, speaking Arabic and Latinía or Aljamía, as the Spanish romance tongue was called. One of the reasons which enabled Christian invaders to push their raids deeply and successfully into Moorish territory was the lack of coherence between the heterogeneous elements of which the Moorish population was composed. This fact, again, the exploits of the Cid will illustrate.

Rodrigo Díaz de Vivar was born of noble parents about 1043 and was brought up at the court of Fernando I of Castile, under the patronage of his eldest son, Sancho. The Gothic kings had been accustomed to keep the sons of their nobility at court and to fit them for their future positions by providing them with some training in letters and in the art of war. In continuation of this custom Fernando I organized a course of instruction for his sons and those of his dependants, in which the youths studied letters under clerical direction and were trained in the use of arms, in riding and hunting. In this environment Rodrigo grew up ; his uncles, Laín Núñez on his father's side and Nuño Álvarez on his mother's, were in constant attendance upon Fernando I and Sancho, and it was Sancho who invested Rodrigo as a knight (caballero) when he came to maturity. His first campaign after this event was undertaken with Sancho, in support of Moctádir, the Moorish King of Zaragoza, against Ramiro I of Aragon who was attacking the frontier town of Graus in the early months of 1063. Zaragoza had been tributary to Fernando I for some two years previously, at which time the King of Castile had captured two of its frontier towns. The joint enterprise was a failure, and Ramiro was killed in the action. This event produced an impression far beyond Spain. The papacy was kept informed by the monks of Cluny of the progress made by Christianity in the task of the Reconquista, and it was felt that the defeat and death of Ramiro, who had shown particular favour to the Church, called for vigorous action. Pope Alexander II, who owed his elevation to the papacy in 1061 to Cluniac influence, proclaimed the cause of Spain in Western Europe, preaching and organizing a crusade on a scale which was to be the model of the Eastern crusades, the first of which set out thirty-four years later. Contingents from Italy and the South of France

joined the Catalan and Aragonese troops at Gerona, under
the command of Guillaume de Montreuil, known as le Bon
Normand, a soldier of fortune in the service of the Pope.
From Northern France was collected a more formidable force,
the backbone of which consisted of troops from Normandy
and Aquitaine ; their leader and the most important personage in the whole expedition was the Duke of Aquitaine
and Count of Poitiers and Bordeaux, who had recently
extended his power to the northern base of the Pyrenees
and was a close friend of the Cluniac monks ; both for religious
and political reasons he was anxious to inflict a blow upon
the Moors. His army crossed the Pyrenees at Somport, and
joined the army concentrated at Gerona in the early part of
1064, when the whole force advanced upon Barbastro.
This town, some thirty-five miles south-east of Huesca, and
half-way between Zaragoza and Lérida, appears to have
been a more important place than it now is. It was a
strategic point between the Ebro valley and the mountainous
lands of Upper Aragon, and its capture was a necessary
preliminary to an attack upon Zaragoza. An accident to the
water-supply obliged the defenders to surrender and the
town was sacked with every circumstance of cruelty and
debauchery. It is said that some fifty thousand Muslims
were killed or captured, the surrounding country was
devastated and enormous booty was divided among the
conquerors ; le Bon Normand obtained five hundred young
women with a corresponding wealth of furniture, clothing
and jewellery as his share. The exploit had no permanent
result, for the Moors recaptured the town in the following
year and slaughtered the garrison which was enfeebled by
a long bout of debauchery. But the moral effects were considerable ; the Moors were profoundly impressed by the
military power of the French, and the French were roused to
enthusiasm for the cause of Christianity in Spain ; henceforward, crusaders were attracted not only by the call of
religious duty, but even more by the prospect of material
wealth in the shape of plunder.

Moctádir of Zaragoza broke his alliance or agreement with
the Castilians in consequence of these events and was attacked
by Fernando I of Castile, who pushed his invasion as far
south as Valencia. Ill-health obliged him to retire ; in the

last month of 1065 he died and was succeeded by Sancho II in Castile, Alfonso VI in Leon and García in Galicia ; the Cid held the post of alférez or standard-bearer at Sancho's court and with it the highest military command.   His prestige was increased in the course of an attack upon Zaragoza by which Sancho attempted to recover his supremacy over that town.   This enterprise brought him into collision with the Kings of Aragon and Navarre who considered him as a trespasser upon territory which they hoped to recover

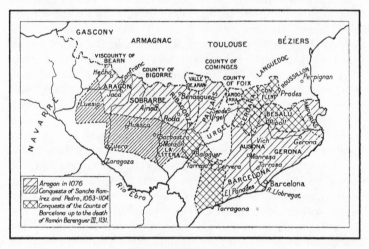

MAP 2. ARAGON, 1063–1131

for themselves ; the resulting conflict, known as the " War of the three Sanchos," ended in no advantage to any one of the combatants and the death of the widow of Fernando I in 1067 removed an influence for peace and allowed Sancho of Castile to turn his energies in another direction, that of uniting Leon with Castile at the expense of Alfonso VI. The events of this fratricidal struggle which continued until 1072 did not immediately affect the position of Aragon. Sancho defeated Alfonso in the battles of Llantada and Golpejera, and took him prisoner in the latter engagement ; Alfonso escaped and took refuge with the Moorish King of Toledo, while Sancho attacked García and drove him out of Galicia and into exile at Seville.   While attacking Zamora, one of the last towns which held out against him, Sancho was killed by a pretended deserter from the town, Vellido Adolfo, said to have been sent by Urraca, Sancho's sister. who held the town. Alfonso returned from Toledo, was recognized as King by the nobles both of Castile and of León, and attacked and defeated his brother García who had returned to Galicia with the help of the Moors of Seville. Alfonso thus became ruler of the united kingdom. He attacked and defeated the Sevillans who had helped García ; the overthrow of the King of Toledo who had befriended him, and had been dethroned by his own subjects, enabled Alfonso to interfere in the affairs of that city which he captured in 1085, an important date in the history of the Reconquista. Numerous petty kings offered their submission ; Alfonso besieged Zaragoza and overran Valencia, upon the throne of which he placed Al-Cadir, the former King of Toledo. These triumphs were ended by the invasion of the Almorávides to whom the Spanish Moors had appealed for help.

Alfonso was not recognized by the nobles of Castile and Leon in 1072 with any immediate show of unanimity. There is no reason to doubt that he was accused of complicity in the assassination of Sancho and that he had to clear himself before an assembly of nobles held at Burgos ; the oath on this occasion was administered by the Cid, Sancho's former commander-in-chief. The Cid appears to have taken the usual oath of allegiance, but memories of the battle of Golpejera and the part which he played in the recognition of Alfonso by the Castilians must have left relations between himself and Alfonso in a state of tension. The King naturally showed favour to his former supporters, such as García Ordóñez, his *alférez ;* but he gave the Cid in marriage his cousin, Jimena, the daughter of Diego Rodríguez, Count of Oviedo, and the wedding took place in 1074 ; it was no doubt a political marriage and one of various measures by which Alfonso hoped to unite Castile and Leon. In the following year the Cid's landed property was relieved of all liability to taxation and the King seems to have been anxious to secure the goodwill of this formidable personage. Trouble began in 1079, when he was sent to Seville by Alfonso to receive the *parias*, the tribute due from the King, Motámid. Rodrigo found Motámid at war with the King of Granada who had in his service certain Castilian nobles, including the Count García Ordóñez of Nájera. These Castilians were probably acting under orders from Alfonso who may have wished to preserve a balance of power between two Moorish rulers ; but the Cid thought that it was his duty to protect Alfonso's tributary when he found him attacked. He completely defeated the forces of Granada and took the Count of Nájera prisoner together with other Christian nobles. He released them after three days, when his victory was secure, returned to Seville, collected the tribute and arrived at Burgos, where the King was holding his court, in May 1080, bringing with the money various presents from Motámid. Rodrigo was then accused, upon what grounds is not clear, of appropriating part of the treasures entrusted to him. The fact that he had engaged in a war against Moors without permission may also have been brought against him. Alfonso further suspected him of an attempt to interfere in his relations with the subject ruler of Toledo. The Cid had numerous enemies of whom García Ordóñez was the leader. The hostility of the court completed the distrust of the King and Rodrigo was sent into exile.

Vassalage was a contract terminable at will by either of the parties to it. If the King removed his favour from a subject, confiscation of property did not necessarily follow ; the exile remained a subject of his King as before and the old relationship might be resumed at a later date. But the fact of exile in the case of a prominent person, affected a number of others who might be in feudal relation to him. The Cid's own vassals thus went into exile with their overlord ; they were men whom he had brought up at his court, endowed with land, or united to himself by marriage, as well as men who had no particular tie of relationship with his family. These formed the *mesnada*, the following of the house, and the principal names mentioned in the *Poema de mío Cid*, Álvar Álvarez, Álvar Háñez, Félez Muñoz, Pedro Vermúdez, the *alférez*, were all united with the Cid as relations of himself or of Jimena. To this nucleus others were attracted ; the disappointed or dissatisfied, the adventurous and those anxious to fish in troubled waters. Thus the Cid left Burgos at the head of a considerable force. The only career open to an exile in his position was one of war for or against the Moors. There was nothing to be done in the west and south, as Alfonso himself was prosecuting various plans for expansion in that direction. The Cid therefore made his way to Barcelona ; he already had experience of war in that part of the country ; he knew that the Aragonese rulers and the Counts of the Spanish mark were striving to secure the valley of the Ebro ; Castile appeared to have abandoned her former efforts in that direction, and he might well continue the policy of Fernando I, in conjunction with one of the local Christian powers.

Barcelona was even then one of the most important cities in the peninsula. Its commerce was considerable and it was a point at which foreign influence could enter Spain both by land and sea. As regards its earlier history and that of Catalonia, for which it formed the centre of gravity, reference has already been made to the formation of the Spanish mark and to the manner in which the local counts made themselves independent of Frankish control; Wifred, known as the Hairy (El Velloso), united the counties of Urgel and Cerdaña to Barcelona : he extended his power to Montserrat and to the mountainous region in which the rivers of Catalonia have their source, and is said to have founded the Monastery of Ripoll. He died in 898 and his successors were able to intervene in the Moorish civil wars and to gain some extensions of territory; but progress was slow until the death of Al-Manzor and the consequent break-up of the Muslim power. At the outset of the eleventh century, the reigning count was Berenguer Ramon I (1018–1035), who did little to extend his frontiers—he is said to have been entirely under the control of his mother—but made some settlement of the political conditions of the country, by recognizing, granting or codifying the fueros and liberties of Barcelona, which at that time included Gerona, Ausona and Manresa. This work was continued by his successor, Ramon Berenguer I, who supplemented the old Gothic laws of the Fuero Juzgo by formulating the celebrated Usatges which reduced to unity the varying customs and laws prevailing in the several *condados* which made up the state of Catalonia in confederation under the leadership of Barcelona. After a preliminary struggle with his grandmother, who established herself in Gerona and claimed the greater part of his dominions as her own, Ramon Berenguer was able to extend his influence in two directions.

He extended his frontiers as far as Barbastro by conquests
from the Moors ; and in other directions, more especially in
the south, Moorish chieftains and governors paid him tribute
and acknowledged his supremacy. By marriage he also
increased his influence north of the Pyrenees ; both his first
wife, Isabel of Béziers, and his second, Almodis de la Marche
(of Limousin), brought him into connection with the nobility
of Southern France, while through his grandmother he
obtained lands in the area of Carcassonne. Thus began an
extension of power which was to prove more trouble than
benefit under Pedro II. His son by his first marriage, Pedro
Ramon, quarrelled with his second wife Almodis and
eventually killed her, in consequence of which he was exiled.
Ramon Berenguer I died in 1076, his last years embittered by
family troubles and by the failure of an expedition into Murcia,
and left his possessions to the twin sons of his second marriage,
Ramon Berenguer II, known as Cap d'Estopa, " towhead,"
from the thickness and colour of his hair, and Berenguer
Ramon II ; his will shows that he held almost as much
territory north of the Pyrenees as in the peninsula itself.

These twin sons were in power at Barcelona at the time of
the Cid's arrival. They do not appear to have accepted the
Cid's estimate of his personal reputation and capacity ; the
exile was affronted by the lack of consideration which he
received and opened negotiations with the Moorish ruler of
Zaragoza, Moctádir Ben Hud, who had been upon the throne
since 1046. He had secured possession of Lérida, Tortosa and
Denia, overcoming the petty kings of those places by force or
treachery, and at the time of the Cid's arrival Zaragoza was
one of the largest Moorish kingdoms in Spain. Moctádir
was, however, not averse from the prospect of securing the
support of the Cid, whose capacity he had observed in the
days of Sancho the Strong. He regarded Aragon as a permanent danger, and there was always the possibility that
Castilian attacks might be renewed ; he was therefore glad
to have on his side a soldier to whom the Christian methods
of warfare were familiar. However, in 1081, shortly after
the arrival of the Cid, Moctádir died ; he divided his kingdom
between his two sons, Mutamin, the elder, taking Zaragoza,
while Al-Mundhir obtained Lérida, Tortosa and Denia. The
inevitable result was a fratricidal war, in which the Christian

rulers intervened in the hope of furthering their own interests. As Mutamin had secured the services of the Cid, the brother turned to Aragon and Barcelona for help ; he also obtained assistance from most of the counts of the Spanish mark and from Languedoc and Gascony. The allies were defeated and Berenguer Ramon of Barcelona was taken prisoner by the Cid. This Arab title (Sidi, lord), is the usual mode of reference to Rodrigo de Vivar by Christian writers who speak of him as Mio Cid ; Muslim writers more often give him the title of Campeador, the Challenger or Champion.

This exploit naturally increased the reputation of the Cid and attracted the attention of Alfonso, who had been induced to interfere in the family quarrels of the Beni Hud. His intervention led to no result, but Rodrigo took the opportunity of meeting Alfonso with a view to reconciliation. Nothing came of it and he returned to Zaragoza. During the years 1083 and 1084 military operations were exclusively concerned with the war between Mutamin and his brother, Al-Mundhir. The King of Aragon, Sancho Ramírez, who had succeeded Ramiro in 1063, was able to capture Graus and other strong points upon the northern frontier of the Moorish kingdom. He renewed his alliance with Al-Mundhir, but the Cid defeated their united forces in August 1084, and made a number of important prisoners. The Cid's inactivity for the next two years may be explained by his reluctance to oppose Alfonso, who was pursuing his imperialist policy in almost every part of the peninsula. While continuing his career of conquest in Andalucía, he was also attempting to secure adherents in Aragon ; to García, the Bishop of Jaca and a brother of Sancho Ramírez, he offered the Archbishopric of Toledo, which city he hoped to make the capital of Christian Spain. In 1083 Alfonso succeeded in capturing Toledo from the Moorish King of Badajoz and in replacing upon the throne Al-Cadir, the grandson of the king who had protected him in his exile. Al-Cadir found his position very insecure ; Alfonso demanded enormous indemnities for the expenses of the war, and the taxation which Al-Cadir was obliged to impose made him very unpopular ; many of his subjects migrated to Zaragoza and induced Mutamin to invade the Toledan territory on the east ; Motámid of Seville grasped the opportunity for an attack in the south. Al-Cadir was obliged to appeal to Alfonso for help and eventually agreed to surrender the city to him upon terms which allowed the Moorish population to remain or migrate as they pleased and secured to them the practice of their religion. Al-Cadir was to be compensated by the possession of Valencia, which his grandfather Mamun had added to the kingdom of Toledo, but which had recovered its independence under Abdal-Aziz; this king died in June 1085, about a fortnight after Alfonso had secured possession of Toledo. It was understood that Al-Cadir would enjoy the protection of the Castilian power, nor was he likely to remain upon the throne without it; the Valencians did not want him; the King of Zaragoza, Mostain, the son of Mutamin, had a strong claim to the throne through his wife, a daughter of Abdal-Aziz, and intended to prosecute it. Al-Cadir was escorted to Valencia by a large force of Christian troops under Álvar Háñez, for the maintenance of which he had to pay heavily; the exasperation of the inhabitants was completed by the outrageous behaviour of the troops and by the taxation which their presence necessitated. The real masters of Valencia were Alfonso and his lieutenant, Álvar Háñez. Alfonso treated Seville and its king to a similar display of imperial aggression; he had for some time been besieging Zaragoza with reasonable hopes of success and its capture would bring every Muslim power in Spain under his sway. These ambitions were shattered by the invasion of the Almorávides.

The Almorávides were originally a tribe of Sahara Berbers, who were converted to Islam by one of the religious fanatics which North Africa periodically produced; in the strength of their new faith they gradually extended their power from Senegal to the northern coast. They were a barbarous, uncultured race of bigots, regarded with considerable apprehension by the civilized Moors of Southern Spain, and it was not without much searching of hearts that Mutamin and others decided that they could not make head against Alfonso without their help. The Almoravid leader, Yusuf, landed at Algeciras with a great force in 1086; the decisive battle was fought near Badajoz, at a spot known as Zallaca by the Muslims and Sagrajas by the Christians, and Alfonso was totally defeated. His authority over the Moorish *taifas* collapsed incontinently; Yusuf had united Islam and it was no longer possible to deal with petty princes separately : there was a distinct possibility that the Christians might be driven back to the mountains of the north. Alfonso, therefore, sent messages to ask for help from the several princes in France ; he also remembered the prowess of the Cid and secured a reconciliation with him early in 1087. The French provinces were fully alive to the danger and most of them sent contingents to a large army which operated, as usual, in the valley of the Ebro, and not where Alfonso would have preferred to see them, south of Toledo. No great result was obtained ; the scanty notices which have survived suggest that the expedition was broken up by internal dissension, and by the end of the year most of the crusaders had returned to their homes. The Spanish Christians were left to provide for their own safety and the Cid undertook the conduct of operations in the east.

The miserably incompetent Al-Cadir of Valencia was once more in trouble ; threatened with expulsion by his own citizens, who were supported by Al-Mundhir of Lérida, the uncle of Mostain of Zaragoza, Al-Cadir applied for help to every one he could think of, including the Cid. Mostain and the Cid arrived at Valencia simultaneously. The case was further complicated by the intervention of Berenguer Ramon of Barcelona. To follow the tortuous intrigues of the business would be waste of time ; the Cid remained master of the situation, and the Almoravid leader determined to advance against him and against the Christian forces which used Aledo as a base of operations under the generalship of García Jiménez. Alfonso summoned the Cid to join him in an attempt to oppose this movement ; the Cid failed to reach the King at the appointed time, and the result was a second quarrel and a second formal dismissal into exile. The Cid had broken with his Moorish allies in loyalty to Alfonso and thus found himself in the position of a private adventurer with no obligations to any one except himself. He established himself in the neighbourhood of Alicante, moved northward in the early months of 1090 and secured from Al-cadir the submission of Valencia. The Moorish King of Tortosa, his old enemy Al-Mundhir, induced Berenguer Ramon of Barcelona to join him in an attack upon the Cid, who completely defeated the confederates in the battle of El Pinar de Tévar and once more took Berenguer prisoner. This victory left the Cid master of the modern province of Valencia ; he exacted an enormous ransom from Berenguer ; he drew tribute from all the chief towns in the district and was able without difficulty to maintain a formidable army of chosen warriors. He also showed sufficient statesmanship to spare the feelings of his Moorish subjects and to rouse among them a strong antipathy to the Almorávides, based upon the contrast between civilization and barbarism.

It was obvious that he could not continue to stand alone in face of the Almoravid power, and as reconciliation with Alfonso was impossible—another attempt in 1091 had failed —he concluded early in 1092 a treaty with Sancho Ramírez, the King of Aragon and with Mostain, his old ally of Zaragoza ; the object of the coalition was the defence of the east against the Almorávides. Alfonso in that year made an attack upon Valencia with the help of the sea-power of Pisa and Genoa, at a time when the Cid was absent in Zaragoza. The Cid replied by ravaging the districts of Nájera and Calahorra and destroying the city of Logroño, and Alfonso was obliged to raise the siege of Valencia and hurry back to the defence of his own dominions. He had, however, caused a crisis in the internal politics of Valencia ; the helpless and invalid Al-cadir was murdered by a hostile faction of the inhabitants who had made common cause with the Almorávides, and the Cid had now a reasonable excuse for securing possession of a city of which he had long been the virtual ruler.

Valencia was now governed by a municipal council with the leader of the revolt, one Ibn Jahhaj, as cadi. In no long time he found the Cid before the walls of the city. Supported by Mostain with men and money, the Cid had started southward as soon as he heard of the revolution. In the last months of 1092 and in the early part of 1093 he succeeded in subjugating the outlying districts of Valencia and began to attack the suburbs of the city ; he was soon able to complete the blockade and the revolutionaries were forced to capitulate in July. Meanwhile Yusuf, the Emir of the Almorávides, unable to acquiesce in the loss of so important a city, was advancing to its recapture. To secure the fidelity of the inhabitants, the Cid made them an offer which is not without parallel in medieval Spain, strange as it may seem to modern ideas ; he

offered Valencia a truce for the month of August, on condition
that the city should accept his rule, if he succeeded in defeating
Yusuf ; but if the Almoravide should be able to defeat him,
he undertook to abandon all pretensions to Valencia. The
condition was readily accepted and the Cid began his preparations to meet the Almoravide attack, by gathering supplies
and men and securing the safety of his communications with
Zaragoza. The enemy advanced slowly and it was not until
November that they were visible from the city, which broke
the terms of capitulation in the expectation of speedy relief.
But a terrific storm of rain and the reputation of the Cid were
obstacles which the invaders could not face ; their army
melted away ; " nimis pavens nocte per umbras fugit," and
Valencia was left to its own resources.

The Cid besieged Valencia for the second time and forced
the Almoravid party to capitulate in May, 1094. The
defending force had seized all the food for themselves and the
unfortunate inhabitants were reduced to the direst straits.
The Cid refused to allow them to leave the town, and those
who were caught in the act of escaping were killed and in
some cases burnt alive before the eyes of their fellow-citizens.
The property of Al-cadir fell into the hands of the Cid, together
with a great amount of booty ; after securing his possession
of the city, he sent to Alfonso of Castile to announce his
success which was the more striking, as Alfonso had himself
failed to make any impression upon the Almoravid power in
the south ; with the announcement came a present and a
request that the Cid might resume the former tie of vassalage ;
he obtained permission for his wife Jimena and his children
to join him in Valencia, all of which details are related at
length in the *Poema*.

In this year, 1094, Sancho Ramírez of Aragon died while
engaged in the siege of Huesca, either from illness or in
consequence of a wound. His successor, Pedro I, renewed
the alliance which had existed between his father and the Cid,
whose attention was then fully occupied by a further attempt
which the Almorávides made to reconquer Valencia. Yusuf
placed his nephew, one Mohammad, in command of a force
said to consist of 150,000 horse and 3000 foot ; compared
with this overwhelming number the Cid's army was insignificant ; nor could Pedro of Aragon help him, as he was

himself occupied in besieging Huesca, which he captured in 1096, after defeating a relieving army sent out by the Emir of Zaragoza.

The Cid remained within the walls, allowing the enemy to expend their arrows upon the fortifications and to grow careless of the possibility of attack upon themselves ; when the favourable moment arrived, he made a sudden sortie which threw the Almorávides into confusion and enabled him to inflict a crushing defeat upon them ; an enormous amount of booty was captured and the danger of invasion was averted for some time to come. The Cid was then able to consolidate his hold of Valencia ; he punished the murderers of Al-Cadir, most of whose treasures he recovered from the hiding-places in which the assassins had concealed them ; he showed considerable leniency towards the Moorish population which was allowed to retain its lands, customs and places of worship, on condition of paying a moderate tribute. This leniency emboldened such of the hostile faction as remained to begin a fresh series of intrigues ; but the Cid averted any danger from this quarter by expelling them from the city. While prepared for a reconciliation with Alfonso, he had a definite policy of his own, of which his alliance with Pedro of Aragon was the outward expression ; the Eastern provinces of the peninsula were to be regarded as a whole and the cause of the Christians was not to be disturbed by the interference of any Western power, whether Christian or Muslim. When Mostain, the King of Zaragoza, persuaded Alfonso of Castile to allow some of his vassals to help in the relief of Huesca, the Cid appears to have given what support he could to Pedro of Aragon, who completely defeated the relieving force in the battle of Alcoraz. Similarly, when the Cid was threatened shortly afterwards by another Almoravid invasion, Pedro came to his help with all the forces that he could collect and helped him to gain another victory. But when Yusuf attacked Toledo in 1097, the Cid sent a force to the aid of Alfonso and with it his son Diego, who was killed in the defeat which the Castilian forces suffered at Consuegra.

In 1098 the Cid captured Murviedro and the possession of this important fortress secured him from any surprise attack by the Almorávides. He had already restored the bishopric of

Valencia and one Jerónimo or Jérome had been appointed to this see ; he was from Périgord, one of a number of French monks whom Bernardo, the Archbishop of Toledo, had brought into Spain to supplement the deficiencies of the Spanish clergy. Jerónimo is represented in the *Poema* as a warrior cleric, who had joined the Cid to take an active part in fighting against the Moors ; when the bishopric was reconstituted, he was the obvious candidate for the post and his election appears to have had the approval both of the Pope Urban II, and of the Archbishop of Toledo, to which Valencia had been suffragan from very early times. About this time the marriages of the Cid's daughters must also have been contracted. The elder, Cristina Rodríguez, married Ramiro, the *infante* of Navarre, which was at that time united with Aragon ; their son became King of Navarre as García IV in 1134, when a final separation of the kingdoms took place. The second daughter, María Rodríguez, married the Count of Barcelona, Ramon Berenguer III. He was the son of Ramon Berenguer II, known as Cap d'Estopa ; the possessions of Barcelona had been bequeathed to him and to his twin brother, Berenguer Ramon II, in 1076. The twins had failed to agree and divided the inheritance between them ; " Towhead " was finally killed while hunting, and popular opinion credited his brother with his assassination. Berenguer Ramon II, who was thus left as sole ruler, fought against the Cid, as has been said, and was twice taken prisoner by him. In 1091 he captured Tarragona, which had previously paid tribute to his father, after which date his history is obscure ; it is said that he was accused of his brother's murder before Alfonso VI of Castile by certain Catalan nobles and that he was defeated in the subsequent ordeal by battle ; there is also a tradition that he went upon a pilgrimage or crusade to the Holy Land and died in Jerusalem. His nephew became Count in 1096 and was some seventeen years of age at the time of his marriage with the Cid's daughter. By her he had two daughters who married the count of Besalú and the Count of Foix ; their mother died about 1105, and Ramon married again, as will be seen later.

The Cid died in July 1099, at the comparatively early age of fifty-six ; campaigns, wounds and anxiety had doubtless worn him out. Jimena continued to rule in Valencia for

4

another three years, after which the Almorávides threatened an invasion with which she could not deal. Alfonso of Castile came to her relief and obliged the invaders to retire ; but he felt unable to retain possession of the city ; much of the crusading energy of Spain was being attracted to the Holy Land and men were anxious to join Godfrey de Bouillon in founding the Kingdom of Jerusalem, though there was an enemy of greater importance to them almost at their doors. Alfonso, therefore, decided to abandon Valencia, which was too far from his dominions to be defended ; the Christian population evacuated the town and retired with the army of Castile in May 1102, taking with them the great stores of booty and treasure that the Cid had accumulated, together with the body of the hero for burial in Castile. Valencia was set on fire, and the Moors returned to find a heap of blackened ruins.

It was thus within the limits of the later kingdom of Aragon that the Cid's energies were displayed ; nor is it mere coincidence that on this side of Spain and not in his native Castile was produced the chief literary document which tells the history of his exploits. Some writers have regarded the Cid as an outlawed freebooter whose victories over the Moors were chiefly inspired by the hope of plunder for himself and his followers. Such a view is entirely mistaken. Nor should he be compared with refractory nobles, such as Bernardo del Carpio, whose defiance of monarchical authority aroused the admiration of a public impatient of subordination for the common good, and intent only upon the aims of individual selfishness. With these the Cid had nothing in common. It is sufficiently plain, in the first place, that he was a military leader of outstanding skill; he was the only general in Spain who succeeded in defeating the Almorávides. While the King of Castile could make no impression upon this Moorish power in the south, Rodrigo Díaz, with resources far inferior, was able to capture a very important city and to defeat the successive Moorish commanders who attempted to retake it. He possessed that peculiar quality of leadership which inspires confidence in followers and misgiving in opponents, and thus gained a reputation to which he owed some of his victories and to which Arab chronicles have borne full testimony. He appears as the foremost strategist of his time. The Almorávides are repeatedly said to have terrified their

foes by the noise of their drums, *los atambores ;* possibly
they were able to direct the movements of their troops at
a distance or to send them information by one of those
systems of drum signals which have been highly developed in
different parts of Africa, and so to use a form of tactics
unfamiliar to the Spaniards ; if this was a reason for their
success, the Cid showed himself able to counter it effectually.
Bold, aggressive, and supported by a small standing army,
he was a statesman as well as a warrior : he had a definite
plan for securing Eastern Spain against Moorish domination, and his very genuine religious belief was strongly
tempered with the ·crusading spirit. Yet he was lenient to
subjugated populations and the situation which ended in the
expulsion of the Moriscos four centuries later would never
have arisen under his methods of administration. His defects
were those of his time ; considerable emphasis is certainly
laid by the early documents upon the amounts of booty
which he acquired, but such references are not surprising
in an age which regarded personal property as the only form
of wealth worth consideration. Occasional outbursts of
anger or the occasional use of cruelty and terrorism to gain
his ends were not sufficiently frequent to break down that
equanimity and sense of proportion known to his age as
mesura and regarded by it as an essential quality of the
knightly character. Remarkable also was his steadfast
patriotism ; unjustly exiled, repeatedly rebuffed and constantly suspected by Alfonso, he none the less remained
consistently loyal to the obligation of vassalage and fully
justified the eulogy of the *Poema :*

¡ Dios, que buen vasallo, si oviese buen señor !

And if his undaunted soul after death may be conceived to
have lamented the abandonment of the crown of his ambition,
Valencia, yet it may have found some measure of comfort to
see his body laid to rest in his own native land, in the
Monastery of San Pedro de Cardeña. Nor was that the end
of his name and fame. His figure became the centre of a folk
poetry and of an epic which is the most precious literary
document of early Spain, and has continually provided
material for drama and lyric in modern Spain, France,
Germany and England.

CHAPTER IV

THE UNION OF ARAGON AND CATALONIA

Alfonso I. Marriage with Urraca. Capture of Zaragoza. Alfonso's death and will. Claimants to the throne. Ramiro the Monk. Petronilla's marriage with Ramon Berenguer IV. Union of Aragon and Catalonia. Earlier history of Ramon Berenguer. Alfonso II. Political and social organisation. The Church. Literature and language.

PEDRO OF ARAGON died in 1104 ; in addition to his conquest of Huesca, he had recovered Barbastro which the Moors had recaptured, and had gained some other strong points in the territory of Lérida. He was succeeded by Alfonso I, the Battler, who was unmarried at that time. In Castile, Alfonso VI, the conqueror of Toledo, the grandson of Sancho the Great and the uncle of the Aragonese king, was anxious about the succession to his crown. His only descendant was a daughter, Urraca, the widow of Raymond of Burgundy, a French noble who had helped in the conquest of Toledo, by whom she had a young son, Alfonso. The prospect of leaving his possessions to Urraca, a woman of no particular abilities and of doubtful character, at a time when Castile was suffering from the defeats of Zallaca and Uclés at the hands of the fanatical Almorávides, caused Alfonso much anxiety ; there was no prospect that his grandson would be fit to rule for many years, and in any case a certain dislike to the late Raymond of Burgundy seems to have alienated his affections from the boy. The Castilian nobles were equally alive to the dangers of the situation, and proposed that Urraca should marry the Count Gómez de Campdespina, one of the most powerful among their number ; it is possible that this union would have legitimized relations which were not above suspicion, while it would certainly have enabled the turbulent nobles to pursue their separatist and selfish ambitions. Alfonso VI solved the difficulty by negotiating a marriage with Alfonso of Aragon ; and when

Urraca's father died in 1109, Castile and Aragon were for the
moment united. Had Urraca been a respectable character
and had the Castilian nobles possessed any tincture of
patriotism and statesmanship, the union might have been a
definite advance towards the work of reconquest. As things
were, a series of domestic, which speedily became political,
troubles were the result. The chronicler Lucas de Tuy described Urraca as " a bold, bad woman," and her behaviour
obliged Alfonso to confine her in one of his castles near Zaragoza ; unable to trust the Castilian nobles, he replaced them
by Aragonese and Navarrese governors, and aroused much
discontent in consequence ; as the Pope declared his marriage
void upon grounds of consanguinity, he lost the support of the
Castilian clergy. The result was a series of petty wars, which
were further complicated by the rise in Galicia, where Urraca's
son, Alfonso, was being brought up, of a party who wished to
place him upon the throne as the legitimate heir. When
Urraca felt indignant at the pretensions of her son, she and her
Castilian friends supported her husband ; when she was on
bad terms with her husband, she stirred up her friends
against him ; one of these was the Count of Lara, by whom
she had a son and whom she is said to have married when her
union with Alfonso was finally dissolved. The struggle was
yet further complicated by the action of her sister, Teresa,
who had married Henry of Lorraine ; Alfonso of Castile had
granted him certain territories in the north of Lusitania,
which became the nucleus of the later Portugal, by which
name were then known the districts between the Minho and
the Tagus. The Count of Portugal considered that the
opportunity for asserting his claims to the throne of Castile
was not to be lost and succeeded after intrigues and struggles
which do not here concern us, in gaining some extension of
territory. It was, moreover, a period in which the towns
were beginning to fight for independence and were forming
alliances or hermandades against the nobles ; thus Urraca
and her *damnosa hæreditas* considerably hampered the
Battler in his struggles with the Moors.

None the less, his enterprise was rewarded with considerable
success. Having cleared the way by the gradual reduction
of various strongholds between his southern frontier and the
Ebro, he prepared to lay siege to Zaragoza. A number of

counts from Southern France came to his support, rather as vassals than as crusaders ; such were Gaston of Béarn, Centullo of Bigorre, Auger of Miramon, Arnauld of Lavedan, the Bishop of Lescar and others. The Count of Toulouse became his vassal in 1116, and Alfonso thus gained help from the whole area of the Narbonnais. The Almorávides attempted to anticipate his operations, but Alfonso defeated their army as it was advancing from Valencia and Zaragoza surrendered on December 18, 1118. This was at least as great an achievement as the conquest of Toledo by Castile ; it secured not merely the possession of the valley of the Ebro, but of a number of places dependent upon Zaragoza, such as Tarazona, Calatayud, and Daroca, and enabled the Aragonese to extend their power as far as Cuenca and Teruel. The obvious culmination of these successes was the capture of Lérida ; but Alfonso's preparations for this purpose were opposed by Ramon Berenguer III of Barcelona, who was equally anxious to secure the town and hoped to gain possession by negotiation with the local chieftain, one Abifilel. Thus, when Alfonso laid siege to Lérida, a battle took place between the Aragonese and Catalan forces, in which the former appear to have been victorious ; but the intervention of the Church induced both kings to abandon the attempt for the moment, and Alfonso was the more ready to accept the arrangement, as he wished to make a raid into Andalucía, with the purpose of helping the Mozárabes who were suffering under the tyranny of the Almorávides. Starting from Zaragoza, he reached Valencia, Murcia and the confines of Granada, ravaging the country as he went and collecting the Mozárabes for settlement elsewhere. He crossed the Alpujarras and captured Málaga, returning by way of Córdoba, Alcaraz and Cuenca ; a Muslim army which attacked him between Granada and Córdoba at Arinzol was defeated, and Alfonso returned to his own state after thus traversing the greater part of Muslim Spain and bringing with him some 10,000 Mozárabes to settle in his new conquests. In 1131, after an absence in the South of France, whither political interests had called him, Alfonso resumed his project of conquering Lérida. It was first necessary to capture the strongholds, Fraga and Mequinenza, which the Moors had reoccupied during his absence ; while advancing upon Fraga he was surprised by a superior force and obliged to fight a rearguard action, in the course of which he was mortally wounded.

Alfonso died in 1134 ; in view of the difficulties with which he was confronted both in his domestic and public life, his achievements were remarkable and placed the idea of reconquest before his successors as a feasible policy. In his hands this policy assumes a definitely religious character, typified perhaps by his quartering of a white cross on a blue field in the arms of Aragon. He was, at any rate, a restorer of

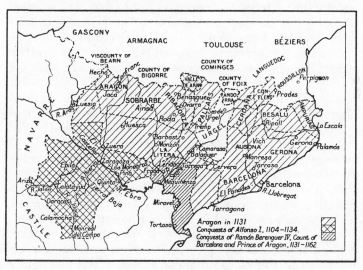

MAP 3.   ARAGON, 1131-1162

churches and monasteries ; in contrast to many of his contemporaries and successors, he left neither bastards nor concubines behind him, and his strange testamentary disposition which bequeathed his kingdom to the two religious orders of the Templars and the Knights of St. John of Jerusalem was probably dictated by religious convictions as sincere as they were unintelligible to those of his Aragonese subjects who did not regard the Reconquista from his point of view. Whether the knights of these two orders took any steps to claim their inheritance is unknown ; in any case, Alfonso's dispositions were disregarded by both Aragon and

Navarre. Three claimants to the vacant throne appeared, the most obvious being Ramiro, the late king's brother, who was proclaimed in Jaca as his successor, in spite of the fact that he was a monk and bishop-elect of Roda. In Monzon, one Garcí-Ramírez, a descendant of King García of Navarre, and in Borja, one Pedro de Atarés, an illegitimate connection of the royal line, both asserted their claims. The last-mentioned candidate soon retired, but Garcí-Ramírez held his followers together and secured his proclamation by the Navarrese as king of that country. A further complication was the interference of Alfonso VII of Castile, who asserted a shadowy claim through his mother Urraca, entered Zaragoza with an army and styled himself King of Aragon. The course of events from this point is far from clear ; certain powerful people met at Zaragoza, including the Archbishop of Tarragona, San Olegario, the confidential adviser of the Count of Barcelona, and the Counts of Toulouse, Comminges and Urgel ; Ramiro then married Doña Ines, a niece of the Count of Toulouse, and Alfonso VII withdrew his claims and retired to his own dominions. Ramiro, who abdicated after a reign of three years, left a daughter, Petronilla, whom he betrothed to Ramon Berenguer IV, the Count of Barcelona. It is probable that the influential personalities who met at Zaragoza, representing the interests of Catalonia and Southern France, informed Alfonso VII that they had no intention of seeing themselves absorbed by Castile ; it was obvious that they could not allow Alfonso to retain the territory of Aragon apart from that of Barcelona ; Catalan ambition was determined to extend southward and the possession of Zaragoza might lead to that of Lérida and of the whole valley of the Ebro. While Aragon and Barcelona thus became united, Navarre resumed its independence under Garcí-Ramírez.

To the Aragonese, Ramon Berenguer must have been practically a foreigner, and his acceptance implied a sacrifice of national feeling and an assertion of statesmanship very creditable to all concerned. Barcelona then, as now, was a far more important country than Aragon in respect both of population and wealth. It had a flourishing trade with the ports of the Mediterranean and was one of the chief points at which foreign influences and ideas could enter Spain. Aragonese stubbornness and conservatism was thus taken into partnership with a spirit of cosmopolitanism, ready for expansion and for commercial and political relations with any country from which advantage could be derived. Ramon Berenguer III, whose first wife, as has been said, was the daughter of the Cid, had done much to increase the importance of Catalonia. After the death of Maria, he married Almodis in 1106 and on her death, Douce of Provence in 1112. These marriages and his relationships enabled him to increase his territory considerably. In 1111 he inherited the county of Besalù, and in 1117 that of Cerdaña ; in 1112 the alliance with Douce brought him territory extending as far as Nice, so that he was in possession of a considerable part of Southern France and of all Catalonia, except the counties of Ampurias, Urgel and Peralada. In 1123 the Count of Ampurias became his vassal ; this was one of the final steps in the process by which the frontier counties created by the Frankish kings were gradually and peacefully absorbed by Barcelona. Ramon Berenguer III also strove to extend his power at the expense of the Moors ; in alliance with the Count of Urgel, he conquered the town of Balaguer in 1106 ; in 1115 in alliance with the Italian republic of Pisa, he attacked the Balearic Islands ; the object in this case was to secure vassalage and tribute from the Moors ; the term Catalan first appears in a Latin poem upon this expedition composed by an Italian, Lorenzo Vernes. The Italians also helped Ramon in an expedition against Valencia ; Lérida and Tortosa were attacked, but none of these towns was captured. Ramon Berenguer's purpose in these operations was to secure his southern frontiers against the Almorávides ; their vulnerable character was demonstrated in 1114, when Ibn al-Hajj of Valencia invaded Catalonia and ravaged the country almost as far as Barcelona. He was decisively defeated at Martorell and the contingents coming to his aid were also destroyed in detail. Ramon Berenguer III died in 1131 ; he had considerably strengthened his power both by land and sea, and to him was due the beginning of commercial and diplomatic relations with Italy, which were to be a strong and fruitful source of influence upon the national life both of Catalonia and of Spain at large in later years.

The dead king left his territories to his two sons, one, Ramon Berenguer IV, taking Barcelona, and the other,

Berenguer Ramon, taking Provence and the other possessions north of the Pyrenees. The new Count of Barcelona continued his father's policy ; he secured his southern frontiers by capturing Tortosa, Lérida, Fraga and Mequinenza, at the expense of the Almoravid King of Valencia and Murcia. This ruler, Abenmerdanix, bought his alliance for four years with the object of resisting the advance of the Almohades and maintaining the independence of his Muslim kingdom. Ramon Berenguer IV supported his brother in France against the house of Baus, which laid claim to Provence, and also against the Count of Toulouse. In 1150 he married Petronilla, as has been said, and thus united Aragon with Barcelona. He died in 1162 and left his Catalonian possessions to his son Ramon, who changed his name to Alfonso in compliment to the Aragonese. The county of Cerdaña and his French possessions went to another son, Pedro. In 1164 Petronilla renounced the crown of Aragon and Alfonso thus became the undisputed King both of Aragon and of Catalonia. The advantages of the union both to Aragon and to Catalonia were obvious ; Catalonia was not much more than a strip of coast-line territory, cut off from communication with the interior of the country and, as such, was not likely to become more than a replica of Pisa, Genoa, or some other Italian maritime republic, and, in a small state, the amalgamation of the several counties which formed its component parts was less easy than when they found themselves parts of a much larger whole. The union thus provided Catalonia with an interior, a hinterland, which could reinforce her armies and stimulate her commerce, while Aragon obtained an outlet to the sea, from which she was cut off upon her western frontier. Before proceeding to follow the fortunes of the united kingdom, some account must be given of the political and social customs and institutions of the two provinces which composed it.

Of the political and social organization prevailing in the territories afterwards known as Aragonese not very much is known of the periods before the eleventh century. Early documentary evidence is lacking or has been insufficiently examined. The Gothic Fuero Juzgo was observed in the eastern as in the western principalities, except that those parts of Catalonia under the Carolingian kings were governed by

Frankish law, and the social divisions of free and serf, with some grading of nobility in the former class, undoubtedly existed. But the Fuero Juzgo applied only to the personal relations of men in civil life and not to the constitution or organized power under which they might be governed. By degrees local customs grew up and obtained the force of law, and were ratified or completed by the grant of privileges in special *fueros* given to particular towns or social classes. The most famous of these is the so-called Fuero de Sobrarbe, a document conceived in the interests of the nobility and long believed to belong to the early years of the Reconquest. Modern criticism has rejected these ideas and regards this *fuero* as a fourteenth-century document. Municipal *fueros* have not been preserved of earlier date than the end of the ninth century and eventually became sufficiently various to impress Ramon Berenguer I with the need for codification. The great difference between the social organization of Aragon and Catalonia as compared with that of the western provinces was the greater intensity of feudalism in the east, and this was due to the greater strength of Frankish influence in this part of the peninsula. As has been pointed out, the Arab invasion drove large numbers of emigrants into France, many of whom passed through Catalonia, and it seems that this province did not contain many of its former inhabitants at the end of the eighth century. With the conquest of Gerona and Barcelona repopulation began under Louis the Pious who divided lands among his military officers, among such of the natives as had remained in the country and a certain number of returned refugees ; the natives were under the old Fuero Juzgo and the Franks under their own legal codes. A feudal hierarchy was soon developed ; the Count of the Spanish mark was the royal representative in his district and enjoyed the usufruct of the land, so far as it was not already in the ownership of a freeman : his holding was styled a *beneficio, fisco* or *feudo.* He could transfer his land to others in return for military service or rent ; thus came into being farmer vassals who paid rent, and viscounts, barons and other subordinates to the count, who might represent him as he represented the King and exercise certain judicial powers, holding their land under the obligation to perform military service when required ; they were known as *beneficiarios*. Frankish kings in course of time, made grants of land freehold and outside of the jurisdiction of the Counts, in return for homage to themselves and acknowledgement of the obligation to military service. These allodial holders were often at variance with the Counts who naturally desired to secure their own territorial supremacy and the Frankish kings were obliged to intervene. As the Frankish power declined, the original life-interest in and tenure of a *beneficio* became hereditary and the Counts of the Spanish mark rose to independence, while most of the allodial holders voluntarily became vassals to a count in return for his protection, and if their holdings were sufficiently great, might themselves grant lands to subordinate holders upon the usual feudal conditions. The rent-paying class or *censatarios* might and did descend in the scale to the position of serfs bound to the soil ; on the other hand, service in the wars against the Moors or the mere need of repopulating a barren district might provide them with entire exemption from the usual rents and tribute. Thus a system grew up much more nearly resembling feudalism than anything that existed in Leon or Castile ; lands were given by the King to the holder as payment for or to secure military service, such gift being irrevocable and, under certain reserved rights, capable of becoming a hereditary property ; the relationship of vassalage implied the fidelity of the holder to the giver ; the vassal had sovereignty and jurisdiction over the inhabitants of his land and stood in the same relationship to them as did his overlord to himself, with the power to make gifts of land on the same conditions and thus to become the head of a feudal hierarchy of his own creation. In Leon and Castile, on the other hand, gifts of land were not made by the ruler upon condition of military service ; in the few cases where such condition is laid down, the gift was usually made by some ecclesiastical corporation to a layman for the purpose of securing his aid against aggressors. The Castilian King also retained control of the legislative and judicial powers, and if a noble exercised such powers, he did so in virtue of some special concession from the Crown and not in his own right. In consequence, though there were subordinate grades of nobility, there was never a feudal hierarchy in the proper sense of the term, and the " lordship " of the western states, though analogous in some respects to the feudalism of the eastern states, must not be identified with it. What has been said of the Aragonese and Catalonian nobility is equally applicable to the Church ; monasteries and churches grew rich through gifts from kings and counts, held land, ruled the occupants and exerted seigneurial rights as did secular lords.

The moral state of the Church before the tenth century was far from edifying, though it was probably no worse in Spain than in other countries in view of the social anarchy which prevailed. Simony and the sale of ecclesiastical posts was frequent, while the attempts of church councils to maintain the celibacy of the clergy were impotent. Clergy lived with their wives or concubines, put their sons into church offices and dowered their daughters with church property. Papal control, though fully recognized by the Spanish bishops, could not always be effectively exerted in an age when communications were slow, difficult and often disturbed by war. The Cluniac movement brought renewed life to the Spanish Church in Catalonia and Aragon, as in the western states. The Cluniac monks, whose object was to restore discipline in monasteries and in the ranks of the clergy in general, and to secure a closer connection with the Papacy, entered Spain early in the tenth century by way of Navarre in the time of Sancho the Great ; thence they spread into Castile and by degrees into the other Christian states. To them was due a revival not only of morality but of learning ; the Latin of church and local records, which displayed a tendency to the forms of the colloquial vernacular, suddenly reverts to a more strictly grammatical style shortly after the beginning of the Cluniac reforms in Spain ; among other effects of their work must be mentioned the stimulus which they gave to the task of the Reconquest by investing it with a definitely religious character. Of the various heretical movements which arose in Spain before the tenth century, the most famous and the only movement which immediately concerned the eastern provinces was the so-called adoptionism professed by Felix the Bishop of Urgel and Elipandus the Archbishop of Toledo, a doctrine which taught that Christ became the Son of God by adoption at His baptism, previous to which He had been as any other man ; similarly, every Christian at his baptism is adopted in like manner, and the difference between him and Christ is one of degree and not of kind ; "et ille Christus et nos Christi" is the catchword of the heresy. It has been regarded by some writers as an earlier form of the Albigeois heresy, which became the occasion of the death of Pedro II, and as such it is not without interest to students of Aragonese history.

Such literary and artistic culture as existed was chiefly ecclesiastical in character. Churches and monasteries maintained schools and collected and copied books ; the monastery of Ripoll was of especial importance in this connection. The schools of Catalonia were in good repute and attracted students from abroad ; they had a particular reputation for mathematical learning ; thus Gerbert, afterwards Archbishop of Rheims and eventually Pope, studied at the school of the Bishop of Vich. Vernacular literature has no examples to show before the time of James the Conqueror and probably there were not many laymen who could read and write. Barcelona, in the tenth century, was an important commercial harbour and an inlet for foreign influences as well as for wares from various parts of the Mediterranean ; but most of the evidence on this point belongs to the following century.

The question of language is a matter for philologists rather than for historians ; the fact remains that Aragon and Catalonia spoke different languages which were not assimilated by their union. The Aragonese dialect, with which must be associated that of Navarre, shows certain divergencies from the dialect of Castile in the earliest documents available for study ; some of these are peculiar to it, as for instance, the Gascon article ero, era, the possessive pronoun lur, lures (also Catalan) ; certain verb forms such as moriet for murió, aduxomos for adujimos ; other characteristic forms reappear in other parts of the peninsula, feito or feto for fecho, pueyo for poyo, muller for mujer, which are seen in Gallego-Portuguese or in the Leonese dialect. These differences were not, however, sufficiently great, so far as can be seen, to impede communication to any great extent between Aragon and the other western or southern states. Catalan presents a different problem ; the question whether it belongs to the Hispanic or to the Gallo-Roman branches of the Romance languages is even yet in dispute. It has obviously been strongly influenced by the dialects of Southern France, as is seen to have been inevitable, when the geography and political history of the country is considered. Certain points are brought forward as proving that Catalan belongs by phonetic development to the Gallo-Roman system; such are its preservation of initial *f* and *g*, the fact that tonic *o* and *e* do not become diphthongs; Spanish has *puerta*, *siete*, which in Catalan are *porta*, *set*. But in Portuguese *e* and *o* are preserved, though they become diphthongs in the geographically intervening dialects; the same may be said concerning *f*. Or consider the case of *O* before a " *yod*," when the vowel becomes a diphthong in many Romance languages; Catalan has *pueyo* against Spanish *poyo*; but the diphthong also occurs in the Asturias, though not in Castile or the Galician–Portuguese area; the same is true of initial *l* which is palatalized in Catalan and Asturian, but not in the two areas of Castile and Galicia–Portugal. The frontier between Catalan and the other Spanish dialects is not abrupt, but the changes take place gradually over a broad band in Aragon and Ribagorza. Catalan is therefore not a language of French origin imported brusquely from Provence, but it takes its stance upon the Latin spoken in Spain in Visigothic times, representing the most easterly phase of a relatively uniform speech—a phase which, on the other side, merges into the Latin of Southern France, though there is a clear line of demarcation between the two, situated to the north of Roussillon. The lack of early documents forbids dogmatic assertion upon the question; but it is not unreasonable to suppose that Catalonians and Aragonese were not unintelligible to one another in the tenth century, whatever the state of affairs may be at the present day. In any case, instances of bilingualism and of trilingualism are known to every medievalist and the difficulty was not one that concerned any large section of the population. Catalan was the language of the Count of Barcelona, the most substantial title held by the Kings of Aragon : the first work of literature in Catalan was the *Chronicle* of James I, who also decreed that Catalan should be used instead of Latin as the official and legal language. The importance which it attained as the Aragonese power increased is probably the explanation of Dante's statement in the *De Vulgari Eloquentia* (I. 8) : " alii *oc*, alii *oil*, alii *si* affirmando loquuntur; ut puta Hispani, Franci et Latini."

Latin documents in the latter half of the tenth century show
Catalan forms and vocabulary which become increasingly
frequent in later years. The first document in pure Catalan is
the *Homilies d'Organyà*, a didactic work which is considered to
be anterior to the *Chronicle* of James I. Provençal troubadours are supposed to have entered Catalonia at the time of
the marriage of Ramon Berenguer III with Douce of Provence
in 1112 ; this is likely enough, but is only a conjecture
unsupported by evidence. In the second half of the eleventh
century was composed the poem of " Sainte Foy," one of the
earliest known compositions in Provençal, which was written
north of the Pyrenees and probably in the Narbonnais :

> Canczon audi q'es bella 'n tresca,
> Que fo de razon espanesca ;
> Non fo de paraulla grezesca
> Ni de lengua serrazinesca.
>
> .   .   .
>
> Tota Basconn' et Aragons
> E l'encontrada delz Gascons
> Sabon quals es aquist canczons.

" I heard a song which is fair in the dance, which was on a
Spanish theme, not of Greek word nor of Saracen tongue.
. . . All the Basque country and Aragon and the country of
the Gascons know what that song is." This prologue suggest
that communication and mutual understanding was constant
between the territories north and south of the Pyrenees.
Ramon Berenguer IV is twice mentioned by the troubadour
Marcabru who sends greetings to Barcelona as also to Castile
and Portugal ; in a crusade song, composed about 1146, he
considers that the help of Barcelona is indispensable, if the
Almorávides are to be defeated :

> Ab la valor de Portegual
> E del rei Navar atretal
> Ab sol que Barsalona.s vir
> Ves Toleta l'emperial,
> Segur poirem cridar : reial !
> E paiana gen desconfir.

" With the power of Portugal and also with that of the King
of Navarre, provided that Barcelona turns to Toledo, the
imperial city, we shall certainly be able to raise our war-cry,
Royal, and discomfit the pagan people." We may thus

assume that troubadours had begun to visit Catalonia about this time and to find there the patronage that was indispensable to them ; similarity of language would make such communications the easier. Catalan was now adopted by the rulers of Aragon as their language and its influence upon Aragonese is clearly marked in the documents of the period. The latter tongue continued in use as a vernacular only.

CHAPTER V

ALFONSO II AND PEDRO II

Alliance with Castile against the Moors. Alfonso's French possessions. Pedro II. His marriage. His submission to the Pope. Social life in Southern France. The Albigeois heresy. Action of the Pope. St. Dominic. The Albigeois Crusade. Simon de Montfort. Spanish affairs. Las Navas de Tolosa. Pedro declares war upon De Montfort. Battle of Muret. Death of Pedro.

IN 1162 the son of Ramon Berenguer IV of Barcelona began his reign as Alfonso II of Aragon. At this time the struggle against the Moors began to be conducted upon a new system, that of co-operation between the several kingdoms in the peninsula. Zones of reconquest were arranged ; in 1151 and in 1179 treaties were made between Castile and Aragon, reserving to each the right of conquest within particular limits ; Valencia was thus reserved to Aragon. Instances occur of help sent from one kingdom to another to accelerate the work of conquest ; apart from the 'more general co-operation in so great a battle as Las Navas de Tolosa, we shall find James I of Aragon helping the King of Castile against the Moors of Murcia and Granada. Such action implies a growing sense of Spanish nationality, which may have been fostered in some degree by the growth of military and religious orders, such as that of the Temple, the organization and administration of which comprehended the whole of Spain.

Alfonso II was in alliance for many years with Alfonso VIII of Castile ; apart from a formal bond of vassalage to Castile acknowledged by Aragon, the two monarchs had certain interests in common. Navarre had separated from Aragon after the death of the Battler, and had extended its boundaries ; both kings wished to reduce it to its former limits, and while Navarre retained its independence, both Castile and Aragon annexed some parts of its frontier lands.

Both kings were besides anxious to push southwards, and the Aragonese ruler advanced his frontier as far as Teruel; the well-known *fuero* granted to this town became a model for others of the kind. Alfonso thus prepared the way for an attack upon Valencia; he twice defeated Moorish armies

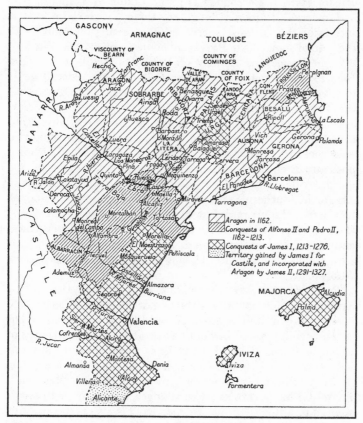

MAP 4. ARAGON, 1162–1327

which invaded the province of Tarragona and finally captured Cuenca; had he not been hampered by the necessity of dealing with incursions from Navarre, he might have been able to push his conquests as far as Valencia itself. In 1179 he made the treaty above-mentioned with the King of Castile, in which the limits of future zones of conquest were fixed :

the water-sheds of the Júcar and Segura rivers were taken as the dividing line, the territory of Denia, south of Valencia, being thus secured to Aragon. Alfonso II also extended his influence and power on the north of the Pyrenees. In 1167 he inherited the County of Provence on the death of his cousin, Ramon Berenguer II ; the Count of Toulouse who had married Ramon's daughter, Douce, laid claim to the succession, but Alfonso succeeded in asserting his rights with the help of some of the Provençal nobles. In 1172 he obtained by inheritance the County of Roussillon while Béarn and Bigorre did homage to him in 1187. These commitments involved Alfonso in various conflicts north of the Pyrenees ; the Viscount of Béziers, for instance, had surrendered Carcassonne to the Count of Toulouse, and when Alfonso compelled the Viscount to do him homage, complications followed with regard to Carcassonne. Alfonso died in 1196 ; he was a poet and friend of the Lion Heart as well as a vigorous and upright ruler, who did not allow the traditional interests of Aragon in Southern France to overshadow those of his Moorish frontiers ; the great defeat of Castile at Alarcos in 1196 by the last wave of Muslim invaders, the Almohades, must have embittered his last days of life. He left Aragon and Catalonia to his eldest son, Pedro II, and Provence to his next son, Alfonso.

Pedro II came to the throne at a critical time. The extension of his dominions to the north of the Pyrenees had brought upon him a number of difficult problems. The several feudal states in Southern France were constantly at variance among themselves, while it was obvious to any one with eyes to see, that sooner or later Northern France would desire to assert her supremacy over the South. Meanwhile Pedro did his best to avert the danger, and in order to secure some guarantee of peace he married his sisters Leonor and Sancha to Raimon VI and Raimon VII of Toulouse ; in 1204 he himself married Maria, the Countess of Montpellier. She was the daughter of William VIII of Montpellier and Eudoxa Comnena, daughter of Manuel Comnenus, Emperor of Constantinople ; Maria had been twice married before she became Queen of Aragon ; her first husband, Barral of Marseilles, had died prematurely and her second, the Count of Comminges, who had two wives living at the time of his union with Maria, had repudiated her. On the death of her father she found herself the heiress to Montpellier, as the sons were illegitimate; the offer of her hand seems to have come from the citizens of Montpellier, no doubt in the hope of extending their commerce with Aragon, while Pedro was glad to secure another outpost against attacks by Northern France. The marriage was not a success; Pedro was a faithless and dissolute husband and the birth of his son, James, is said to have been the result of a deception by which his wife was substituted for another lady of his fancy. He repudiated Maria, and she appealed to Rome and obtained a decision in her favour; she died in 1213, a few months before her husband was killed in battle.

Pedro took a further measure of precaution which aroused much dissatisfaction among his subjects; he acknowledged the feudal supremacy of the Papacy and was crowned at Rome by Innocent III in 1204, undertaking to defend the Catholic faith, to respect the privileges and immunities of the Church and to fight against heresy; he also promised that his kingdom should pay an annual tribute to the Papacy as a feudal vassal, in return for which the Pope and his successors were to defend Pedro and his subjects with their apostolic authority. Pedro received or assumed the title of *Católico*, but his action was greeted with unanimous disfavour by both his Aragonese and Catalan subjects, who declined to ratify it. His ostensible reason was his desire to secure the support of the Pope and the help of the Genoese for an attack upon the Balearic Islands; there is little doubt that his real purpose was to strengthen his position in the South of France. The numerous petty lords in that region were constantly at variance with one another; the complicated claims and grievances that arose from the interconnection of feudal obligations and marriage alliances were never at rest and the settlement of them would have taxed the wisdom of Solomon to the uttermost. Court quarrelled with court and cities were sometimes divided within themselves; Toulouse was torn by internal sedition from 1181 to 1188, and similar disturbances at Arles in 1191 were so violent that Pope Celestin II was obliged to order the local Archbishop to intervene. At the same time the general character of society both in courts and towns was in keeping with that of the degenerate Roman society which they had replaced. Towns were wealthy, courts were luxurious ; an aristocratic and leisured class existed with time and taste for art and literature, which, like commerce, was stimulated by communication with the Mediterranean countries. Trouba-dour poetry, which depended for its existence upon a class of cultured patrons, flourished in such an environment ; and the fact that lyric poetry was developed to the highest degree of technical perfection, while epic poetry forms no real part of Provençal literature, was the natural result of existing conditions. There was a certain general enthusiasm at the time of the Crusades ; there was a certain general opposition to Northern France ; but there was no sense of nationalism because there was no central *point d'appui* round which any tendencies to unity could centre. Particularism or parochialism was the prevailing political tendency, and was reflected in a literature entirely personal, artificial to a degree and intensely aristocratic.

Those circumstances which favoured the spread and development of art and literature in Southern France also stimulated the growth of more sinister influences. The twelfth century had seen an intellectual renaissance, a growing interest in the study of philosophy and law, which led to freedom of speculation upon matters ecclesiastical and religious. Throughout the eleventh century wandering teachers of strange doctrines had been perambulating Europe ; in course of time some of these succeeded in founding sects and the South of France was invariably the most fruitful field of their labour. This is not the place to discuss the obscure and difficult problem of the origin of the so-called Albigensian heresy ; its enemies almost invariably regarded it as a variety of Manichean dualism ; others have retraced it to the early centuries of the Christian era and suggest that it was a development of the adoptionism which has already been noted as appearing in Spain, and which appears to have passed from Armenia to the Balkan peninsula and thence to Italy and Germany. In any case, the heresy was not an isolated movement, but was in continuity with beliefs prevalent in other parts of Europe. It was a poor man's heresy and emerged into the light of history only when it happened to attract large masses of people or aristocratic adherents. It was also a pre-Reformation movement, essentially in opposition to Roman catholicism and sustained by popular indignation against the dissolute and scandalous character of the Roman Catholic clergy. Albi was the first headquarters of the heresy, but Toulouse soon became the real centre of it. The Vaudois heresy which appeared at Lyons about the same time was a schismatic, not a heretic movement. The Vaudois objected to the profligacy and worldliness of the orthodox clergy, but did not quarrel with Church doctrine. The Albigenses were no less zealous than the Vaudois in reproving Church abuses and in setting an example of purity of life ; but they also differed profoundly from the Church in matters of doctrine.

Pedro's own dominions south of the Pyrenees were by no means free from this infection ; but in Southern France it was clear that the authority of the Church was doomed, unless she took vigorous measure to assert it. The evil was of long standing. Pope Calixtus II had attempted as early as 1119 to check the spread of it by decrees issued at a council held at Toulouse and since that date a regular series of councils had called attention to the growth of the movement. Innocent III was fully aware of the danger ; he sent two commissioners in the summer of 1199 with full powers to act, but little effect was produced. They were replaced in 1202, but the local clergy were jealous of them or anxious not to be disturbed in their own manner of life ; the Archbishop of Narbonne, whom Innocent rebuked in one of his most violent letters, declined even to accompany them on their journey, and other bishops were no less refractory. Pedro felt that he must intervene and a public conference was held in February 1204 at Carcassonne between the heretics and the orthodox prelates under his presidency ; he was obliged to admit that the charge of heresy was proved. Innocent was convinced that spiritual weapons were useless and determined to use force. He increased the number of his legates and proclaimed a state of martial law throughout the country. He required Philippe Auguste and his son Louis with the barons and nobles of Northern France to take up arms against the heretics, and indulgences and absolutions were liberally promised to all who should join in the crusade. It was the last stage in the development of the crusade movement; originally begun to recover the Holy Sepulchre, it had been extended against the avowed enemies of Christianity in other countries. Now the movement was to be turned against erring members of the Church, and henceforward, in a metaphor much abused at that time, the crusader was not only to destroy the wolf, but to drive the vagrant sheep back to the fold of the Roman Church.

Innocent's appeal was fruitless. Philippe Auguste had already gained an indulgence as a crusader to the Holy Land; he was occupied with the provinces which he had regained from John of England and did not wish to incur further responsibilities for the moment. In June of 1205 Innocent attempted to attract Pedro by a promise of all the territory that he might acquire from the heretics, and in 1206 he raised the bribe by the addition of all property owned by heretics. Pedro rescued the castle of Escure, a papal possession, from the hands of the Albigenses, but did nothing further. He was apparently resolved to temporize; as feudal lord of Provence and other districts, he could not tolerate foreign interference; but since such an attitude would identify him with heresy, he had made his submission to Rome, in the vain hope that some means might be found of separating the religious from the political question. His brother-in-law, Raimon of Toulouse, was no heretic himself, and like most of his nobles, was indifferent to the claims of religion; living in the most brilliant and cultivated court of Europe, a protector of troubadours and jongleurs, popular among his subjects and surrounded by every luxury that the civilization of the age could provide, he could not be expected to plunge his territories into civil war for the benefit of a Church in which he felt no special interest and the venality and corruption of which were patent to all the world. Pedro could not but admit the cogency of such considerations.

In the summer of 1206 the papal legates met at Montpellier, admitted that their mission had been fruitless and proposed to abandon their efforts. At this moment a Spanish prelate entered the town, Diego de Azevedo, Bishop of Osma, accompanied by the sub-prior of his church, Domingo de Guzmán, afterwards the famous St Dominic. Both were returning from Rome to Spain and hearing the despondent accounts of the legates, Diego urged them to persevere, to put away the retinues and rich apparel which exposed them to the derision of the heretics and to go preaching from town to town in apostolic poverty. The privilege of preaching was guarded by the Church and the itinerants were obliged to apply to Innocent for permission ; his consent began the movement which was to produce the famous order of Dominican preachers. Their efforts met with little success ; the Pope excommunicated Raimon of Toulouse and laid an interdict upon his territory ; but his letters and the representations of his legate, Pierre de Castelnau, were disregarded ; the King of France was unwilling to consider fresh proposals for a crusade, and the situation seemed to be hopeless, when it was profoundly changed by an unexpected event of which the Papacy took full advantage. Pierre de Castelnau had accused Raimon of perjury and treachery to the Church and had so wrought upon his feelings that Raimon invited the papal legates to a conference at Saint-Gilles, at which he promised to submit to the ruling of the Church. From this point the narratives of either side are so contradictory that the truth will never be determined ; but the fact is clear that the Count and the legates parted in anger and that the next day, January 15, 1209, Pierre de Castelnau was murdered, when about to cross the Rhone, by a member of Raimon's court. The general excitement was comparable only with that aroused by the murder of à Becket thirty-eight years previously, and the Pope, though not convinced of Raimon's guilt ("*valde suspectus*" was his phrase four years later), had no hesitation in turning the murder to the advantage of the Church. He sent letters to the King of France and to his principal nobles, calling on them to take the cross in defence of the Church ; he undertook to arrange a two-years' armistice between France and England ; the Cistercian order resolved to preach the crusade in every country likely to send help and numbers of monks travelled through Europe, stirring up popular fanaticism and offering salvation upon easy terms to every crusader ; criminals, debtors and needy adventurers flocked in numbers to the invading host to secure immunity for their persons or profit for their purses. The long-standing jealousy between the North and the South, amounting practically to racial antagonism, now came to definite expression. It was inevitable that sooner or later an attempt at the unification of France should be made, slow as the French king was to seize the opportunity afforded by the growth of the heresy and the appeals of the Pope. For nearly a century the material for a conflagration had been accumulating and the murder of the papal legate proved to be the torch which fired the pile. This racial difference was soon apparent in the course of the crusade ; while there are many instances in which orthodox southerners helped heretics to repel the invaders, cases in which they joined the side of the crusaders are comparatively rare ; heretics are even found depositing money and jewels with churchmen for safe keeping. The crusade soon lost its specifically religious purpose and assumed the character of a racial struggle.

The crusaders concentrated at Lyons in the summer of 1209 and, after the capture of some insignificant places, covered themselves with infamy by the notorious massacre of Béziers, after which they proceeded to attack Carcassonne. At this point Pedro II intervened and attempted to secure a pacific settlement, but without success ; the town was captured after a resistance which inflicted much loss upon the crusaders and the Viscount, Raimon Roger, Pedro's vassal, was imprisoned until his death which occurred shortly afterwards. The conquered territory was refused by several of the chief nobles among the invaders, who were disgusted by the cruelty and treachery with which the campaign had been conducted ; eventually Simon, the fourth Count of Montfort, was recognized by the crusaders as Lord of Béziers and Carcassonne and as the future leader of the crusade, a position which he held until his death in 1218. A tall, well-built and commanding figure with regular features and long hair is the picture drawn of him by the chroniclers ; to courage, ambition and tenacity, he added military talents of no mean order, as he had shown in the course of the Fourth Crusade. He was the second son of Simon III of Montfort and Amicia, daughter of Robert Beaumont, third Earl of Leicester ; the earldom had passed to Simon in 1203. His immediate anxiety was to secure recognition of his rights from Pedro, and to do homage to him for the Viscounty of Carcassonne ; Pedro seems to have thought that he could secure the defeat of the crusade, if he made proper use of his advantages. The Pope was well disposed towards him, and had shown a leniency towards Raimon of Toulouse which had disappointed the fanatical crusaders ; there was no enthusiasm in the South for the cause of the Church as such ; it was difficult to keep the crusaders together ; after serving the forty days which qualified them for an indulgence, they were anxious to return home, and De Montfort could never be certain how many efficient soldiers he would have at his command. Pedro thought that he might both defeat the crusade and tighten his hold over the provinces which already acknowledged his dominion, perhaps even adding to their number. He therefore put De Montfort off with promises and fomented revolts in the territory which the crusaders had overrun. But in 1211 he found that his hopes were not likely to be realized ; affairs in Spain also demanded his attention and he therefore made a convention with De Montfort, whom he recognized as the Lord of Béziers and Carcassonne, and agreed also that his son James should marry De Montfort's daughter ; James, then three years of age, was left in De Montfort's care, and Pedro returned to Spain.

After the crushing defeat of Alarcos which the Almohades inflicted upon Alfonso VIII of Castile on July 19, 1195, that King had succeeded in repairing his shattered fortunes. His quarrel with Leon had been settled by a marriage alliance ; in conjunction with Aragon, he had reduced Navarre to impotence. The advance of Aragon in Valencia and incursions made by the Castilians in Andalucía had alarmed the Moors who began to concentrate their forces for a decisive battle. Alfonso sent appeals for help to all the Spanish kingdoms, to Portugal and to the Pope. The Pope proclaimed a crusade and a great number of foreigners came to Castile, but are said to have withdrawn as soon as the campaign began, disheartened by the heat and the hardships of Spanish warfare. All the Spanish kingdoms, with the exception of Leon, were represented in the forces of Alfonso, which fought the great battle of Las Navas de Tolosa on July 16, 1212. Alfonso gained a complete victory which placed most of Andalucía in his power and accelerated the internal discord which was beginning to undermine the power of the Almohades. Pedro II took a prominent part in this battle which finally determined the success of the Reconquista and marked an important step in the path to some kind of national unity in Spain. Events in France then obliged him to return across the Pyrenees.

De Montfort and his party had renewed the war against Raimon of Toulouse whom they were determined to drive out of his possessions. Raimon had retired to Toulouse, his strongest fortress, with the Counts of Foix and Comminges and sent an urgent appeal to Pedro for help. The Pope, in an attempt to satisfy Pedro, ordered that a council should be held at Lavaur, where the parties were to consider if any settlement were possible. Pedro attended the council which began on January 15, 1213, and requested the crusading party to restore to the counts the lands which had been taken from them. The assembled prelates declined to consider any proposal of the kind and Pedro therefore appealed to the Pope. His representatives were able to show that the crusade party were acting rather in their own interests than in furtherance of the Catholic faith ; clerics and laymen alike had seized livings and lands to which they had no shadow of claim. Innocent wrote a vigorous letter to De Montfort, accusing him of unnecessary aggression and suggesting that the time for pacific measures had come. Pedro also succeeded in inducing the King of France to stop the expected contingents of crusaders from setting out, on the ground that the Pope intended to enforce a peaceful settlement. But De Montfort's party hastened to Rome and told a very different tale ; the Pope, in perplexity, ordered both parties to suspend operations until he could send a trustworthy legate to examine the situation and deal justly with both sides. Pedro, relying on the fact that De Montfort would gain no reinforcements from France and convinced that his party was determined to ruin Raimon of Toulouse, while papal action might be indefinitely delayed, resolved upon war. By August 1213 he had reached Toulouse with a considerable army which included two thousand of the Aragonese and Catalan nobility. The nobles who upheld the cause of Toulouse were not roused to any great enthusiasm by the arrival of their Spanish ally. They doubtless suspected him of a design to secure the suzerainty of Southern France, but they were too far pledged to withdraw, and accordingly the allied force advanced upon Muret, a little town on the

Garonne, some three leagues from Toulouse which was held for De Montfort by a small garrison. A number of boats brought up munitions of war and supplies and were moored a short distance above the town. The numbers of the allied troops are far from certain; the lowest estimate of contemporary writers puts the infantry at 30,000, while the garrison of Muret is agreed to have consisted of no more than

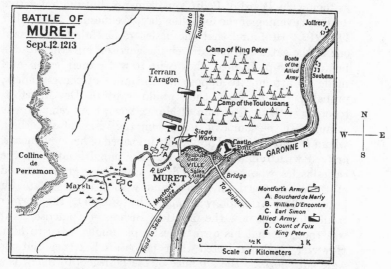

MAP 5. BATTLE OF MURET, SEPTEMBER 12, 1213

A full description of the battle is given by Oman, *The Art of War in the Middle Ages* (London, 1924), vol. i, p. 453 ff. His account is near to the truth as we are now likely to get and provides the best explanation of the discrepancies among the several narratives which he discusses.

some 700 men, ill-armed and badly provisioned. The crusading cavalry (the battle as usual at this period was a cavalry action) was barely 900 strong, while that of the allies must have amounted to 3000 at least.

The town of Muret lay in the angle formed by the confluence of the Louge with the Garonne, was surrounded by walls and was also protected by a bourg or citadel of considerable strength which lay at the apex of the angle formed by the two rivers. On the left bank of the Louge a plain extends northwards bounded by the Garonne on the east and by the rising ground of Perramon on the west; the central portion of this plain was marshy in winter, but covered with grass in summer; its character is still attested by its name, Les Pesquiès, the Marshes. On the north-east of the marsh rises a little stream which runs into the Garonne through a depression some thirty yards wide with steep banks. In this plain was fought the battle of Muret, the decisive conflict of the crusade. Pedro and his allies reached Muret on September 10; De Montfort had started in the same direction as soon as he heard of Pedro's movements, but did not arrive until the evening of the following day, Wednesday, September 11, 1213. He found that the besiegers had already secured one of the gates and had driven the garrison into the citadel, but as he approached they withdrew to their camp and made no attempt to oppose the entrance of the crusaders, probably hoping that they would capture De Montfort, together with the garrison of Muret, when they renewed the assault. In the course of the evening the Viscount of Corbeil, whom De Montfort had previously informed of his movements, arrived with reinforcements; but the papal legate and the ecclesiastics who accompanied the crusaders, grew alarmed at their numerical inferiority and wished to negotiate for peace. The attempt was made by Folquet, the former troubadour and now the fanatical Bishop of Toulouse, as it was thought that his own townspeople might listen to him. However, Pedro rejected their proposals and negotiations were cut short by the advance of the besiegers to renew the assault. De Montfort assembled his forces in the market-place of the town and after delivering a harangue, in which he especially urged them to charge in close order and to avoid single combats, led them out of the walls through the gate on the road to Sales. They then crossed the Louge and found themselves on the plain of Muret, facing the enemy. Raimon, who knew that the provisions of the besieged were exhausted, wished to continue the assault upon the west side of the town and if De Montfort should make a sortie, to await his attack in the fortified camp. Pedro, however, rejected this cautious proposal as unworthy of a knight and proposed to offer battle in the plain; he even changed armour with one of his knights that he might fight in the front rank, instead of directing operations at the head of the reserves. His confidence in the issue of the conflict was boundless.

De Montfort had divided his troops into three squadrons and the first of these began by charging the infantry and cavalry who were assaulting the town. Taken by surprise, the latter were scattered and fell back upon Pedro's army in the plain, upon which the same squadron immediately charged ; at the same time a second squadron rushed forward and crashed into Pedro's ranks almost simultaneously with the first. During this struggle Pedro was killed and his cavalry began to retreat ; De Montfort then led forward his remaining squadron against a body of troops which he could see on the enemy's left. From these he was separated by some marshy ground ; but a crossing was found and this movement decided the victory ; Pedro's forces were driven from the field in hopeless confusion. Meanwhile, Raimon's militia had turned to resume the assault upon the town. They had not been permitted or were unwilling to engage in open battle with the knights and presumed that their Spanish allies had been victorious. They were speedily undeceived. De Montfort's knights, returning from the pursuit, surprised and scattered them in all directions. Many were killed, some attempted to regain their camp, and the greater part fled to the ships which had brought up provisions and materials of war from Toulouse. The number of killed and wounded cannot be estimated ; the chroniclers assert that some fifteen or twenty thousand were killed when De Montfort's cavalry returned towards the town, a number impossibly large. Most of the Aragonese knights are said to have fallen ; among them was Huc or Hugo de Mataplana (a mountain castle near Ripoll) ; he was a troubadour himself, three of his compositions remain to us, and was perhaps even better known as a patron of poetry in his sumptuous court, where troubadours were welcomed and rewarded, as Raimon Vidal de Besalú describes in one of his versified *nouvelles*.

De Montfort's victory was entirely unexpected and the moral effect of it was immense. Not only had he defeated a far superior force, but one commanded by a king who had enhanced a great military reputation at the battle of Las Navas de Tolosa in the previous year ; such was his renown that the victors themselves were ready to ascribe their success to divine intervention. They were pious men, who had received absolution at the hands of Folquet and had gazed upon a fragment of the true Cross, exhibited by him before the battle ; the Aragonese had spent the night in debauchery and Pedro, according to his son's chronicle, was too sleepy in the morning to listen to the reading of the Gospel. The fact is, that De Montfort was the only leader who showed some glimmering of tactical ability ; he succeeded in attacking his enemy in detail, and was able to make his force charge home, disregarding the medieval habit of selecting an opponent for individual combat. His men were also inspired with religious enthusiasm and with the further knowledge that they were fighting with their backs to the wall ; there were no provisions in Muret and no chance of support if they were defeated. They had the advantage of fighting under an energetic and determined leader, whereas the counsels of their enemies were divided and some of them had no great faith in the disinterestedness of Pedro. By this victory the ultimate domination of the North over the South of France and the ultimate unification of the country was made possible ; the pretensions of Aragon were also ended ; in spite of the fact that the war dragged on for many years the kings of Aragon made no serious attempt to recover what they had lost ; their energies were fully occupied in other parts of the Mediterranean world.

CHAPTER VI

JAMES THE CONQUEROR

Childhood and accession. Struggles with the nobles. Conquest of the Balearic Islands. Conquest of Valencia. Policy in Southern France. The treaty of Corbeil. Wars with the Moors. Marriage of Pedro with Constance of Sicily. Death of James. His character and literary interests.

PEDRO II left as his heir his only son, James, whom he had entrusted to the keeping of De Montfort in 1211 as a guarantee of the promise that the boy should marry the Count's daughter when he came of age. There was no desire to dispute his succession, and the Aragonese at once took steps to release him from the custody of De Montfort ; a show of military intervention and the despatch of an embassy to Pope Innocent III were necessary to induce De Montfort to yield. James was handed over to the Aragonese representatives at Narbonne in 1214 when he was nearly six and a half years of age. He was given a splendid reception in Barcelona and Cortes were held at Lérida to provide for the government during his minority. Guillen de Montredo, the Master of the Temple in Spain and Provence, was appointed as tutor to the young King ; Count Sancho of Roussillon, a great-uncle of James, was made procurator-general of both states, and four subordinate governors were appointed, two for Aragon, one for Catalonia, and one for Montpellier. These arrangements were made by the papal legate in Languedoc, Pedro of Benevento ; their continuance was a matter of uncertainty. Sancho, the procurator-general, and Fernando one of the young King's uncles, were plotting to usurp the throne ; the Aragonese nobles were traditionally insubordinate and impatient of authority, characteristics which now became more than ever pronounced ; the extravagance of Pedro the Catholic had reduced the royal revenues to the verge of bankruptcy. James himself, with unusual precocity, seems to have felt that strong measures were required. In 1217 the loyal party enabled him to escape from the fortress of Monzon where Sancho kept him in practical captivity. Though only nine years of age, he was able to disown the regent and to gain the support of the towns and of a considerable number of the nobility ; that of the Church and of the Templars he already enjoyed. The gradual restoration of authority and order seems to have been largely the work of the Templars, and it was probably on the advice of such leaders among them as Ximeno Cornel and Guillen Moncada that a marriage was arranged between himself and Leonor, the daughter of Alfonso VIII of Castile, which was celebrated early in 1221 when James was little more than thirteen years of age.

For the next six years James was occupied in struggles with refractory nobles, who sometimes fought among themselves with unconcerned disregard of royal authority, or formed leagues in direct opposition to the crown. Guillem de Moncada, Pedro Ahones, Pedro Fernández of Azagra, Lord of Albarracín, were among the most troublesome of his opponents. James was twice held prisoner by such enemies, but presence of mind bordering upon effrontery enabled him to escape ; he also bore in mind the principle of policy which a later Castilian ruler affirmed, to keep on good terms with the towns and the Church. It was probably the towns which brought about the peace of Alcalá, when the rebels agreed on March 31, 1227, to give up a struggle of which all parties had become weary and the disastrous results of which were increased by a famine in the early part of the year. In the following year, however, James was involved in a war with Guerao de Cabrera, who had taken possession of the county of Urgel, an important province which occupied most of the north-west Catalan frontier and separated Barcelona from the northern districts of Aragon. The former Count, Armengol VIII, had died in 1208 leaving one child, a daughter Aurembiax ; her cousin, Guerao, claimed the succession on the ground that a female could not inherit. Her mother, Elvira, had applied to Pedro for protection, and had also married a second husband. On her death, in 1220, Guerao was able to overrun the county while James was occupied with the troubles of his minority. He appears to have bought Guerao out, under condition that Aurembiax might redeem her terri-

THE BALEARIC EXPEDITION 83

tory from himself, and in 1228 she appeared before the king at Lérida to claim her right. It is pretty clear that Aurembiax was one of the earliest of that impressive list of mistresses with whom James was associated. A kind of mock trial was staged ; Aurembiax undertook to hold the county in fief and to surrender Lérida to the Crown, while James was to restore the towns that the cousin had seized. Guerao was driven out and a husband was found for Aurembiax in Pedro of Portugal, who had been obliged to leave his country owing to family dissensions. The marriage took place in 1229 ; in 1231 Aurembiax died and Pedro was induced to cede the whole province to James, receiving the Balearic Islands in return ; these he later exchanged for certain towns in Valencia. Thus James gained possession of the county for a time. The Cabrera family renewed their attempts to recover it and the county was plunged in a series of troubles which were not finally settled until 1278.

James was well aware that an excellent means of restraining the unruly spirit of his nobles was to find them occupation elsewhere, and his thoughts turned to the Balearic Islands, on which his father had also had designs. Accusations of piracy and reprisals for it were of constant occurrence between the Balearic Moors and the Catalans, and an incident of this kind provided James with an excuse for action. The expedition was given a religious character and the Catalan clergy made generous contributions to the cost ; it was almost entirely Catalan in origin and character as the Aragonese declined to support it, and suggested another outlet for military enterprise. In 1229 James went to Lérida to meet the papal legate ; he wished to divorce Leonor and was allowed to do so by a council held by the legate at Tarazona ; Leonor was sent back to Castile, the separation being justified upon the usual excuse of consanguinity ; she was given many presents and James legitimized their son Alfonso and declared him heir to Aragon. In the course of this business the Aragonese nobles attempted to persuade him to invade Valencia instead of attacking the Balearic Islands. The King of Valencia, Zeid Abdurrahman, had been driven from his throne upon a charge of favouring Christians and arrived at James' court asking for help at that moment. James agreed that his Aragonese subjects might give Zeid assistance in return for the cession of certain districts, and the Valencian secured the support of Azagra and other nobles. But James was himself too far committed to the maritime expedition to withdraw and spent the next few months in preparation for it, eventually starting early in September 1229.

The expedition consisted of over 150 sail, including vessels from Genoa, Marseilles and Narbonne, and carrying a force which may have amounted to 1500 horse and 15,000 foot. The moment for the attack was opportune. The Almohade King, Abu Yahya, had received news of the impending attack, had raised a force to meet it and had also sent to Africa for help, but a palace conspiracy against him, led by his own uncle, was discovered almost at the moment when the Christian fleet was sighted. Under these circumstances a peace was patched up, and when the Christians landed on the Island of Dragonera, which lay across the bay of Palomera at the southern end of the north-west coast of the island, they found themselves confronted by a considerable force. A landing was forced at the harbour of Santa Ponza, some ten miles to the south-east, before the Moors could offer any serious opposition, but two days later a pitched battle took place with their main body; James defeated the Moors, though with the loss of several knights, among them Guillen and Ramon Moncada, two of his most valued helpers, and was then able to advance to the siege of Mallorca. This operation lasted for three months; overtures for capitulation were declined, and when the walls had been adequately breached, the town was stormed on the last day of 1229. Some 30,000 Moors are said to have escaped to the mountains, but nearly as many were massacred and the city was sacked. Several of the local Moorish chieftains had already made their submission during the siege, and one of them had provided James with a welcome supply of provisions. The task of reducing various scattered bodies of the enemy was then undertaken, the land and booty were divided and one Berenguer de Santa Eugenia was left in command of the island. James was then able to return to Tarragona in October 1230. The next two years were spent in negotiations with the old King Sancho of Navarre, who wanted help against his nephew, Theobald of Champagne, and in two further expeditions to the Balearic Islands, in the course of which

Menorca was captured and the islands completely subdued. Ibiza was captured in 1235 by expeditions from the larger islands.

James was thus able to turn his attention elsewhere, and to satisfy the ambitions of his Aragonese subjects who were anxious to advance upon Valencia. The Cid's conquest had been recovered by the Almorávides in 1102 ; when the Almohades overcame them, the province became an independent kingdom under Zeid, who had been driven out by Zaen and had attempted to enlist the help of the Aragonese. The beauty and fertility of the province, apart from other reasons, was enough to make it a most desirable possession ; the industry and ingenuity of the Moorish population, the remains of whose system of irrigation can be seen even to-day, had raised its productivity to the highest point, and the "garden" of Valencia was famous for its flax, rice, wine, oil and fruit of every kind. Zaen had provided James with an adequate excuse for invasion by the fact that he had raided Christian territory as far as Tortosa and had refused to pay outstanding instalments of tribute. One of the Aragonese nobles, Blasco de Alagon, relying upon the permission given by James before he had started upon his Balearic expedition, had attacked and captured Morella, an important frontier town and stronghold. James hastened to the spot and obliged Blasco to surrender the town to himself, though he allowed him to hold it as a fief. He then prepared for an invasion of Valencia in 1233 ; a papal bull was secured from Gregory IX, making the war a crusade ; money was voted by the Cortes both of Catalonia and Aragon,· and Zeid made over all his claims upon Valencia to James, who summoned his nobles to meet him in Teruel early in May. The response was not great, but James was able to overrun the northern part of the province and to capture Burriana, Peñíscola and other places. For the remainder of this and for most of the following year, James was occupied by affairs at home. Early in 1234 he was betrothed to Yolande or Violante, the daughter of Andrew II of Hungary and the granddaughter of Peter Courtenay, Count of Auxerre and Emperor of Constantinople ; the marriage took place in September. There were difficulties about the succession of Theobald Count of Champagne to the throne of Navarre and the Pope was obliged to intervene. A misunderstanding arose with France, apparently connected with the claims of James upon Carcassonne while his relations with Castile were not improved by his projected marriage with Violante ; there was also a dispute with Pons Cabrera concerning the possession of Urgel. These matters were all settled by the end of 1235 and James was free to continue his Valencian campaign.

He was already master of most of the country up to the Mijares but he required a base of operations nearer to Valencia itself and on the other side of the river ; for this purpose he selected the Puig de Cebolla, a height about twelve miles from Valencia and near the sea. The Moors had foreseen the strategical advantages of " Onion Hill " and had dismantled the fortress on its summit. James rebuilt the fort, left Entenza with a hundred knights in command and returned home to collect men and money for the final stroke. The Moors made a vigorous assault upon the Puig in the following year, but were beaten off with much loss ; James meanwhile found that enthusiasm for the invasion had died down ; but he set out for the Puig with such forces as he could collect. Entenza had died, the garrison was disheartened and the nobles of Ferdinand's party urged the abandonment of the undertaking on the ground of expense. James declined to listen to any proposals of the kind, swore that he would not return north until he had captured Valencia and sent for his queen and daughter whom he lodged in Burriana. By the middle of 1238 he was able to advance to Valencia itself and, when the prospect of a formal siege was opened, reinforcements came to him in large numbers ; the Archbishop of Narbonne sent 40 knights and 600 foot, and Henry III of England is also said to have sent a contingent. Valencia surrendered in September 1238, under an agreement which allowed Zaen and all who wished to follow him to leave the town with such articles as they could carry, their security being guaranteed for twenty days. Some 50,000 Moors are said to have thus evacuated Valencia, to the disgust of many in James' army who were anticipating a week of pillage and slaughter ; James, however, obliged his followers to observe the terms of the convention in full. The land was divided among the nobles after a good deal of wrangling, as James

had previously distributed more than there was to divide ;
arrangements were made for the government and protection
of the town, a cathedral was endowed and a bishop installed.
From this date until 1258 much of the King's attention
and energy was occupied by affairs in the South of France
and it will be convenient to summarize here the events which
ended his prospects of forming an empire extending from the
Maritime Alps to the southern border of Valencia. In 1229,
Raimon VII of Toulouse had been obliged to accept the Peace
of Paris, which practically reduced him to dependence upon
Louis VIII, to whom Amauri, the son of Simon de Montfort
had transferred rights and claims which he was himself too
weak to enforce. James was alarmed by the encroachments
of the French Crown and was ready to come to any arrangement with Raimon which might check the progress of Louis ;
a union of Toulouse and Provence seemed to be the best
beginning of this policy. Sancha, the wife of Raimon of
Toulouse, was James' aunt ; she had ceased to live with her
husband and had retired to Provence. The Count of Provence, Raimon Berenger, had a daughter also called Sancha.
James proposed that his aunt should be divorced from Raimon
of Toulouse who should then marry Sancha of Provence, with
the idea that any issue of this marriage would eventually
marry a member of his own family. James undertook to
secure the necessary papal dispensations, to pension the
divorced wife and to gain absolution for Raimon for his
share in the Albigensian wars. When these negotiations had
been brought to the point of performance, Pope Gregory
died and the papacy remained vacant for some eighteen
months, in the course of which Sancha of Provence married
Richard of Cornwall. In 1241, the Count of Toulouse joined
a number of southern lords in revolting against the French
rule ; exasperation with the cruelties of the Inquisitors was
the immediate cause of this movement. Hugo de Lusignan,
Count de la Marche and Henry III of England were the chief
leaders and were joined by Trencavel of Béziers, who had
been living in exile at the court of Aragon and now appeared
with a considerable force. The rebels overran the Narbonnais,
but were defeated by Louis at Taillebourg in July 1242.
Henry III had been drawn into the movement by his mother,
Isabella of Angoulême, who had married Hugo de la Marche ;

after the defeat, Henry returned to England in 1243 and took
no further action. Troubadour sirventes of the time couple
his name with that of the King of Aragon and there seems to
have been a general idea that the Capetian monarchy could
only be held in check by their alliance, and if troubadour
poetry can be considered to express popular opinion, there is
no doubt that general feeling was antagonistic to the Northern
French who were regarded as barbarians in comparison with
the cultured southerners. There is, however, no evidence to
show that James took any part in the revolt.

By 1244 the Count of Toulouse had made his peace with
Rome and his submission to Louis ; he then conceived the idea
of marrying Beatrice, the fourth daughter of Raimon Berenger
and heiress of Provence. Unfortunately her father died in
1245, at the moment when all obstacles seemed to have been
removed, the French Court intervened and induced the Pope
to refuse dispensation for the marriage and in the following
year Beatrice married Charles, the brother of St. Louis. Thus
another opportunity of uniting Provence and Toulouse was
wrecked and the hopes of preserving the independence of
the South were further diminished. In 1249 the Count of
Toulouse died and his son-in-law, Alphonse of Poitiers, seized
his possessions before James could intervene ; with this
event, the prospect of a united Southern France vanished
entirely, and it remained for James to press his personal
claims. This matter did not come to a head until 1255,
when James had occasion to assert his rights to Montpellier ;
the French crown put in a counter-claim to Barcelona and
its dependencies, a claim which went back to the days of
Charlemagne. A commission was appointed to consider the
question, which was not settled until 1258 when the treaty
of Corbeil was signed by which St. Louis renounced his claims
to the territory composing the former county of Barcelona,
while James abandoned his rights in the South of France ;
a contract was signed for a marriage between his daughter
Isabella and Philip, the second son of the King of France.
The treaty is noteworthy as it was based upon the principle
of natural frontiers as opposed to that of feudal claims.
James certainly retained the Roussillonais and the Cerdagne.
As they approach the Mediterranean the Pyrenees divide into
two ranges. The modern frontier lies along the crest of the

southernmost range, but in this treaty the northern line of the
Pyrenees (which is also, roughly, the linguistic frontier) was
adopted. Thus the general principle is clear, that Aragonese
influence north of the Pyrenees was to cease. It may be considered that James made a bad bargain ; the claim of France
to Barcelona, if historically correct, was in practice obsolete ;
whereas the claims of Aragon to parts of Southern France
had been repeatedly acknowledged in recent years and were
recognized by the countries concerned. But James was a
statesman of some penetration ; he realised that he had
difficulties enough to occupy the whole of his resources and his
attention in the Spanish peninsula, and that to waste his forces
and distract his energies in attempts to keep a footing in
France could only end in disaster. Spain would have been
more powerful and prosperous if later monarchs could have
realized this fact.

Home affairs had, in fact, prevented James from giving that
attention to France which the prosecution of any imperialist
scheme demanded. In 1247, at the Cortes of Huesca, he
promulgated his legal code, the Customs of Aragon, part of
his much-needed legislative work. He had already conquered
the whole province of Valencia as far as the borders of
Murcia in 1245 ; in 1247 a revolt broke out, and after crushing
it James proposed to guard against this danger by expelling
the Moorish population. This edict stirred the revolt to
fresh life and the nobles in occupation of Valencian estates
protested vigorously, using the arguments that reappear
when Philip II proposed the expulsion of the Moriscos ; they
and their Christian dependents could not hope to cultivate
the land as the Moors had done. A hundred thousand Moors
are said to have left the kingdom, but the eviction was not
thoroughly carried out ; some nobles seem to have secured
exemption and in 1610 there were about 200,000 Moors in
the province for Philip III to deal with.

The later years of James's reign were largely filled with
struggles against the refractory nobility, a trouble endemic
in the country. Of other events one of the most important,
in view of its future consequences, was the marriage between
his son Pedro and Costanza, the daughter of Manfred, King
of Sicily. As Manfred was at war with Charles of Anjou and
the papal party, the Pope naturally regarded this as a very

unholy alliance ; he urged St. Louis to break off the proposed match between his son Philip and James's daughter Isabella, and James could overcome the French King's scruples only by giving a definite undertaking not to help Manfred in his struggle with the papacy. The French marriage took place in July 1262 ; the alliance with Manfred had been celebrated about a month earlier at Montpellier. James appears to have been anxious to conciliate the Pope and made some show of starting upon a crusade, an undertaking which he resumed at a later date. In the same year he received an appeal for help from his son-in-law Alfonso of Castile. In 1260 the Moors of Andalucía had risen against the Castilians and had gained considerable successes ; in that year Alfonso had appealed to James, who gave his subjects permission to serve against the Moors, if they wished, on condition that their action did not disturb relations with the King of Tunis, upon whose goodwill an important part of Catalonian commerce depended. Alfonso resented the offer of help under such restrictions, but in 1262 he induced his queen, James's daughter, to plead again for help. There was no love lost between the two kings, but James thought well to help Castile, for the obvious reason that he would himself be next attacked, if the Moors were successful ; nor could he well desert his daughter and grandchildren. A frontier commission was appointed to settle the points in dispute between Aragon and Castile and James announced to the Cortes his intention of declaring war upon the Moors ; the nobles seized the opportunity to try and extort various concessions and privileges and it was not until 1265 that James was able to invade Murcia. Early in the following year the capital surrendered under an agreement which left the Moors in the enjoyment of their religion and laws, with part of the town as a Moorish quarter. A strong force was left in the country, which submitted without difficulty to the new rule.

Early in 1267 James received an invitation from the Khan of Tartary to undertake a crusade. It was a project which he had long entertained, and he had proposed it to Pope Clement IV while he was occupied with the campaign in Murcia ; the Pope informed him that he was too scandalous a character to offer himself as a crusader. Alfonso, his son-in-law, tried to dissuade him, but to no purpose. James made peace with the Moorish King of Granada, went round various parts of his dominions collecting funds, arranged for the conduct of the government during his absence and concentrated a considerable fleet at Barcelona; he set sail in September 1269. James never went to sea without meeting a storm and on this occasion was driven into Aigues Mortes; he then gave up the attempt and returned to Spain by way of Montpellier, "por l'amor de sa dame Berenguiere," according to the continuator of the *Chronicle* of William of Tyre; but the reason for his return has not been satisfactorily explained; part of the fleet reached Acre and there seems to have been no material reason why James should not have gone after it. When his sons Pedro Fernández and Fernán Sánchez, who were in command of this part of the fleet, found that no one at Acre was prepared to give them any assistance, they returned home, touching at Sicily on the way, where Fernán Sánchez was knighted by Charles of Anjou. Pedro was the son-in-law of Manfred, the enemy of Charles, and the result was a bitter quarrel between the two brothers, which was not composed until 1273. James was also involved in further disputes with the Catalan nobles who were stirred up by Fernán; a serious revolt followed, which was not ended until Pedro captured Fernán and killed him, an action which apparently met with his father's approval.

No sooner had the revolt of the nobles been quelled than James was confronted with a series of Moorish aggressions. The King of Morocco, Ibn Yusuff, invaded Andalucía early in 1275, in spite of the fact that he had concluded a treaty with James in the previous year and knew that James was on terms of alliance with Alfonso. Alfonso was absent from the country as he was a candidate for the imperial throne, and in his absence the Castilian forces suffered a series of defeats. James sent a contingent to their aid, but in the following year he had himself to deal with a serious revolt of the Moors in the district of Alicante; they were helped by bands of invaders from overseas and the revolt spread to Xátiva. While James was preparing to attack the rebels, he was taken ill and died at Valencia on July 27, 1276, at the age of sixty-nine, after a reign of sixty-three years.

Upon James and his work historians have passed the most varied judgments; he has been eulogized as the pattern of

chivalry; he has been condemned as an illiterate and
licentious barbarian. Yet there is no doubt that he was the
great figure and mark of his age. His personal character displayed great defects, even when judged by the moral standards
of his own time; the list of his illegitimate children is sufficient to explain why his amours became the scandal of
Christendom; his infatuation for his queen Violante allowed
her to exert a disastrous influence upon his policy, as in the
partition of his kingdom by his will; his occasional outbursts of devastating anger led him into excesses which
were difficult to excuse; the story that he ordered the Bishop
of Gerona's tongue to be torn out for revealing to the Pope a
secret of the confessional seems to be well founded. There
was also a certain strain of hypocrisy in his character, a strain
which was not uncommon in men of his period. He considered that his championship of the Church should condone
his shortcomings in morality and that he might excuse or
explain acts of cruelty by regarding himself as the instrument
of Divine vengeance. A pattern of chivalry he certainly was
not; for chivalry implies above all things an unselfish
readiness to serve, and with James his own interests and
desires were usually the first consideration. Yet with these
defects, and, perhaps, in part because of them, he was an
attractive human character. Tall above the average and
powerfully built, expert in all bodily exercises of peace and
war, he seems to have been able to exert that personal
magnetism upon invididuals which is one of the attributes
of leadership. Like other great men, he was interested in
detail as well as in principle; the man with a grievance could
always feel that his affairs were of absorbing interest to the
King, whether he secured redress or not, with the result that
James was undoubtedly popular; "nunqua rey era tant
amat per son poble com aquest."

James was a great legislator and a great administrator.
These qualities were strained to the uttermost by the task of
reducing a turbulent and selfish aristocracy to some kind of
obedience and preserving unity between two proud and
independent nationalities. His struggles with his nobles
continued intermittently throughout his reign; yet if the
condition of affairs at the time of his accession be considered,
it will seem unlikely that another ruler would have been

any more successful in restraining feudal separatism. Loyalty, patriotism and unselfishness are qualities not acquired in a day ; James could do little more than provide an occupation for his restless nobility by his attacks upon the Moors, and check their opposition by supporting the Church and the towns. His foreign policy is said to have been a failure ; it is true that Aragon had the chance of forming a great southern empire under her rule and that James realized this possibility ; but when the chance had gone through no fault of his, he was sensible enough to realize that natural and not political frontiers were the true limits of nationality and that a consolidated kingdom was likely to be more powerful than a loosely-knit empire of states in varied degrees of dependence.

James was a patron of letters and has derived no small reputation in this respect from the *Chronicle* which bears his name. Whether he wrote this book himself is doubtful ; some have denied that he could write at all, as his signature has not been found upon any document of the period ; but in any case, it is likely that he would have dictated the book to one of his scribes. James was not the kind of man to keep a private diary with any sort of regularity, and many of the inaccuracies and inconsistencies in the narrative are best explained by assuming that it was written or dictated some time later than the events which it describes. Traces have been found in it and in Desclot's chronicle of a poem in deca- syllabic verse on the conquest of Mallorca, James's own exploit. While it cannot be regarded as reliable history, it remains a very readable narrative, informed by an artless sim- plicity and a vigorous straightforward style which suggest a definite personal authorship ; and there is no sufficient reason for denying that James was that person, nor for refusing to him the honourable position of the first of the Catalan prose writers. His Book of Wisdom (*Libre de la Saviesa*) is an anthology of maxims and proverbs from various writers, ranging from Solomon down to Albertus Magnus and the Arab moralists ; many were taken from the *Apophthegmata Philosophorum* of the learned Honein ben Ishak (809–873), of which a Hebrew translation was made in the thirteenth century ; from this James derived his selections through one of his interpreters, Jehuda, who made other translations into Catalan at the King's orders. There is no evidence that

James wrote in verse, though he could appreciate troubadour
poetry, to the influence of which Catalan poets were entirely
subject.　The Albigensian persecution had driven troubadours
into other lands, and the court of Aragon had been hospitable
to them of old ; Alfonso II was a composer himself and was
known in consequence as *El Trobador*.　Peire Cardenal, the
famous satirist of the Roman Catholic Church, retired to
Aragon when the cause of Toulouse was lost ; Aimeric de
Belenoi ended his life in Catalonia.　Of the native poets of
the time, the best known to us are Serveri de Gerona and
Guillem de Bergedan ; Arnaud Catalan, Hugo de Mataplana
who fell at Muret, and Guillem de Cervera were also in repute.
James, no doubt, was obliged to be cautious in this matter ;
he did not wish to offend the Church and he could not entirely
disregard the representations of Ramon de Penyafort, his
confessor and a prominent Dominican, who regarded troubadours and their activities as the prime cause of heresy.　He
persuaded James to introduce the Inquisition into Aragon
and in 1233 to prohibit the circulation of any romance
translation of the Scriptures in his dominions.　Certainly
before that date James was renowned as a patron of poetry ;
an eloquent tribute to him appears at the outset of the epic
poem *Jaufre*, which was written between 1225 and 1228 ;
the author says that he heard the story told—

> En la cort del plus honrat rei,
> Que anc fus de neguna lei.
> Cho fon lo bon rei d'Aragon
> Paire de pretz e filltz de don
> E seiner de bonaventura,
> Umils e de leial natura,
> Qu'el ama Deu e tem e cre
> E manten lealtat e fe,
> Patz e justicia ; per que Deus
> L'ama ; car si ten ab los sieus,
> Qu'el es sos noveltz cavaliers
> E de sos enemies guerriers.
> Anc Deus non trobet en el faillia,
> Aintz fon la primeira batailla
> Per el facha, e a vencutz
> Cels, per que Deus es mescresutz ;
> Per que Deus l'a d'aitant honrat,
> Que sobre totz l'a essauzat
> De pretz e de natural sen,
> De gaillart cor e d'ardimen.

Anc en tan jove coronat
Non ac tan bon aib ajustat ;
Qu'el dona grantz dons volontiers
A joglars e a chavaliers ;
Per que venon en sa cort tut
Acels, que per pros son tengut.

—" in the court of the most honoured king that ever was of any king. This was the good King of Aragon, father of worth, son of liberality and lord of happiness, of kindly and loyal nature who loves, fears and believes in God and maintains loyalty and faith, peace and justice ; wherefore God loves him for such is his conduct with his subjects that he is God's foremost knight and the warrior against His enemies. Never did God find in him defect ; indeed the chiefest of battles was wrought by him and he has conquered those by whom God was scorned. Wherefore God has honoured him, to exalt him above all in worth and native sense, gallantry and bravery. Never upon any young crowned king were so many virtues shed ; for he readily gives great gifts to jongleurs and to knights, so that all those come to his court who are accounted good." This is in pleasing contrast with the virulent lampoons directed against James by Bernard de Rovenhac and other troubadours who were dissatisfied with his policy in the struggle between Northern and Southern France. Giraut Riquier, " the last of the troubadours," was in Catalonia in 1270 and wrote a cheerful *retroencha* in praise of the country and its inhabitants ; he had suffered disappointments at Narbonne ; his lady would show him no favour ; he would therefore go to Catalonia—

Quar dompneys, pretz e valors,
Joys e gratz e cortesia,
Sens e sabers et honors;
Bels parlars, bella paria,
E largueza et amors,
Conoyssensa e cundia
Troban manten e secors
En Cataluenha a tria,
Entre.ls Catalas valens
E las donas avirens.

—" For courtesy, valour and worth, joy, favour, courtliness, sense, learning and honour, fair speaking, fair fellowship,

liberality and love, knowledge and refinement, these find
abundant support and protection among the valiant Catalonians and their charming women." It was not the first
time that troubadours had praised the land and its people.
Bertran de Born praises his lady by comparing her with a
Catalan : " E de solatz mi semblet Catalana." Raimon
de Miraval speaks of a journey " entre.ls Catalas joyos."

James, as has been said, made Catalan the official language
of his kingdom ; in this tongue was written the great legal
compilation formed during his reign, the famous *Libre del
Consulat de Mar*, a collection of maritime laws and customs.
The *Chronicle* of Ramon Muntaner and the voluminous
writings of Ramon Lull are evidence of the impulse given to
the development of prose composition, but these writers
really belong to the next generation. James, in pursuance of
this policy, was naturally prepared to support education ; the
University of Montpellier owed much of its development to
his support ; he founded a *studium* in Valencia in 1245 and
secured privileges for it from Pope Innocent IV ; but little
is known of this foundation. Nor were architecture and art
neglected ; the cathedral of Lérida was built and consecrated
during his reign. Though now out of use as a cathedral,
the building shows that the transition from Romanesque to
Gothic was not yet accomplished and that the influence of
the Moors upon this kind of architecture was inappreciable.

The death of James marks the end of a period. With the
next reign begins a new epoch both of domestic and foreign
policy. In the course of the struggles with the nobility, a
regular constitution had been developed in its main out-
lines. Within Spain itself the limits of expansion had been
reached, and the wars against the Moors had attained their
purpose. The connection with Sicily brought Aragon into
the world of European politics, and her influence in the
Mediterranean became of increasing importance.

CHAPTER VII

PEDRO III

His accession. Disaffection of the nobility. Relations with Castile. Inter-
vention in Sicily. Guelfs and Ghibellines. Charles of Anjou, Manfred
and Conradin. The Sicilian Vespers. Pedro's preparations. John of
Procida. Pedro invades Sicily. Charles challenges him to combat.
Action of the Pope. Pedro's difficulties in Aragon. French invasion of
Catalonia. Pedro's victory and death.

JAMES had divided his territories in his will, leaving
Aragon, Catalonia and Valencia to Pedro, the Balearic
Islands, Roussillon and Montpellier to James. Pedro
was now forty years of age and had obtained a good deal of
military experience during his father's wars with the Moors.
His first act was to arrange for his coronation at Zaragoza in
November 1276 ; he and his wife Constance received the
crown from the hand of the Archbishop of Tarragona, but
at the same time he reversed the obligation of vassalage to
the papacy undertaken by his grandfather Pedro II, and made
a solemn declaration before the nobles that he did not receive
the crown from the Roman Church to which he acknowledged
no feudal obligation. His son Alfonso, then aged five, was
acknowledged as his heir by the assembled estates of the
realm, and after distributing presents and honours to the
nobles, Pedro returned to Valencia to conclude the war which
had been interrupted by his father's death. By September of
the following year he had driven the enemy out of their
strongholds into Montesa, where they surrendered and the
pacification seems to have been complete.

Meanwhile, a serious revolt had been begun in Catalonia
by certain disaffected nobles led by the Viscount of Cardona
and the Counts of Foix, Pallas and Urgel. Pedro had made
himself unpopular with the nobility by previous acts of
severity ; the excuse for revolt upon this occasion was the
fact that he had omitted to summon the estates of Catalonia

7   97

upon his coronation and to confirm their privileges. The
succession to the county of Urgel was also in dispute. The
manner in which James the Conqueror had gained partial
possession of the county has been already related. The
claims of Guerao, whom James had dispossessed in favour of
Pedro of Portugal, were revived by Guerao's son, Pons, who
could count upon the support of any noble at variance
with James and succeeded in recovering a number of towns.
In 1236 it was agreed that James should keep Lérida and
Pons should retain what he already held, both rulers holding
the. title of count, an arrangement which lasted until the
death of Pons in 1243. He was succeeded by his son Álvaro,
aged four, who was betrothed to Costanza the daughter of
Pedro Moncada of Béarn, in 1255, the bride being aged ten
and the bridegroom fourteen. The marriage was not con-
summated, the children disliked one another, and in 1256
Álvaro married Cecilia, a daughter of the Count of Foix.
The result was a quarrel between the Moncada and Foix
families. An action for divorce was referred to the ecclesiastical authorities, while James the Conqueror made a further
attempt to get possession of the whole province. Successive
ecclesiastical courts ended by crediting Álvaro with two wives,
and his death in 1268 left the county at the mercy of two
opposed factions. Álvaro's eldest son, Armengol, made
repeated attempts to recover his patrimony, some parts
of which were in pawn with the King, while others were held
by the Count of Cardona ; eventually, in 1278, Armengol
regained possession of the county on condition of holding it
as a fief from Pedro III. Few more dismal examples of the
results produced by feudal separatism and ecclesiastical
muddling can be found in the records of the Middle Ages.

When this matter had been settled, the King attacked the
refractory nobles in 1280 with an army drawn from the
towns, drove them into Balaguer, a stronghold in Urgel, and
obliged them to surrender after a month's siege. The leaders
were imprisoned in Lérida, but were released in the following
year on giving guarantees of future loyalty, with the exception
of the Count of Foix who was not released until 1284. About
this time the King's brother, James, signed a declaration
that he held his states in fief from Pedro whose authority was
to be binding upon him and his successors. The connection

between the Balearic Islands and the Aragonese kingdom was thus reaffirmed. The subjects of James were displeased with his action and he himself asserted at a later date that he had signed under compulsion. Pedro continued friendly relations with Castile and Portugal ; he arranged a marriage between the Infanta Isabel of Aragon and King Diniz of Portugal ; in the quarrels concerning the succession to the Castilian throne, his reception of the Infantes de la Cerda, the grandsons of Alfonso X and the direct heirs to the throne, when they took refuge in Aragon with Pedro's sister Violante and her daughter-in-law, their mother Blanche, sister of Philip III of France, led to no immediate breach with Castile.

The chief event of Pedro's reign is his intervention in Sicily and consequently in the struggles between the Papacy and the Empire, for the comprehension of which a brief reference to the political situation is necessary. On the death of Lothair II, Emperor and King of the Romans in 1137, two candidates appeared for the Imperial Crown, Conrad of Hohenstauffen, Duke of Swabia, and Henry the Proud, Duke of Bavaria ; the family of Conrad was known by the name of Waiblingen, from one of their estates in the diocese of Augsburg ; the house of Bavaria had had many princes of the name of Wölf, which thus became a regular appellation. These names were italianized as Ghibellino and Guelfo, and became the titles of the opposed factions during the struggles between the Empire and the papacy during the twelfth and thirteenth centuries. In general, the Ghibellines were for the Emperor and the Guelfs for the Pope ; the Ghibellines were supporters of authority and of a universal empire of which Italy was to be the head, whereas the Guelfs stood for liberty, self-government and the principle of nationality. The struggle was, or professed to be, one between a temporal and a spiritual power, but the Popes claimed temporal hegemony in the Italian peninsula and attempted to secure it by calling in the help of foreign princes. In the latter half of the thirteenth century the distinction between the parties was by no means so clearly cut as the above description might seem to imply ; the watchword of one generation often becomes the catchword of the next, and Guelf and Ghibelline became mere party cries, confused

with memories of ancestral feuds and inherited hatreds,
labels for the leaders of bloodthirsty vendettas. In the
North of Italy the formation of leagues enabled the great
towns to maintain a certain independence ; in the South,
Naples and Sicily remained under the dominion of the
Stauffen. After the death of the Emperor Frederick II in
1250, Manfred his natural son was appointed by his will to
govern the province on behalf of his legitimate son Conrad,
who was to remain in Germany. Pope Urban IV, a Frenchman of humble birth, who succeeded to the papacy in 1261,
strove to revive the Guelf party and opposed Manfred by
every means in his power. As has been seen, he was unable to
prevent the marriage of Manfred's daughter Constance with
Pedro of Aragon, a union which might be regarded as counter-
balancing that of Beatrice, the Countess of Provence, with
Charles of Anjou, the brother of St. Louis, to whom the Pope
proceeded to offer the crown of Naples.

Charles was to turn out the German power and to hold the
kingdom as the Pope's vassal. Charles was certainly the
ablest and probably the most unscrupulous of the sons of
Louis VIII. In Provence he had succeeded in establishing
Northern methods of government and Northern ideals of life.
The feudal nobles lost their independence and the cities their
muncipal franchises ; the prelates of the Church ceased to be
temporal sovereigns and the troubadours migrated to other
countries. But Charles provided justice and settled government ; the towns found that their commercial interests were
considered and the country gradually became reconciled to
the new régime. His wife Beatrice, the daughter of Berenguer
IV of Provence, in whose right he held the county, was no
less ambitious than himself, and at the time when the Pope
called him to Naples, Charles might consider himself at least
as powerful as most of the reigning sovereigns of Europe.
Urban IV died as Charles was about to march into Italy, but
his successor, Clement IV, was no less ready to support the
French, being by birth a Provençal from Narbonne, and gave
the invasion the character of a crusade. Manfred was completely defeated at Benevento on February 26, 1266, and was
himself killed, while his wife and children were thrown into
prison ; Constance of Aragon was the only member of the
family left at liberty.

Conradin, the grandson of the Emperor Frederic II, inherited his father's claim to the kingdom of Naples, a claim which Manfred had never denied, though he had shown no inclination to retire in Conradin's favour. This young man was now persuaded by the Ghibelline party to attack Charles the usurper. His cousin, Frederick of Austria, was prepared to join him in the adventure. Conradin was defeated by Charles at Tagliacozzo in August 1268, and was captured with Frederick by one of the Frangipani, as he was trying to escape to Sicily. Charles beheaded both of them after a form of trial as rebels against himself, and as Pedro of Aragon was, through his wife Constance, the only possible claimant to the throne, and the last hope of the Ghibelline party, it appeared that Charles might now enjoy his new possession in peace. His position was to some extent dependent upon the sympathies and the policy of the Pope for the time being ; his supporter, Clement IV, died a month after the execution of Conradin and a successor, Gregory X, was not elected until 1271. This pontiff was anxious to recover the Holy Land and for this purpose to keep peace between the various powers of Europe ; he died in 1276, at the moment when he had prepared the way for a united crusade against the infidels, and after a rapid succession of three popes within a year, Nicholas III was elected in 1277. His policy was that of Gregory X and Charles found that any projects of self-aggrandisement were impossible. On the death of Nicholas, Charles worked the papal election in his own interests and secured the elevation of a Frenchman, Simon de Brie, who took the title of Martin IV. Charles kept the new Pope under his own supervision at Viterbo, and was able to make himself the predominant power in the Italian peninsula. He was then preparing to attack Constantinople, when the outbreak occurred which is known as the Sicilian Vespers.

James the Conqueror had been in receipt of an annual tribute from El Mostansir, the Moorish King of Tunis. When Mostansir died, one of his sons seized the throne and denounced the treaty with Aragon, and Pedro proceeded to secure a footing in Northern Africa. He sent an expedition in 1280, under the command of a Sicilian, Conrado de Llansa, and established what amounted to an Aragonese protectorate over Tunis. In 1281, Pedro prepared to extend his influence yet further upon the coast of Africa, and gathered a fleet of 140 ships and an army of 15,000 men at the mouth of the Ebro. The King of France was not unnaturally alarmed by these extensive preparations and sent ambassadors to inquire into Pedro's intentions; they were informed that the expedition was destined to proceed to Constantine, the Governor of which had asked the King of Aragon to help him against the King of Tunis. A landing was made in 1282 at the town of Alcoyll, where the Aragonese troops fortified themselves and began some desultory operations against the natives. Then came an embassy from the Sicilians who had revolted against Charles of Anjou. On Easter Monday, March 30, 1282, as people were streaming out of Palermo to Monreale to hear vespers in the monastery church, a French soldier insulted a girl under pretence of searching for concealed weapons. A shout was raised, " Muoiano i Francesi," the soldiers on the spot were killed and the population, exasperated by years of brutality and insolence, began a massacre of the French which continued for twenty-four hours and is said to have cost the lives of four thousand victims.

Pedro accepted the invitation of the Sicilians. He was within easy reach of the island, at the head of a powerful and well-equipped force, and it is difficult to believe that his presence in North Africa at that particular moment was the result of mere coincidence. Fugitives from Sicily had constantly appeared in Aragon; the leader of the previous expedition to Tunis had been a Sicilian; and these arrivals were so many reminders of his wife's claim to the crown and of his own duty in the matter. There was the prospect of gaining a kingdom which would compensate Aragon for what she had lost in the South of France; in command of Sicily and with a footing on the African coast, Aragon would dominate the western part of the Mediterranean. Doubts have been thrown upon those narratives which relate the activities of the secret service agent, John of Procida, but the story has no inherent impossibility. John of Procida was the physician, the friend and counsellor of both Manfred and Conradin; after the defeat of Tagliacozzo, he escaped to Aragon and devoted himself to the task of overthrowing

Charles and of establishing the rights of Manfred's daughter. He visited Sicily, found the island seething with discontent and urged the leaders to await the suitable moment which he would prepare. He went to Constantinople and warned the Emperor Palæologus of the designs of Charles, and promised that a diversion would be made by Aragon, if an adequate subsidy were forthcoming. The Greek Emperor was unwilling to act without the approval of Pope Nicholas III, which John succeeded in obtaining ; Nicholas viewed the ambitions of Charles with some alarm and was not averse to a project which might increase the power of the papacy. John of Procida had completed these negotiations and returned to Barcelona, when Nicholas died ; his successor, Martin IV, was the creature of Charles. But the work had been done, Palæologus provided funds and the carefully planned scheme was brought to fruition. Pedro must have realized that his enterprise involved a breach both with France and with the papacy, but he seems to have thought it worth while to run this risk, after discussing the matter carefully with his councillors.

Amid the general enthusiasm of the Sicilians he landed at Trapani on August 30, 1282 ; at Palermo he received the homage of the Sicilians and confirmed their laws and privileges. He sent a force to relieve Messina, which Charles was besieging and obliged him to evacuate the island by the end of October. The Pope excommunicated the invaders, but the fulminations of the Church did not help Charles, who had lost command of the coast of Calabria by February 1283. Charles then, in full medieval style, sent Pedro a letter by the hand of two Dominican monks, accusing him of treachery to God and the Church and challenging him to decide the issue by single combat. Pedro, a powerful and expert warrior, readily accepted the challenge and Charles went to France to make arrangements for the event, after the Pope had vainly tried to dissuade him from leaving Italy at such a critical moment. Six knights were chosen by either side to determine the time and place of the combat which was fixed at Bordeaux for June 1, 1283, when each king was to appear attended by a hundred knights ; it was hoped that Edward I of England would act as umpire, but in obedience to the papal prohibition, he declined any participation in the business. Pedro explained the situation to the authorities at Messina, left John of Procida in charge of administrative matters, while the conduct of the war in Calabria was entrusted to the famous admiral, Roger de Lauria, and returned to Aragon on his way to Bordeaux. He then heard that Charles had no intention of meeting him in open combat but had prepared an ambush to capture him and his following. In order not to break his word, he entered Bordeaux in disguise, revealed himself to the seneschal of Guienne, under whose direction the combat was to be held, and returned in safety to Aragon, evading the French pursuers who had heard of his movements. Here considerable difficulties awaited him. On November 18, 1282, the Pope had declared him to be deprived of his kingdom, had relieved his subjects of their oath of fidelity and had conferred his possessions upon Charles of Valois, the third son of Philip III of France, who was now preparing to invade Aragon with an expedition to which the Pope had given the character of a crusade. Pedro found his subjects in a state of dissatisfaction and anxiety; it was unjust that a papal interdict should be laid upon a country which had always been foremost in the struggle against the Moors; as France was in possession of Navarre, there was every prospect of an invasion from more than one point; and this, while the possession of Sicily was by no means assured. The nobles considered that their advice should have been sought before the enterprise had been begun, and the additional taxation rendered necessary by the cost of the war aroused much discontent among the people at large. Stormy meetings with the estates of the realm took place at Tarragona and Zaragoza; a formidable combination of nobles, with the support of some municipalities, threatened revolt, and formed a " Union " with an armed force of its own. Pedro was obliged to recognize this body and to grant a number of concessions, known as the *Privilegio General*, which defined the immunities and privileges of nobles and municipalities. His successor, Alfonso III, was driven further upon the same path and forced to recognize that the nobles had a constitutional right to form a union and that the Cortes might even depose the King, if he failed to fulfil his obligations. The inevitable struggle was fought out by Pedro IV, as will be seen hereafter. In October 1283, Pedro

DEFEAT AND DEATH OF CHARLES 105

was able to go to Catalonia and take measures for placing his country in some posture of defence against a French invasion.

This task was considerably lightened by the success with which Roger de Lauria had conducted the war in Sicily. On leaving Bordeaux, Charles of Anjou had collected a fleet in Provence and had sent a squadron of it in advance to Naples. This was intercepted by Lauria and destroyed off the island of Malta, which he also captured from the French. By plundering the neighbouring coast-line, he then induced the son of Charles, the Prince of Salerno, to leave Naples with every available ship and attack him in the open sea ; Lauria again won a complete victory and returned in triumph to Messina with the Prince of Salerno, Charles the Lame, and other important persons as his prisoners, and forty-two captured vessels. It is possible that an attack upon Naples might have been successful at that time ; a series of disturbances broke out which were suppressed only by the timely arrival of Charles with reinforcements. Pedro was able to strengthen Lauria's forces and Charles was prevented by the insecurity of his position in Italy from undertaking a campaign against him. The Angevin's defeats and the loss of his son are said to have preyed upon his mind and in January 1285 he died, leaving the Italian war without a leader. Shortly afterwards the French began their invasion of Catalonia, perhaps the most unjust, unnecessary and calamitous enterprise ever undertaken by the Capetian monarchy.

Meanwhile, Pedro had been occupied in securing his frontiers. He had first to deal with a Castilian noble, Juan Núñez de Lara, who held through his wife the stronghold of Albarracín within the territory of Aragon, and had been stirred to revolt by French influence. Expecting that Pedro would be unable to leave Catalonia, he had made no special provision for the defence of the town and when the King of Aragon suddenly appeared before it with a considerable force, the place was obliged to surrender. Pedro then renewed his alliance with Sancho of Castile and attacked Tudela, for the purpose of strengthening his position on the side of Navarre, but the approach of winter obliged him to abandon the attempt. As the domestic dissensions of the country were by no means abated, he summoned the estates of the realm to Zaragoza early in 1285, to try and secure some unity in the face of the imminent danger. His concessions were met with fresh demands, and at length he was obliged to tell nobles and citizens that the moment when a great and formidable army was threatening their very existence was no time to be squabbling about constitutional privileges, that these questions must await a more suitable moment and they must support him as loyal subjects against the common enemy. He then went to Barcelona, where he suppressed a revolt among the lower orders by hanging their leaders, and prepared to meet the French, who had now finished their concentration. Few more formidable armies had been seen in France. A fleet of 100 ships was ready in the southern ports, large supplies had been accumulated in the chief towns near the Pyrenees and a force of 16,000 knights, 17,000 crossbow men and 100,000 infantry was ready to take the field. The Aragonese nobles declined to help and some of them even opened communications with the enemy ; Pedro was obliged to rely chiefly upon the Catalans. His brother James, the King of Roussillon and the Balearic Islands, had recognised the supremacy of the French King over Montpellier as early as 1283 and now granted him a free passage through his lands. Pedro, however, suddenly appeared before Perpignan and captured James and his family in the castle of the town. He asked his brother to surrender the frontier strongholds for purposes of defence, promising to return them when the danger had passed. James, however, suspecting some further design, abandoned his family and fled ; Pedro therefore carried the wife and children into Catalonia, left the defence of the Navarrese frontier to the local forces and himself undertook responsibility for the passes into Catalonia. The advancing French captured and plundered Elne on May 27, but were held up at the Col des Panissars (now superseded by the Col de Pertus to the east of it), where the Catalonians harassed them considerably. Eventually a knight provided by King James betrayed the fact that there was another passage ; this was insufficiently guarded and the invaders were able to advance into Catalonia in the month of June. Pedro retreated, ravaging the country as he went, to Gerona, the defence of which was undertaken by the Viscount of Cardona, during the siege which began on June 21. At the same time, the French fleet appeared off the Catalan coast to provision the army and take possession of the harbours. The Catalan fleet was still in Sicilian waters, but Barcelona was able to man eleven ships with which the Admiral Ramon Marquet defeated a squadron of twenty-four French vessels. The garrison of Gerona offered a desperate resistance ; the besiegers were constantly harassed by guerilla bands which cut their communications, and the numbers of men and horses crowded round the town engendered an epidemic which inflicted severe losses. The garrison suffered from the same cause, and when their walls had been battered down by the engines of the besiegers, agreed to surrender with the honours of war at the end of August. They had, however, gained the necessary respite for the country. In September the invincible Roger de Lauria suddenly appeared off the Bay of Rosas, where the French fleet was concentrated ; he had called at Barcelona, picked up such reinforcements as were there and attacked the French without delay. By the end of the day the French fleet was destroyed and the supply and treasure ships were in Lauria's possession. This disaster ended the invasion ; the King of France had himself been attacked by the prevailing epidemic and at once ordered a general retreat. Pedro had now persuaded the Aragonese to support him effectively, proposed to hamper the retreat of the French as much as possible, and reoccupied the Col des Panissars. The French left a garrison in Gerona, abandoned most of their baggage and plunder and struggled across the frontier with heavy losses. In October King Philip III died in Perpignan and the garrison left in Gerona was forced to surrender. Pedro then determined to punish his treacherous brother and equipped a fleet for a descent upon the Balearic Islands ; at this moment he fell ill and entrusted the expedition to his eldest son Alfonso. Feeling that death was near, he summoned the Archbishop of Tarragona with other prelates and nobles and declared that he had attacked Sicily merely to defend the rights of his family and with no hostile feelings to the Church ; when he had declared his readiness to submit to the ruling of the Church, he was given absolution, and his declaration was naturally interpreted as a statement that he would return Sicily to the Pope. He died on November 2, 1285.

Pedro III was known as the Great, and the title was not ill-deserved : in the words of his contemporary Dante, " d'ogni valor portò cinta la corda." Like his father, he was a man of great stature and strength, expert in all knightly exercises and probably more than a match for Charles of Anjou in single combat ; he was also a clever and cautious ruler who could wait for his opportunity and display patience under difficulties. To have defeated Charles of Anjou, the French kingdom and the Roman Catholic Church at a time when his own realms were far from united is no small title to fame. By his will his eldest son Alfonso became his heir, to be followed, should he be without issue, by his second son James, who received the kingdom of Sicily, to be followed in the succession, failing issue, by the remaining son, Fadrique or Frederick.

CHAPTER VIII

SOCIAL AND CONSTITUTIONAL ORGANIZATION

Grades of nobility. The clergy. Relations with the Papacy. Heresy and the Inquisition. The middle classes. Moors and Jews. Municipal government. The Cortes. Powers of the Crown. The Justicia. Military organisation. Revenues. Agriculture, industry and commerce.

REPEATED reference has been made to the struggles of the Crown with the nobility, struggles which occupied much of the next reign, that of Alfonso III. The constitutions of both Aragon and Catalonia had by this time assumed settled forms, some description of which is necessary, if the nature of the differences between Crown and nobility is to be understood.

Feudalism and the social distinctions which it implied were especially tenacious in Aragon. Four grades of nobility were eventually recognized. The first were the *ricoshombres de natura*, who regarded themselves as descended from the original conquerors of the county of Aragon, and were possibly in origin vassals holding lands in the Spanish mark directly from the Frankish King. Such was their relation to the Crown in historical times : the statement that their number was limited to nine contains no more truth than the fact that they strongly objected to an addition to their order made by James I. They received lands from the King on life tenure in return for military service ; these *honores* became, in course of time, hereditary and the term was also applied to the rents of particular towns assigned to each noble by the King to enable him to maintain a proper number of knights in his service. The *ricoshombres* were thus noble by tradition and birth as well as by tenure, in which respect they differed from the Catalan nobility. The name has been regarded as of Gothic origin ; the simpler explanation is that the bravest and most competent warrior in early times obtained the largest share of the conquered land and

109

thus became the richest. Among their privileges were exemption from corporal punishment and the right to trial by their peers ; they were under obligation to serve for two months in the year and for a longer time, if the King paid their expenses. James I introduced a new order, *ricoshombres de la mesnada*, specially attached to his household, but the innovation caused so much ill-feeling that he promised at Exea in 1265 to confer *honores* only upon those who were noble by birth. Until 1196, the Crown had the right of redistributing the *honores* at the beginning of each reign ; Pedro II agreed to regard these as herditary, in return for the cession of supreme judicial power. *Ricoshombres* were also known as barons, though a baron was not necessarily a *ricohombre ;* of the sons of a *ricohombre* only one could inherit the dignity ; others belonged to the lower class of nobility.

These were the *caballeros*, also known as *mesnaderos*, knights attached to the *mesnada* or royal household. They might be no less important and powerful than the *ricoshombres*, but differed from them by the accident of birth. Originally vassals only of the King, they were allowed in course of time to hold lands as vassals of the *ricoshombres*, and if their possessions and influence were sufficient, could rise to the dignity of baron. Below these were the *infanzones*, who were competent to receive knighthood and were in the position of esquires ; they were exempt from taxation and were bound to serve in war for three days. A valued right of every class of nobility was that of *desnaturalización*, of renunciation of allegiance to the Crown upon giving due notice. A noble who wished to attack one of his own standing was obliged to issue a formal defiance ten days beforehand in the presence of witnesses. Nobles who did not take the field when summoned for military service were liable to a fine and could also commute their service for a payment analogous to the English scutage. Apart from any tax that they might themselves vote in a Cortes, they were under no other pecuniary obligation to the Crown. In Catalonia the feudal classes were known as *condes, vizcondes, valvasores* and *vasallos*, the first three of which were nobles and were also known generically as *barones*. The *valvasor* was the holder of a fief who could maintain at least five knights.

The general organization of the Church, which was represented in the Cortes as a separate estate of the realm, was uniform throughout the peninsula ; the Bishop governed his diocese under the Archbishop, who was responsible to Rome ; the monastic and mendicant orders governed themselves under their own abbots, priors and provincials. The Crown, as a rule, was anxious to secure the support of the Church ; James I advised his son-in-law Alfonso of Castile to " keep the Church in his love," and also the towns, as a means of checking the nobility ; the court Chancellor was usually a bishop and bishops performed other governmental functions for the Crown. The Church had its own courts ; but Aragon was free from the abuses that ecclesiastical jurisdiction aroused elsewhere, the general rule being that actions of clergy against laity came before a secular court and actions of laity against clergy before a bishop's court. Clergy enjoyed immunity from taxation, their persons were under the royal protection, and they are not found at any time at variance with the King as the nobles often were. The Crown, however, was jealous of any attempt upon the part of the Church to acquire landed property ; James I was censured by Clement IV for demanding to see the title-deeds to ecclesiastical estates, and for restricting the endowments of the Church in Valencia. The legal codes declared that persons entering religious orders without the consent of their parents were liable to be disinherited, nor could any landed property be transferred to the Church without the consent of the Crown. The relations of the Church with the papacy were, to some extent, dependent upon those of the King with that power, and these varied from time to time. Pedro II made himself tributary to Rome ; James I owed his crown to Rome ; Pedro III broke with the papacy entirely. In general, the Aragonese kings were willing to acknowledge papal supremacy in spiritual matters and to go their own way in temporal concerns ; James, for instance, accepted the Pope's objection to a nominee of his own for the Archbishopric of Tarragona in 1234, and Pedro III allowed the papal interdict to take effect without opposition. Reference has already been made to the Cluniac reforms ; while they raised the standard of discipline to some extent, the general morality of the Church during this period can be described only as low. The rule of celibacy was continually disregarded ; clergy lived openly with women as their wives, an arrangement known as *barragania*, and even left bequests to their children in their wills, or secured their legitimization by other means. The cruelty which refused to accept the surrender upon terms of Moorish garrisons, as at the siege of Mallorca, may be excused as due to fanaticism ; but in 1254 the Bishop of Urgel was degraded for simony, incest, adultery and other crimes ; in 1257 the famous monastery of Ripoll was hopelessly in debt to the Jews, while provincial councils and synods issued canons and measures against profligacy and luxury of living and dress. In the South of France, conditions were even worse, as might be expected during the period of the Albigensian wars, and some of the disorders among the Spanish clergy were doubtless due to the example of clerical immigrants from beyond the Pyrenees. Both Pedro II and James I forbade heresy and James permitted the establishment of an inquisition in Catalonia in 1269 which is said to have burned many heretics and exhumed the bones of others ; in Aragon inquisitions were forbidden by the *fueros*. At the same time, the Church produced pious and learned men. The famous saint Ramon de Penyafort was chaplain to Pope Gregory IX shortly after 1230 and drew up a collection of papal decretals ; after declining the Archbishopric of Tarragona, he was at Barcelona in 1238 when he was appointed General of the Dominicans, an office which he resigned in 1240 to devote himself to the conversion of the Moors, which he hoped to do by promoting the study of Arabic. Other well-known missionaries were Pedro Nolasco and Ramon Nonnatus of the Order of Mercy, an association formed for ransoming Christians from captivity among the Moors, which released many slaves from Granada and Africa.

As to the middle classes, they were divided in Aragonese towns into *burgueses*, citizens following the liberal professions, and *hombres de condicion*, who were artisans, shopkeepers and the like. In Barcelona and probably in other towns where commerce was highly developed, the second class was subdivided ; those occupied as bankers, doctors, advocates and the like formed the *mà major*, the greater hand ; the ordinary merchants, the *mà mitjana*, the middle hand, and the artisans and workmen the *mà menor*, the lesser hand. Peasants and slaves were known as *mezquinos*, and in documents as *peitarii, villani, casati, collatii ;* until the thirteenth century they were able to move about the country, but became by degrees attached to an overlord and to the soil, and their condition grew steadily worse. Moorish slaves were not, as in Castile, personal property but were bound to the soil and were known as *exaricos*. In Catalonia and probably in Aragon the property of a serf fell to his lord upon his death ; the custom was then introduced of allowing his family to continue to cultivate his land and to pay his dues, with the result that the labourer was regarded as a part of the land and was sold with it. On the whole, he was probably worse off under the more developed feudalism of Aragon and Catalonia than in Castile.

The remaining portions of the population were the foreign elements represented by the Moorish *mozárabes* and *mudéjares* and the Jews. The *mozárabes* had increased as the line of Christian conquest advanced ; mention has been made of the favour shown to those of Andalucía by Alfonso I. But they, like the Jews, were regarded, as everywhere in the Middle Ages, as royal serfs with no rights of their own ; " Judei servi regis sunt, et semper fisco regio deputati " (*Fuero* of Teruel, no. 425, in the year 1176). Thus James I refused to allow the taxation of Jews in Montpellier, as being an infringement of the royal prerogative. The King could transfer this right to a noble, if he so wished. Jews were not allowed to leave the country, and if they travelled abroad for commercial purposes, they were obliged to leave adequate security behind them to guarantee their return ; the Crown, however, seems to have had no legal claim to their personal property, but they could not sell land without royal permission and were obliged to surrender a third of the price to the Crown. They were subject to the same taxation as the Christians, but paid taxes as communities, not as individuals ; such annual payments were known as *peita, questia, tallia* or *tributum* and are first mentioned in 1254. Whether the Jewish communities paid more than the Christian towns is uncertain ; the poll-tax, or *cabessagium* was levied as a general rule only upon Moors. The policy of the Crown towards the Jewish and Moorish elements was directed by a desire to support the Christian religion,

8

to safeguard the interests of Christian subjects and to enrich
the royal treasury. The fourth Lateran Council attempted
to secure the first of these objects, by ordering that Jews
should wear a special dress ; this regulation was not always
strictly enforced in Aragon and Jews were able to secure
relief from it by monetary payments. Under James I and
his successors the royal finances were largely in the hands of
Jews, who were often the creditors of the Crown ; court
secretaries and doctors were generally Jews. Repeated, if
spasmodic, attempts to convert them were undertaken under
the stimulus of exhortations from Rome and the Dominican
Order. The Crown was concerned to see that these efforts
did not impair the pecuniary value of the Jewish communities, for which they had a considerable respect ; in 1247
James I offered protection to all Jews who settled in his
territory ; he and Pedro III attempted to colonize Valencia
with Jews ; James II in 1306 offered a home to the French
Jews who had been expelled by Philip the Fair. These and
other efforts of the Crown to protect Jews and their property
were actuated solely by self-interest ; the royal methods of
realizing this interest were arbitrary in the extreme ; if the
Crown was in extremities, heavy loans or taxation might be
demanded ; in 1372 Pedro IV drove the Jews of Barcelona
by his excessive demands to seek help from their co-religionists
in France. Territorial lords and such knightly orders as
those of Calatrava and the Temple held rights over Jews
within their territory, analogous to those of the Crown ; but
the Crown could claim a share of any taxation which they
levied, so that some Jews were subject to two masters. The
towns (with the exception of Tortosa for reasons unknown)
could not tax the Jews for communal purposes, as such action
would have infringed the rights of the Crown. They could,
however, exact from Jews a share of the expenses incurred
upon works of public utility, such as the erection or repair
of walls and defences. From the end of the thirteenth
century the towns obliged the Jews to live in a separate
quarter, a *judería,* where they formed an *aljama,* a community
of their own, and were distinguished from the Christian
population by various regulations affecting dress and other
matters. In general, the towns were suspicious of the Jewish
communities and it was through town influence that Jewish

officials were removed from the financial departments of
Pedro III and Alfonso III. Barcelona secured from Alfonso V
the privilege of refusing admittance to would-be Jewish
immigrants ; on the other hand, cases occur of small towns
which invited Jews to settle within their walls, in the hope of
increasing their commerce.

No reliable estimate is possible of the number of Jews
within Aragonese territory ; they were more numerous in
Barcelona than anywhere else. In general, they were allowed
to observe their religious practices without restraint and were
protected by the kings against the Church and the Inquisition,
which could proceed only against relapsed Jewish proselytes
or against Christian converts to Judaism. In the fourteenth
century the Inquisitors gained more power and Jews were
constantly brought before their courts, while in times of
famine or heavy taxation they were often the objects of
popular animosity. Jews were not without legal rights.
They had their own courts of justice and cases occurred
when Christians were obliged to plead in these ; a Christian
who killed a Jew was not liable to capital punishment, but
might be heavily fined. In the thirteenth and fourteenth
centuries Jews were allowed to possess land, which they held
in theory from the Crown, a practice which continued for a
longer time in Aragon than in Castile, where they were
expropriated by the end of the fourteenth century. Apart
from liberty of buying and selling, Jews were also allowed to
lend money at interest ; James I forbade compound interest ;
the usual rate was 20 per cent per month and 16 per cent if
the loan was made for a longer period than a year ; the
interest was never to exceed the amount of the loan, though
exceptions to the rule were allowed in some towns, notably
Montpellier and Perpignan. The money-lender was obliged
to swear obedience to the law concerning loans before a
public court and was then given a licence, without which he
could not recover at law.

Moriscos and *mudéjares* were under regulations very
similar to those which settled the social position of the Jews.
They had their own courts and magistrates and were protected
by the Crown from Christian oppression. To their labours
was due much of the productivity of the country and in
some cases their overlords stimulated their efforts by allowing

them a modified ownership of the soil which they paid for on a metayer system ; such holders were known as *exaricos*. The papal decrees which obliged them to wear a special dress to distinguish them from the Christian population were not at first strictly enforced and there was little restriction upon intercourse between Moors and Christians. But as time went on, barriers were raised by ecclesiastical influence and the Moors were obliged to live in quarters of their own within the towns.

Reference has been already made to the reasons which induced the Crown to grant special privileges, *fueros*, to particular towns. Such towns or *universidades* were outside the powers of the Church or nobility and were responsible to the King alone ; they became, as in Castile, a political power of inestimable value to the Crown in its struggles with the nobility. Municipal government was in the hands of a body of *jurats*, chosen by the citizens or, in some cases, choosing their own successors. They were expected to consult the general assembly of the townsmen, the *concell*, upon any matter of importance to the whole community. The alcaldes appear as judges in civil cases, and were generally appointed by popular election ; with them were the *judices*, judges in criminal matters, usually appointed by the Crown. The King was represented by a batlle or bailiff who was responsible for collecting the royal revenues, and towns of importance had a supreme judicial authority known as the Justicia (in Zaragoza as the *zalmedina* and in Valencia as the *alcait*). While local variations of these arrangements are found, the general principle is uniform ; the Crown is permanently represented in each town, but local government is in the hands of the municipality. The Crown is the fount of justice and cases can be carried to the royal courts of appeal ; but the local magistrate, in giving his decisions, must consider the opinion of the jurats ; as there was no system of circuits bringing judges to hear appeals, the powers of the local courts were extensive. There was no mayor or other official to act as the figure-head of the municipality, nor does the need of such a functionary seem to have been felt. Towns formed unions among themselves, for mutual protection, trade or other purposes ; these unions were known as *comunidades* and took the name of the leading town in the union, for the formation of which the royal permission was required. In the thirteenth century such unions were usually formed for police purposes and were known as *juntas ;* they were under the command of a *sobre-juntero* whose business was the maintenance of public order. The force thus raised was known in Catalonia as *sometent,* the members of which were allowed to possess arms and were bound to answer any summons for joint action.

Representatives of the upper classes had been accustomed to meet in Aragon from the year 1071, and from these were developed the Cortes. The lower classes were not represented until the towns had risen to some importance and the date of their appearance in the Cortes is uncertain. The Aragonese Cortes were composed of four *brazos* or estates, the *ricoshombres,* the *caballeros,* the clergy and the towns ; not all of the nobles had the right of representation and in course of time the right was restricted to those towns which contained at least four hundred households (*fuegos*). The Cortes could be convoked only by the King, who was bound to summon them once every five years, and, after the union of Aragon and Catalonia, every other year ; but the kings did not strictly observe this obligation. The business of the Cortes was to receive the King's oath that he would observe the laws and *fueros* of the realm ; to swear allegiance to the heirs to the throne ; to put forward complaints of individuals or towns concerning the administration ; to vote service in money or kind, as the needs of the Crown required, and to approve of legislation initiated by the King. Unanimity, not majority, was required to secure the adoption of any proposal ; and it may be noted that the larger towns had several votes, while the smaller had but one. The Catalan Cortes consisted of three estates only, clergy, nobles and townsmen ; it is probable that the subdivision of the Aragonese nobility which gave their Cortes four estates did not take place until after the union. The first general Cortes of the two countries were held in 1162, but both the Aragonese and Catalan Cortes continued to meet independently after this date ; Valencia also had Cortes of its own after the conquest of the province. The usual place of meeting was Zaragoza or Barcelona, which towns each enjoyed the privilege of five votes in the Cortes, but the King was at liberty to summon meetings elsewhere.

Contrary to the practice in Castile, redress must precede supply; the Cortes could make the grant of any unusual request for supplies conditional upon royal compliance with its wishes. In any case, the Crown could not afford to disregard national sentiment as expressed in such an assembly, and it also found the Cortes useful as a means of adding to the prestige of the towns in opposition to the refractory nobility, who were more anxious to secure the triumph of baronial privilege than of parliamentary independence, as was seen in the famous Cortes of Exea. Thus, when large supplies were needed to meet some general emergency, the Crown was forced to recognize the general principle that what " touches all should be approved by all," and the fact remains that popular representation was of more ancient institution in Aragon than in any other European monarchy.

The powers of the Crown were thus far more limited than in other monarchies of the time. In Castile, the King was regarded as the vicegerent of God upon earth; in Aragon, he was *primus inter pares*, and his authority was the object of jealousy and suspicion on the part of nobles and townsmen alike. The kings themselves considered that they ruled *Dei gratia*, but the concessions extorted from so absolutist a ruler as James I by his nobles at the Cortes of Exea in 1265 are enough to show that he was considered by his barons as no more than their feudal superior, a claim reinforced by reference to the mythical *fuero* of Sobrarbe, which stated that the Aragonese elected their king upon condition that he swore to maintain their territorial rights and privileges and to make neither war, nor peace, nor treaty with other powers without the knowledge and consent of the *ricoshombres*. Such is probably the origin of exaggerated statements concerning the weakness of the King's position; when, for instance, Argensola says that in Aragon, " hubo antes leyes que reyes," he is overstating the case. James I came into collision with his nobles, because he was an absolutist who ruled constitutionally only when it .suited his purpose; Pedro III embarked the kingdom upon the Sicilian adventure without consulting his subjects, as secrecy was necessary to his purpose, and was obliged in consequence to grant the General Privilege to the Cortes of Zaragoza in 1283, which declared that absolutism was entirely foreign to the constitution of Aragon. In short, adventurous and ambitious kings were hampered by the democratic character of the constitution and people, and were naturally inclined to govern according to the practice of other contemporary monarchs.

The Crown of Aragon had certain powers which made the holder of them a formidable antagonist to the most refractory of nobles. The King, in the first place, was the fount of legislation, in the sense, that if he failed to initiate legislation or opposed it, laws were not likely to be passed. He could confer upon towns and individuals " privileges," such as municipal charters, grants, legitimations, exemptions and the like ; while the Cortes could sanction or reject laws presented for approval, those laws must have been introduced by the King and drawn up by his lawyers. His executive powers were also great ; he was the supreme judge and held the final court of appeal ; as a feudal superior, he could summon any subject before him to answer for an offence. He could deprive nobles of their fiefs or " honours " and impose certain dues upon them. The King was thus chief judge, legislator and commander, with powers of initiating action which the Cortes never possessed. The checks upon him were the fact that he was dependent upon the Cortes for any considerable grant in aid, and that he must submit any differences with the Aragonese nobility to arbitration, the arbitrator being the Justicia of Aragon.

The existence and the peculiar position and functions of this official have always been regarded as a feature unique in medieval constitutions ; in the plenitude of his power, the Justicia undoubtedly acted as an intermediary between the Crown and its subjects ; he was the keeper of the King's conscience, the highest interpreter of the law and the final referee in cases of dispute ; he was a permanent counsellor of the King whom he accompanied everywhere as a kind of Lord Chancellor. Aragonese tradition regarded the office as created by the *fuero* of Sobrarbe, which is said to have provided a " judex medius . . . qui judicaret et esset judex inter regem et ejus vasallos," in the words of the unreliable Blancas who is inclined to accept traditions as historical which had before his time won their way to the fabulous. The fact that the Justicia was appointed by the King himself would inevitably impair his authority as an independent referee. His mediatory powers were conferred upon him at the Cortes of Exea in 1265, when the nobles secured that he should always be a knight, as a *ricohombre* was exempt from corporal punishment and could not easily be called to account. The Justicia was, in origin, the most prominent member of the body of lawyers and judges who formed the royal curia, and his function was to promulgate the sentences and decisions of that court ; in arbitration cases between king and nobles or between nobles themselves he merely pronounced the sentence decided by his assessors, nor could he try any suit of importance without the help of assessors. The Cortes of Exea made personal to the Justicia functions which he had previously performed as merely delegated to him, and from that time his powers of arbitration increase. The General Privilege, secured by the nobles from Pedro III in 1283, made the Justicia the judge in all cases where the rights granted by earlier *fueros* or customs had been infringed by the Crown. During the unfortunate reign of Alfonso III, the nobles extorted a new charter, the Union, which greatly increased their influence ; the King undertook to proceed against no member of the Union, unless the Justicia had pronounced against him with the approval of the Cortes, which were to be held annually in Zaragoza, and if the King infringed the terms of the Union, disobedience to him was not to be considered as treason. In short, as Alfonso put it, " en Aragon había tantos reyes como ricoshombres." James II succeeded in revoking these privileges, but until his time the purpose of the Justicia was to watch over the privileges of the nobles under their supervision, rather than to mediate between them and the Crown. Until the end of our period it was also his business to preserve two privileges concerned with the penal law, the right of *manifestación*, which enabled a defendant to claim a right of asylum with the Justicia, who protected him from annoyance of any kind until his case was decided, and the right of *firmas*, which enabled the Justicia to secure immunity for the property of a litigant until sentence had been passed.

Other royal functionaries of importance were the Chancellor, who was treasurer for the whole kingdom, and the Major-domo of Aragon, who possessed judicial powers in a court of appeal, and commanded the cavalry in battle. The Major-domo of the Palace was a Catalan office, the holder acting as steward to the royal household in Catalonia ; he was appointed by the Seneschal of Catalonia, who was the commander-in-chief of the Catalan army, an office hereditary in the Moncada family.

The military organization of the kingdom did not differ materially from that of any other medieval state. The army was composed of feudal levies, municipal troops and mercenaries. The townsmen were probably not obliged to serve outside of the kingdom and nobles occasionally refused obedience ; it was perhaps to overcome this danger that James I instituted the *mesnaderos*, a class of nobility in close relation with himself. Of the mercenaries, the most notable were the Almogávares, who became for a short time the terror of Anatolia, when the Catalans made their expedition to the East. The name is said to be a corruption of the Arabic *al-mughawir* or " raider." They were light armed foot-soldiers and cavalry, armed with darts which they threw with great force and accuracy and with a sword or other weapon for fighting at close quarters ; defensive armour they had little or none and relied for success upon their bodily agility. Extremely mobile and unencumbered with baggage, they could march immense distances and live upon the country as they went. The Aragonese army possessed the usual supply of rams, mangonels, towers on wheels and other devices for attacking fortifications. Their fleet was provided by the Catalans, whose wide maritime experience made this arm of the service as efficient as any in Europe. The military orders, such as the Templars and the Hospitallers, had settled in Aragon at an early date and proved a valuable military support to the Crown, though the wealth and influence which they acquired made them a source of occasional trouble, as was the case in Castile.

The Crown revenues consisted of the income from the royal domains throughout the kingdom ; salt was a royal monopoly and mines were worked near Zaragoza and Xátiva ; there were taxes on cattle, known as herbage and carnage, and upon Jews and Muslims ; dues upon merchandise and the proceeds of the administration of justice, fees, fines and confiscations ; the coinage also produced a profit. The collection of these revenues was generally farmed out in return for a lump sum, an iniquitous system in vogue also in Castile. To these regular sources of revenues were added extraordinary revenues, aids voted by the Cortes, which usually took the form of monage, a property tax, in Aragon, and of bovage, a tax upon each yoke of oxen, in Catalonia ; voluntary grants for some special enterprise might be made by towns or individuals, and in time of war redemptions for default of service were exacted. There were many exemptions ; nobles and clergy paid nothing except such sums as they chose to vote from time to time or the redemption money in lieu of military service, and certain towns enjoyed immunities from particular forms of taxation ; Barcelona and Valencia were free from taxes on merchandise ; Figueras was free from bovage, herbage and dues on merchandise ; Villanueva from all feudal dues, while the Temple and Hospital had the right to free trade. The wasteful system of farming the taxes also tempted kings to anticipate their incomes by pledging them to money-lenders and creditors ; the Crown was at times reduced to financial straits ; we hear of James I pawning his shield and jewels, and paying his tailor with an exemption from taxation.

The condition of agriculture, industry and commerce was naturally reflected in the royal revenues. In Aragon, the olive appears to have been cultivated even earlier than in Castile, wines, corn and rice were also produced in considerable quantities and supplied the deficiencies of Catalonia in these commodities. Much of the Aragonese land was and is of quality too poor for cultivation, and stockbreeding or sheep-farming was developed upon a considerable scale ; there was some manufacture of leather and woollen textiles. In Valencia and Mallorca, agriculture was the principal industry and was carried on by the numerous *mudéjares* who had remained there. Fabrics of wool, cotton and silk were manufactured, and a large trade developed. Catalonia was chiefly occupied with commerce, and agriculture was there of less importance than in other parts of the Aragonese kingdom. Wine and cereals were produced, but the energies of the province were largely given to manufacture which had been learned in part from the Italian republics. Gerona, Lérida, Vich and especially Barcelona produced iron-ware, wine barrels, leather, glass,

cordage, textiles of every kind and objects of luxury, jewellery
and art pottery. The dyeing of cloth was an important
industry. Commerce overseas was in the hands of the Catalonians and Barcelona was the chief centre of trade, while
Montpellier was not far behind it. Barcelona was a town in
which trade was never considered derogatory, as it was in
Castile ; all trades of any importance were represented in the
town council no less than the learned professions, such as law
or medicine. The port was visited by vessels from France,
Italy, Greece, Sicily, Syria, Africa, and in general from all
parts of the Mediterranean. Commercial relations were
closest with Pisa and Genoa and a series of commercial
treaties with these towns was concluded. The extension of
trade necessitated the maintenance of a fleet of warships to
protect the merchant-men ; under James I began a system of
sending commercial representatives (*consules*) to foreign ports
to watch over Catalan interests, and *consulats de mar* were
established for the same purpose in the chief ports of Catalonia
and Valencia. This traffic was regulated by a body of custom
which gained the force of law as time went on and was
eventually codified in the famous *Llibre del Consulat de mar*
at some unknown date. A similar compilation at Tortosa
belongs to the thirteenth century. Trade was not free,
except in the case of towns which had been granted immunity,
and port or excise duties contributed regularly to the royal
revenues. The amounts received show a steady increase,
but the Crown was generally in debt and the Aragonese
kingdom was not regarded abroad as particularly rich, if we
may judge by a remark made by Clement IV to the King of
France in 1268, when he asserted that the total tithe in
James's dominions did not amount to more than a sum
equivalent to £100,000 of our money.

CHAPTER IX

ALFONSO III AND JAMES II

The successors to Pedro's dominions. Quarrels with the nobility. Alfonso and Edward I of England. Breach with Castile. Negotiations on the Sicilian question. The peace of Tarascon. Death of Alfonso. Succeeded by his brother, James II. Peace with Castile. The claims to Sicily. Boniface VIII. James abandons the Sicilians. They elect Fadrique as king. War with Castile and Sicily. The peace of Caltabellota. Invasion of Sardinia. The Act of Union. Death of James.

PEDRO III left four sons and two daughters by his wife, Constanza. Alfonso, the eldest, succeeded to the kingdom of Aragon; James, the second son, became King of Sicily. The third son, Frederick, generally known as Fadrique, became King of Sicily when James succeeded to Aragon upon the death of his eldest brother. The fourth son, Pedro, who bore his father's name, married Constanza of Moncada. The elder daughter, Isabella, became Queen of Portugal, while the younger, Violante, married Robert, the King of Naples. At the time of Pedro's death, Alfonso was sailing to Mallorca with Roger de Lauria to reduce the Balearic Islands to subjection. Pedro III had declared upon his death-bed that he was ready to restore the kingdom of Sicily to the Pope, but his sons had no intention of abandoning the new acquisitions, and, when Alfonso had completed the subjugation of the Balearic Islands, he sent the Admiral to Sicily to maintain the rights of his brother, James. The conquest of Mallorca was no difficult task. The inhabitants had suffered under the oppression of the King, James, and his officials, and Alfonso was regarded as a liberator. He was able to return to Valencia early in 1286, and summoned the Estates of the Realm to Zaragoza for the coronation ceremonies. He found the nobles in no amiable spirit. In the despatches in which he had announced the conquest of Mallorca, he had already assumed the royal title, and had made donations and conferred titles before he had received

124

the crown and taken the coronation oaths, all of which was regarded by the nobles as a gross infringement of their rights. They therefore requested him to swear to observe the laws and privileges of Aragon, as his predecessors had done, and to refrain from further exercise of royal rights until his coronation had taken place. Alfonso returned a mild answer to these representations, asserting that he had only used the royal title because the Catalan barons and towns had already addressed him in that style. But this dispute was only the prelude to a lengthy series of discussions and recriminations which it is convenient to recount in connection, although they were spread over a number of years. Some historians stigmatise the Aragonese and, to some extent, the Catalan nobles as selfishly concerned only with the maintenance of their own privileges. On the other hand, the fact seems to be undoubted that many of them were impressed with the dangers to which the realm was exposed by the actions of an absolute monarch. Pedro III had plunged the kingdom into an exhausting and expensive war, had brought down upon his country papal excommunication and had committed it to a policy which was likely to involve much further military effort and expenditure, and the nobles wished to be assured that in such matters as concerned the whole kingdom they should at any rate have the right of representing their views. On the other hand, Pedro III, like James I before him, probably felt that the oligarchic constitution which the Aragonese nobles desired to maintain implied a serious loss of efficiency in the diplomatic and military world of his time. The success of his Sicilian adventure, for instance, was due almost entirely to the secrecy with which it had been conducted, and, in an age when so much depended upon personal relations between individual monarchs, it was unreasonable to ask that every decision should be submitted to the approval of Cortes, which could only be collected with difficulty, were exasperatingly slow in their methods of deliberation, were often ill-informed, and inspired in many cases by individual prejudices and petty partisanship. This was really the contradiction which lay at the root of the subsequent disputes, the question whether an oligarchic or democratic state could hold its own amid a number of kingdoms and principalities governed under an absolutist system.

The nobles began by demanding that the King should take into his royal household a number of councillors nominated by themselves. The King was prepared to agree to this, provided that he had a right of veto, but it then appeared that the Union of the Nobles was by no means unanimous, and that an opposition party in favour of the King was exerting a strong influence. Alfonso's presence was also required upon the northern frontier, as James of Mallorca was preparing forces in Roussillon for an invasion of Catalonia. Negotiations therefore ended until the month of June, when another meeting in Zaragoza was held. The nobles then reaffirmed the objects of the Union, insisting that the King should accept certain councillors, nominated by themselves, as permanent appointments, and should revoke certain donations which he had made since his father's death ; in case of refusal, he would receive no help or support from them, either with money or men. They also declared themselves prepared to attack any noble or combination of nobles opposed to their policy. As will be seen, Alfonso was occupied by foreign negotiations of considerable importance, but in October he summoned Cortes at Huesca, and again informed the nobles that, in view of the divisions among themselves, it was impossible for him to arrive at any conclusion. It appeared, in fact, as if the state of Aragon were being divided into a royal and a baronial party, and that civil war would be the outcome. Alfonso, however, in view of the dangers which threatened his kingdom from abroad, was anxious to secure some measure of peace, and proposed to hold a court at regular intervals, to call his councillors together for daily consultation, and to secure a regular administration of justice, but he insisted upon retaining the appointment to the most important offices, and upon this point negotiations again broke down. The Union met once more in Zaragoza in December, and summoned a general meeting to be held in Teruel in the following month, at which pressure would be brought to bear upon those barons and individuals who declined to support them. Alfonso met the Estates once more in May 1287. He was then involved in important negotiations with Edward I of England, and informed the nobles that he could only allow two days for their discussions. This proved to be insufficient, and the Union in exasperation proceeded to send ambassadors to the Pope, and to open negotiations with France and Castile and even with the Moors in Spain, with the object of forming an alliance against their own King. Alfonso, with the knights and barons who supported him, began by attacking the Union in Tarragona, but, after some desultory fighting and the execution of some of the leading citizens, the Prior of the Dominican Monastery in Zaragoza, one Valero, succeeded in bringing the disputants once more together, and eventually an agreement was secured at a meeting in Zaragoza on December 20, when Alfonso conceded two privileges. He promised, in the first place, not to proceed against any baron, knight or other member of the Union until the Justicia had pronounced sentence upon him, with the concurrence of the Cortes. As a guarantee for the fulfilment of this promise, he was prepared to surrender to the Union sixteen castles, the commanders of which were to hold them in the name of the kingdom, but were not to be regarded as guilty of high treason, should they transfer their allegiance elsewhere, in case the King failed to fulfil his side of the agreement. In the second place, Alfonso promised that general Cortes should be held in November every year at Zaragoza, that the Estates should appoint certain councillors whom he and his successors would accept, and whose views should have full consideration in directing the policy of the realm. The councillors upon appointment to office were to swear that they would give the King loyal advice in accordance with the laws of the realm, and would avoid the giving or taking of bribes. They could be removed from office and replaced by others at the will of the Cortes. These were the so-called Privileges of the Union. They were not submitted to the kingdom as a whole, but were extorted from the King by a confederation of powerful barons. They were consequently not confirmed by following kings, and were revoked by Pedro IV as a danger to the good government of the kingdom. At the end of January 1288, the Union made use of these privileges, and appointed various councillors and members of the King's household who were received by him without further demur.

While these wearisome and indeed dangerous negotiations were in progress, Alfonso was also engaged in important matters of foreign policy. During his father's lifetime, he

had been betrothed to Eleanor, the daughter of Edward I
of England, but the Pope had forbidden the marriage, as
Aragon was then excommunicated in consequence of Pedro's
quarrel with the Pope. Edward I was anxious to secure a
general peace, and was the only mediator in Europe to whom
all the parties were prepared to listen. He sent ambassadors
to the Pope, and invited the Kings of Aragon and France to
send their plenipotentiaries to him at Bordeaux. Pope
Martin, the creature of Charles of Anjou, had died in March
1286, and was succeeded by Honorius IV, who was no less
anxious than his predecessor to maintain the sovereignty of
the papacy, and excommunicated James of Sicily with
threats of war, if he continued to remain in occupation of
his kingdom. Alfonso was also confronted with the possibility
of an attack upon his frontier by James, the King of Mallorca,
who had been collecting troops for that purpose in Roussillon,
and obliged him to maintain a considerable force in the neighbourhood of the Pyrenees. He undertook to send ambassadors
also to Rome as soon as circumstances allowed him to do so.
Edward of England had used his position to secure an
armistice with France which was concluded in Paris in July,
and was accepted also by the King of Mallorca, although
Philip hesitated to give his final consent until the Pope's
approval had been secured. However, the armistice was
observed, Alfonso assured the Pope of his obedience, and the
Archbishops of Ravenna and Montreal came to France to
begin the final negotiations. Alfonso utilized this interval
of peace to subjugate the Island of Menorca. The local
chieftain had opened negotiations with the Moors,
thrown open his harbours to the French and generally
shown himself hostile to Aragon. The appearance of the
Catalan fleet put an end to all resistance, and in January
1287 the island capitulated.

While the efforts of Edward I appeared to have opened a
reasonable prospect of peace, difficulties arose for Aragon
on the side of Castile. In 1275, while Alfonso X of Castile
was in the South of France soliciting the support of Pope
Gregory to his candidature for election as emperor, his heir,
Ferdinand, died, and the problem arose whether the successor
and heir to the Crown of Castile should be Ferdinand's son
or his younger brother, Sancho. By the King's own code of

laws, the Siete Partidas, the claims of the grandson were undoubted. But the provisions of the code were of a permissive character, and the Cortes, acting on the older Germanic elective principle, decided in favour of the son, Sancho, who was proclaimed heir to the throne. Ferdinand had married Blanche, the sister of King Philip of France, who naturally objected to this decision which disinherited his nephews, and declared war upon Castile. The young princes, with their mother and Alfonso's own queen Violante, fled to Aragon, where they were kindly received at the court of Pedro III. Pope Nicholas III threatened to excommunicate Philip of France if he interfered in a family quarrel. When Alfonso died in 1285, Sancho assumed the Crown and was naturally anxious to secure the persons of his nephews, the Infantes de la Cerda, who were then resident in Xátiva, and whose claims might reasonably involve the validity of his own. When Alfonso of Aragon refused this request, Sancho began an alliance with the King of France, and thus disturbed the negotiations that were proceeding under the mediation of Edward of England. It then became clear that there was no prospect of peace until Charles the Lame of Naples, the Prince of Salerno, who had been taken prisoner by the Catalan admiral and was then held in confinement in Catalonia, was set at liberty. The Kings of England and Aragon, therefore, met at Oléron in Béarn, and agreed that Charles should be set free, after giving his three eldest sons to Alfonso as hostages, and paying a ransom of 30,000 silver marks. Alfonso was also to hold the eldest sons of sixteen Provençal knights as hostages. Charles, in return, had promised the Kings of Aragon and Sicily to secure a three years' armistice with France and the Church, which interval was to be used in the arrangement of a peace satisfactory to all parties. Should he fail to secure this object, he undertook to return to imprisonment and to leave the hostages in Alfonso's power. He had already considered the possibility of some such arrangement. Before he left Sicily he had negotiated with James, the King of the island, the vital point of the discussion being that he would induce the Pope to revoke the donation of Aragon to Charles of Valois which Pope Martin had made. These negotiations had broken down through the refusal of the Pope to continue.

9

At the present moment the situation had changed for the better, from the Aragonese point of view, thanks to the exploits of the Catalan admiral, Roger de Lauria. In April, Count Robert of Artois, who had been made governor of the kingdom of Naples by the will of Charles I, had fitted out a numerous fleet, made a descent upon Malta, captured Augusta on the Sicilian coast, and retired to Brindisi. James of Sicily then proceeded to besiege the town, while Lauria cut off his communications with Naples. Count Robert, therefore, collected sixty galleys in his capital, which were to unite with the fleet in harbour at Brindisi, and sail with a numerous army to Sicily for the relief of Augusta. In June, however, Lauria appeared off Naples, enticed the inexperienced French barons to attack him, and completely destroyed this part of the fleet. This victory placed Aragon in a stronger position, but the eventual conclusion of the peace was delayed by the death of Honorius IV in April 1287, after which the Papal Chair remained unoccupied for some time. Nicholas IV was not elected until February 1288 ; as general of the Franciscan order, he had visited Barcelona and was acquainted with the chief men of the district ; he was also inclined to favour the Ghibelline cause and had little affection for the French dynasty. He showed, however, no great partiality for the Aragonese. He exhorted the Sicilians to return to their obedience to the Roman Church, ordered James to give up his illegal possession of the island, and Alfonso to set Charles the Lame at liberty without delay. He also flatly refused his consent to the conditions that had been agreed upon at Oléron. However, at his request, Edward of England continued his efforts, and, at the end of October, he met Alfonso at Canfranc in Aragon, on the frontiers of Béarn. Charles was also present, and swore to observe the compact concluded at Oléron. The hostages were handed over, and Alfonso released his prisoner who returned to Italy in 1289 and was crowned as King of Sicily at Rome by the Pope. The Pope had already declared the conditions of the agreement null and void, on the ground that they were extorted by compulsion. He now relieved Charles, the King of England and the Provençal princes of the obligations of their oath, solemnly excommunicated Alfonso, and made a grant to the King of France of the Church tithes for three

years, on the understanding that he would put his brother
Charles in possession of the Crown of Aragon. Alfonso was
shortly afterwards attacked on the frontiers of Navarre, and
was also threatened with an invasion by King Sancho of
Castile who, as we have said, had secured an alliance with
France. Sancho's Castilian subjects were by no means agreed
upon this policy, which had been concluded without their
consent, and one of them, Diego de Haro, went to Aragon,
and induced the King to set the Infantes de la Cerda at
liberty, and to permit the eldest of them, Alfonso, to be
proclaimed in Jaca in 1288 as King of Castile and Leon. He
promised the Infante his help in securing his restoration to
the throne, and explained that the internal dissensions in
Sancho's kingdom afforded every prospect of success. He
was able to conclude an alliance with Alfonso, and to declare
war upon the King of Castile. In the spring of 1289 he
invaded Castile and besieged the town of Almazan in Soria,
while Sancho was obliged to retreat. The Aragonese were
obliged to raise the siege, as the King of Mallorca had invaded
Catalonia. Sancho then took the opportunity of invading
Aragon, and ravaged much of the Province of Tarragona,
while Alfonso was busy on his northern frontier.

In the same year King James of Sicily continued his war
against the Italian coasts, and attacked Gaeta. A collision
between his forces and those of Charles II was prevented by
the arrival of an English ambassador, Odo of Grandison,
who interviewed the Pope telling him that the war was the
scandal of Christendom and that he would incur the anger
of all Christian princes if peace were not secured. The Pope
arranged an armistice for two years. In the year 1290,
Alfonso also sent ambassadors to the Pope, and negotiations
with France were reopened. Thanks to the indefatigable
offices of the King of England, peace was eventually concluded, after various meetings at Tarascon, in February 1291,
under conditions which obliged Alfonso to abandon the cause
of his brother in Sicily. The contracting parties were thus,
on the one side, the King of Aragon, and, on the other, the
Church, the King of France and his brother Charles. It
was agreed that Alfonso should offer his obedience to the
Pope, that the Pope should return his kingdom and remove
the interdict. The King of Castile was to be included in the

peace, if he so desired. Charles was to recover his sons and the other hostages he had given, and there was to be an exchange of conquests and prisoners. The King of Aragon also undertook to withdraw all support from his brother James, to order his subjects to quit the kingdom of Sicily and to prevent any of his family from holding possessions in Sicily without papal permission. The kingdom of Mallorca was to be held as a fief of the Crown of Aragon. Alfonso desired to celebrate the conclusion of this long-desired peace by his marriage with Edward's daughter, Eleanor, and the necessary festivities had been arranged in Barcelona when he died after a sudden illness in June 1291, and peace was once again endangered by this unexpected occurrence. It was a peace for which Alfonso has incurred the reprobation of historians. He undertook to turn his mother and brother out of Sicily, to hand over to their bitter enemies a courageous people who had won their independence, and to abandon that supremacy in the Western Mediterranean which had been gained at the cost of so much blood and treasure. On the other hand Alfonso had to face the hostility of the papacy and the Guelf party with the power of France behind them : he was threatened by a war with Castile and his hands were often tied by internal dissensions in his own kingdom. He was known as " el Liberal," and appears indeed to have been unable to refuse the request of any petitioner if he could possibly grant it. He possessed neither the overbearing personality of James I nor the cool and dogged perseverance of Pedro III, and his extravagance seems to have been one of the causes that aroused the indignation of his nobles.

Immediately after Alfonso's death, a deputation of Catalan nobles went to Sicily and invited James, the King of that island, to assume the Crown of Aragon. James appointed his brother Fadrique as Governor of Sicily, a violation of the treaty of Tarascon, to which, however, he had not been a consenting party. He landed in Barcelona in August and met the Cortes at Zaragoza, when he swore to observe the laws and privileges of the kingdom which his predecessors had conceded, and accepted the crown under the declaration that he took it as the eldest surviving son of King Pedro III, and not as the heir of his deceased brother. Alfonso had nominated Fadrique as the heir to Sicily, but

James was apparently anxious to unite Sicily and Aragon under his own government. King Sancho of Castile then came forward with proposals for peace which James was the more inclined to accept, as he had to expect a struggle with France and the papacy sooner or later. Sancho was anxious to secure his own position by inducing Aragon to abandon the cause of the Infantes de la Cerda, and the peace then concluded was confirmed by the betrothal of James to Sancho's daughter Isabella, who was only eight years of age. Sancho also did his best to compose the quarrels of the Aragonese barons, which were then distracting the kingdom, and persuaded them to submit their difficulties to the Justicia, and to swear allegiance to their king. Domestic peace was the more desirable as the Pope had forbidden James to accept the crown of Aragon during the continuance of his interdict, and had ordered the population of the Balearic Islands to refuse obedience to any ruler except their own King, James, who had been driven out. The clergy within the Aragonese territories were also strictly forbidden to recognize James as King. Charles of Valois declared that he had abandoned his rights in favour of Alfonso and not of James, and the brother of Charles, Philip of France, begged the Pope to proclaim a crusade against James, with the object of putting Charles of Valois upon the throne of Aragon. The Pope, however, who was projecting a new crusade in the East, declined to interfere until he had received a definite answer from James. He did, however, urge the King of France to oppose the incessant attacks of the Sicilians. The maritime war in Calabria was continued almost without interruption. Roger de Lauria won further successes and James had deprived Charles of his most powerful maritime supporter by concluding a peace with Genoa. Meanwhile, Sancho of Castile exerted himself to secure a peace between Aragon and France, as he was afraid that King Philip might give his support to the Infantes de la Cerda. In April 1292, the Pope died ; in the following year the Sicilians entreated James not to abandon their cause, and if he could do no more, to instal Fadrique as king. James shortly afterwards met Charles of Anjou, his former prisoner, and seems to have been convinced that the abandonment of Sicily was inevitable, if any permanent settlement was to be made. Sancho continued his negotiations and in 1294 persuaded James to meet him at Logroño, and extorted from him, under a veiled threat of captivity, an agreement to his conditions. James afterwards declared that he considered himself relieved of any obligation in the matter. Meanwhile the papal chair had been vacant for two years. The papacy in the pursuit of temporal power and self-interest had become so closely associated with contending factions in Rome that in 1292 the cardinals were equally divided : after many attempts to secure an election, they had agreed to elect a hermit of the Abruzzi, famed for his holiness, who assumed the name of Celestine V, " che fece per viltate il gran rifiuto." But the papal policy required an astute politician and diplomatist. Celestine knew nothing of business or diplomacy and was helpless in the hands of the King of Naples. It was a profound relief to the cardinals and a sorrow to the people when he abdicated after a pontificate of five months. He was succeeded by a statesman, Boniface VIII, who realized the importance of the papacy as a political institution, whatever his estimate of its spiritual significance. Scandal has left a slimy trail across the personal life of Boniface : it is clear that he was a megalomaniac, with a profound contempt for his inferiors which was openly expressed in his dealings with them by a display of bad manners almost communistic in its crudity. The best-hated man in Europe, he regarded himself as the possible president of a great European confederacy, as the guardian of its one religion and as the administrator of its international law. The papacy had defeated the Empire and proposed to exercise imperial power. Such was the policy of Boniface VIII : it was everywhere unsuccessful. Everywhere he interfered and everywhere he met with opposition or disobedience. Charles of Valois at his instigation attempted to restore the unity of the Sicilian kingdom and merely brought upon himself and the papacy the hatred of the Italians : Edward I of England and Philip IV of France refused to recognize any papal supremacy over their temporal affairs and when in 1303 Philip was threatened with a bull of deposition, he commissioned Sciarra Colonna to seize the Pope's sacred person. Boniface was made prisoner at Anagni, the prestige of the papacy was broken and its supremacy over the rising states of Western Europe was no longer recognized. But in June 1294 Boniface was influential enough to conclude a peace at Anagni with Charles of Sicily, with King Philip of France and Charles of Valois. The Pope removed his interdict, and confirmed James II in possession of his territories, to which Charles of Valois resigned his claim. James agreed to divorce his wife Isabella upon the usual medieval excuse of consanguinity, to marry Blanche, the daughter of King Charles of Naples, and to return all the territory that he had taken from France or from the Church. Nothing was said about the position of Mallorca, but the Pope extorted a half-promise from James that the island should be returned to its former ruler. The Pope also promised to give James the islands of Sardinia and Corsica in exchange for Sicily, and James further promised to help Philip in his war with England with a fleet of forty galleys, the expenses of which France was to pay. The terms of the peace were confirmed at Cortes held in Barcelona. James has been bitterly reproached for his abandonment and betrayal of the Sicilians, who were apparently contented under his rule, and were deeply grieved by his desertion of them. It must have been clear to him, even then, that the prospect of a war between himself and his own brother was no remote possibility, and the gift by the Pope of two islands which he did not possess, and which would have to be conquered from their immediate owners at considerable expense and trouble, could hardly be considered a compensation for the loss of Sicily.

Pope Boniface was equally aware of these possibilities. He induced Fadrique to visit him, and though the citizens of Palermo warned their prince to distrust any assurances offered by the Pope, he went to the meeting accompanied by John of Procida, Roger de Lauria and other distinguished Catalans. The Pope then promised that he should marry Catharine, Philip's daughter and the granddaughter of the Emperor Baldwin II of Constantinople, and that the papacy would then support the claim to the Byzantine Empire which he would thus acquire. These plans were shattered by the indignation and grief of the Sicilians at the conclusion of the peace. As soon as the Catalan and Aragonese nobles in Sicily heard the news a general meeting of all the local leaders was held ; an embassy was sent to James, which arrived in the midst of the festivities with which his marriage was celebrated in October 1295. As no satisfaction could be gained, the Sicilians chose Fadrique as King of the island and crowned him in March 1296. Though James recalled his subjects, they determined to remain in Sicily, stating that Fadrique was the rightful King of the island, according to his father's testamentary dispositions. The efforts of the Pope to prevent this election were entirely fruitless. His ambassadors were obliged to save their lives by rapid flight, and the Sicilians asked for nothing better than to take the field against Charles and the papal forces. Fadrique did not delay. He collected an army, and soon overran the whole of Calabria, and Charles could do no more than defend the coastline of Apulia. James of Aragon had been invited to Rome by Boniface in February 1296 ; the Pope offered him the post of commander-in-chief of the papal forces against the enemies of the Church, but the position of affairs in Castile gave James a reasonable excuse for declining the invitation.

Sancho had died in April 1295, and, though his son, Ferdinand IV, who was only nine years of age, had been recognized as his successor, the kingdom was in a state of considerable confusion. Ferdinand was said to have been born out of wedlock, and his brother Juan therefore assumed the royal title and entered into an alliance with the Kings of Granada and Portugal. At the same time, Alfonso de la Cerda put forward his own claims and agreed to divide the kingdom with Juan, Alfonso taking Castile, Córdoba, Toledo and Murcia, while Juan was to have the remainder. Alfonso secured the support of King James by ceding to him the province of Murcia, and in April 1296 a considerable Aragonese army invaded Castile and was joined by the forces of Juan, who had secured the support of Navarre. They captured the town of Leon without difficulty, and Juan was there crowned. At the same time, James invaded Murcia, the population of which was for the most part Catalan, and gained possession of the province without much difficulty. After this, he returned to Valencia to obey the Pope's repeated summons to Italy. He reached Rome in March 1297, where he was received with great honour by Boniface, and the wedding of his sister Violante with Duke Robert of Calabria was then celebrated. King Charles of Sicily was present, but Fadrique, who declined to come in person, was represented by Juan de Procida and Roger de Lauria. In April the Pope invested the King of Aragon and his descendants with the kingdoms of Sardinia and Corsica, to be held as fiefs of the papacy. James then returned to Catalonia and prepared to send an expedition against his brother, who vainly attempted to dissuade him, and had already made for himself a dangerous enemy by quarrelling with Roger de Lauria who went to the side of King Charles. James was unable to prosecute his designs upon Sicily for some time, as he was deeply involved in the disturbances of Castile, and also in negotiations with the Kings of France and of Mallorca. When peace had been finally concluded with Philip and the King of Mallorca had received his kingdom, to be held as a fief of Aragon, James returned to Rome with eighty galleys, and sailed for Naples where he held a council of war with King Charles. About the end of August 1298 the allies moved against Sicily. Fadrique was not able to offer any successful resistance at sea, but the invaders were unable to make much progress by land; Syracuse was besieged for several months without result, and the desperate resistance of the Sicilians, together with the demand for his supervision of affairs in Spain, induced James to give up the attempt for the moment. He returned to Barcelona early in 1299 and collected means and men for further operations. The brothers met face to face in the naval battle of Cabo Orlando : after a desperate conflict the Sicilians were defeated : but James, either disheartened by his heavy losses or influenced by the grief of his mother Constanza, abandoned his designs upon Sicily and returned to Barcelona at the end of the year.

Hitherto, James's government in Aragon itself had been continuously peaceful. The King had had no occasion to infringe the laws and privileges of the nobles. He had maintained peace and order, and had even inspired some sense of nationalityinto a considerable number of his subjects. A quarrel, however, arose which came to a head in April 1301, concerning the sums due to particular nobles for military services rendered. Those who considered themselves aggrieved formed a union, and some hostilities began in the neighbourhood of Zaragoza. James, therefore, summoned the Cortes to Zaragoza to discuss these difficulties, and also to secure the recognition of his eldest son James as his successor to the Crown. The King then declared that such combinations of nobles to secure payment of debts, the justice of which he did not acknowledge, were in any case treasonable, and he suggested that the matter should be referred to the decision of the Justicia. This proposal was accepted, and a decision was given in the King's favour. The Cortes also acecpted James's eldest son as successor to the Crown. The internal peace of Aragon was thus once more secured.

Domestic peace was the more desirable as Castile was now in a position to threaten Aragon with reprisals. Pope Boniface had declared Ferdinand to be the legal son of Sancho, and the lawful heir to the throne. Juan had resigned his claim, and was prepared to support Ferdinand, and the Queen Mother Maria, to whose energy these combinations were chiefly due, had secured the support of some distinguished Aragonese barons, and was proposing to reconquer the province of Murcia. James offered to give up the province if he could retain the town of Alicante. The Queen hesitated to accept this condition, but Ferdinand proposed to submit the matter to arbitration. The decision gave that part of Murcia to Aragon which was divided from the rest of the province by the River Segura, and peace was thus made between Aragon and Castile. Alfonso's son James was betrothed to Eleanor, Ferdinand's daughter, and Ferdinand suggested that Castile and Aragon should unite for an attack upon the Saracen kingdom of Granada. The Pope gave his blessing to the undertaking, and at the end of July Ferdinand began the siege of Algeciras, while James attacked Ceuta and Almería. The King of Granada, who came to the relief of this town, was beaten in a pitched battle, but James was unable to take Almería, the inhabitants of which defended themselves desperately. Differences broke out between the Castilians and the Aragonese, and the former (with the exception of the famous Alfonso Pérez de Guzmán, a constant friend) withdrew from the undertaking, so that James, confronted by the whole of the Moorish power, was obliged to abandon his enterprise in January 1310; in that year his queen, Blanca, died. However, friendly relations between Castile and Aragon were not broken off, and were strengthened by the marriage of Maria, James's daughter, with Pedro, the brother of Ferdinand.

Meanwhile, Sicilian affairs had been settled by the Peace of Caltabellotta, which was concluded in August 1302. The war which had continued with varying successes upon either side was concluded by the mediation of Violante, the Duchess of Calabria and sister of Fadrique. Charles of Valois was tired of the struggle, and the peace provided that Fadrique was to reign over Sicily during his lifetime as independent king, that he should marry Eleanor, the daughter of King Charles of Naples, and that his sons by Eleanor, if no principality could be found for them by the papacy, should be allowed to inherit the kingdom of Sicily, though King Charles and his heirs should have a right of purchase. There was also to be a general amnesty and an interchange of prisoners, and the Church property in Sicily, held before the revolution, was to be restored. The conclusion of this peace set at liberty the numerous mercenary forces which the King of Sicily had at his disposal, and the difficult question of their employment was finally solved by the famous expedition of the Catalans to the East. Shortly after the conclusion of peace, the celebrated admiral, Roger de Lauria, died in Valencia. He was one of the great figures of his age, and made Aragon for a time the chief naval power in the Mediterranean. His victories were often marred by ferocious acts of cruelty to the conquered, a fault due as much to the age in which he lived as to himself. But for his brilliant strategy and tactics, and the energy and rapidity of his movements, Aragon would have been brought at least once to the verge of collapse.

Hitherto James had refrained from asserting his rights to Sardinia. The island had been captured from the Moors in 1050 by the combined forces of Genoa and Pisa, the latter town claiming a general sovereignty ; quarrels soon began and the island had for some time been a bone of contention between the two towns. When Boniface gave the islands to James in 1303, he had ordered the inhabitants to submit to the King of Aragon and had sent a similar admonition to Pisa and Genoa. As these commands were not obeyed, James determined to conquer the islands as soon as his quarrel with Castile had been settled, and began to make preparations for this purpose in 1309, inviting Florence, Lucca and other Guelf towns in

Tuscany to join him against Pisa. However, nothing was done at the time, as the citizens of Pisa induced him to abandon the enterprise in return for a large sum of money, and the Guelfs in Italy were obliged to combine for their own defence against Henry VII. James was also occupied by the attack upon the Order of the Templars, initiated with the support of the Pope by Philip the Fair of France. The atrocious charges brought against the French Templars were not sustained in Aragon ; none the less, the influence of the papacy and the bishops induced the King to suppress the Order and in 1317 most of its possessions in Aragon were taken over by the Order of St. John.

In 1321 James was induced to resume his designs upon Sardinia, by an invitation from Hugo de Sera, the judge of Arborea and a Guelf who was more anxious to exterminate the Ghibellines than to help the claims of Aragon. In 1322 an outbreak between the Guelfs and the Ghibellines in Genoa had thrown the town into such confusion that no resistance was to be expected from that quarter. James, therefore, revised his plan and commissioned his son Alfonso to conquer Sardinia, and to attack the inhabitants of Pisa, who held the best part of the island. His subjects, especially the Barcelonese, readily supported the undertaking, and a great army was prepared. King Robert of Naples, then at war with Fadrique of Sicily, became alarmed for the safety of his own kingdom, and the citizens of Pisa once again attempted to purchase peace by offering to indemnify James for all the costs of the expedition. However, on this occasion the expedition started and James solemnly sent Alfonso forth with the command to conquer or to die. He had already secured the adherence of some of the chief land-holders in Sardinia by promises that they should not be disturbed in their tenancy, and Alfonso was able to effect a landing without difficulty, and to besiege Iglesias and Caller (or Cagliari), two of the chief towns. These were captured in 1324 and an attempt from Pisa to raise the siege was completely defeated. In that year a peace was signed, Pisa ceding the sovereignty of the island to Aragon, but continuing to hold in fief the town and territory of Caller. This victory is said to have cost the lives of 1200 Aragonese and Catalan soldiers and for years to come a succession of rebellions and disturbances cost the rulers of Aragon dearly.

Of the legislative acts of James's reign mention should be made of the Act of Union passed in December 1319, by which the kingdoms of Aragon and Valencia, the county of Barcelona and the feudal territories of Mallorca were united under one rule, on condition that these realms should never be divided by testamentary disposition or by donation, though the King reserved the right to himself and his successors to make donations of individual castles and properties. It was resolved that this law should form part of the rights and privileges of the realm to which the Kings swore obedience at their coronation. Apart from the disturbances which we have mentioned, the Aragonese kingdom enjoyed an unusual period of peace and order under the government of James. His careful regard for law and justice secured him from his subjects the name of the Just, to which his foreign policy hardly entitled him ; his desertion of Sicily, his war against his brother and his suppression of the Knights Templar do not redound to his credit.

CHAPTER X

THE CATALAN EXPEDITION TO THE EAST

THE peace of Caltabellota, concluded in August 1302, ended the twenty years of struggle known as the War of the Vespers. Fadrique of Sicily was then confronted with the problem of finding maintenance or occupation for the Almogávares who had largely helped him to secure his independence. These troops lived for war and plunder ; a menace and a plague in times of peace, like the White Companies in Southern France at a later date, they were a very formidable force of ferocious ruffians whom impoverished Sicily was unable to maintain or employ, and it was a relief to Fadrique, who felt that he owed them a debt of gratitude, when an opening was found for their undoubted capacities in the Byzantine Empire. Relations between Constantinople and Aragon had been begun when Charles of Anjou developed his projects of conquest in that quarter : and such was the position of the Byzantine power at the moment, that the help of the Catalan forces was more than welcome. The prospect which had attracted Charles of Anjou was no novelty : the crusades had familiarized Western Europe with the problems of Byzantine civilization and the Venetians had been especially interested in the commercial advantages enjoyed by Constantinople. The Fourth Crusade was directed by the Venetian Enrique Dandolo against Constantinople, in spite of the remonstrances of Pope

Innocent III, and in 1204 he had secured possession of the Byzantine capital. In 1261 the Genoese, the continual rivals of Venice, enabled Michael Paleologus to return, and Genoa became the most influential power at the Byzantine court. Continual attacks by the Turks upon the eastern side and by Bulgars and Serbs on the west, necessitated the maintenance of a strong military force : the danger became imminent in the time of Michael's son and successor, Andronicus II, who recruited mercenaries from the tribes on the Danube and Dnieper, generally known as Alans. The eventual successor of Andronicus, Michael IX, attacked the Turks in 1301 with an army of Byzantine troops and mercenaries and was utterly defeated. The Turks advanced to the Sea of Marmora, and the Byzantine Empire seemed to be on the brink of ruin when Michael received an offer of help from the Catalans.

The proposal was made by the Catalan leader, Roger de Flor, who knew something of the dangers which beset the Byzantine power. He was the son of one Richard Blum, a German falconer to Frederick VI who had married an Italian woman, and was killed in the battle of Tagliacozzo. Rutger von Blum was translated as Ruggero della Fiore and hence Roger de Flor. He had gained high distinction as a sailor or licensed pirate, brought up in the excellent school of Roger de Lauria. With the permission of Fadrique, he went to Constantinople to settle the conditions of service under the Byzantine Empire : his demands as regards payment of his troops were readily conceded, as also was his wish to receive the title of Megaduc and the hand of Maria, the Emperor's cousin. Among other outstanding figures of the expedition, mention must be made of Ramon Muntaner, its historian. His work is excellent reading ; he speaks as an eye-witness to hearers in a simple unaffected manner and there is no reason to doubt his veracity : he was no scholar, confuses Thrace with Macedonia and makes Helen of Troy the wife of a duke of Athens ; he is inclined to exaggerate numbers, especially of the enemy whom his compatriots defeated, but he remains a chief authority for the narrative of the expedition which the partiality of the Byzantine chroniclers has somewhat obscured.

The conditions proposed by Roger de Flor were accepted by Andronicus and the expedition sailed from Sicily, reaching

its destination in September 1303. Sicily was in too
impoverished a condition to offer any financial help, but
provided a fleet of transports and some provisions. Roger
expended his personal fortune and borrowed 20,000 ducats
from the Genoese, a loan guaranteed by Andronicus. The
numbers according to Muntaner, whose figures are not
contradicted by the Byzantine historians, were 1500 cavalry
(who were to be horsed in Constantinople), 4000 foot, 1000
sailors with the women and children of many : in all some

MAP 6. GREECE IN 1384, WITH THE ROUTE OF THE CATALANS IN ASIA MINOR,
THRACE AND MACEDONIA

8000 persons. The court gave them a flattering reception and
the marriage of Maria with Roger de Flor was celebrated
without delay. The Genoese, however, who had long been
established in Galata, resented the presence of the new-
comers, and a quarrel became a riot in which numbers of
Genoese were killed. To avoid trouble with the Republic
of Genoa, Andronicus decided to hasten the departure of
his new allies as soon as possible. Supported by some
Greek and Alan mercenaries, the Catalans set sail for Cyzicus
where they established themselves on the isthmus on which
the town is situated. The Turkish forces which had been
ravaging the district were encamped at no great distance.

The Catalans after a night march, surprised and completely defeated them : no quarter was given, women and children alone being spared, and 10,000 of the enemy are said to have fallen, while much valuable booty was captured. Constantinople was thus relieved of fears for the immediate future, but a strong party within the capital, headed by Michael the heir-apparent, were strongly opposed to the policy of Andronicus and regretted the success of those whom they regarded as barbarians in comparison with themselves, the inheritors of Hellenic culture and civilization. This feeling found no open expression for the moment, as the Catalans spent the winter in Cyzicus ; the Megaduc, Roger, who had sent to Constantinople for his bride, organized their winter quarters and did his best to preserve discipline among the troops and prevent excesses.

Early in April 1304 Roger de Flor prepared to continue operations against the Turks. He was delayed by a conflict between his own troops and the Alan mercenaries, the outcome of which reduced the mercenary force on which he could rely. When this matter had been settled, he advanced to relieve Philadelphia, which was besieged by the Emir of Caramaria, one Ali Shir, a notable figure among the Turkish chieftains, who then divided Anatolia among themselves. The Catalans completely defeated a force of 12,000 foot and 800 horse with a loss to themselves of less than 200 men : Philadelphia was occupied and Roger then advanced upon Magnesia. His troops were accustomed to live upon the country and were unencumbered with baggage, but Roger wished to keep in touch with his fleet and therefore remained within reach of the coast. The Byzantine Empire was divided into districts governed by *strategoi* and the governor of Magnesia had declared himself independent. The arrival of the Catalan forces brought him back to a show of allegiance : he went to Constantinople, and while declaring his loyalty accused the Catalans of terrorizing the district and exacting tribute from the populations : he found supporters among the court party who objected to the introduction of the Catalan mercenaries. But Maria, the wife of the Megaduc, made her influence felt, Roger received the Emperor's thanks for his achievements and his opponents were discredited and disgraced. His next advance was to Tyrranim (Tyra), some

10

forty miles from Magnesia ; the inhabitants begged him to help them against the Turks who were devastating the country and threatening the town. Here again a complete victory was won, with the loss of Corberan de Alet, an officer of rank who was killed in the pursuit. His place was taken by Bernard de Rocafort, who had arrived at Constantinople from Sicily with 200 horses and 1000 foot and had been ordered by the Emperor to join Roger de Flor. The reinforcements travelled by sea and met the main body at Ephesus, which Roger had already entered. The advance continued southwards as far as Mount Taurus, the Turks retiring before them until a fresh victory at the Cilician Gates scattered them completely. Some members of the expedition wished to continue the advance and to push on as far as Palestine. Roger, however, realized the risk of advancing further into difficult country without guides and with the prospect of facing the winter season. He gave his troops a week's rest and began the return journey. The Byzantine historians assert that the Catalans inflicted more damage upon the country than the Turks had ever caused. Some plundering was certainly committed by the Alan mercenaries, who had been left behind to garrison Magnesia and who revolted in order to secure the rich booty which Roger had stored in the town.

Roger had begun the siege of Magnesia when he was recalled by an urgent message from Andronicus, who wished him to support his nephew Michael in a war against the Bulgarians. The legitimate heir to the Bulgarian throne, John Assan III, who was the father-in-law of Roger de Flor by his recent marriage, had been deprived of his inheritance by a usurper, Teter. Michael was the son of the dethroned Assan and consequently the brother-in-law of Roger, and was prosecuting his claim, with the result that Thrace was menaced by a Bulgarian force. The quarrel was eventually ended by a marriage between Teter's son and one of Michael's daughters, and it has been suggested that Andronicus machined an unimportant dispute into an excuse adequate for recalling the Catalans. There is no doubt that, like every one else, he was astonished by their amazing success and began to fear that the new ally might become a positive danger to himself, suspicions no doubt fomented by the Genoese in

Constantinople. The Catalans rejoined their fleet at Anea,
and disembarked on the Thracian Chersonese, making the
town of Gallipoli their centre and finding excellent winter
quarters in the Gallipoli peninsula. Muntaner speaks of
it as the most fertile country in the world, there being bread,
wine and fruit of every kind, while the towns provided good
houses and other amenities of life. When Roger de Flor had
settled his troops in their winter quarters he went to Constantinople and was warmly received by the Emperor Andronicus.
The emperor's satisfaction was somewhat damped by a
demand for arrears of pay which he had not expected, as he
supposed that the Catalans would be satisfied with the booty
they had collected in Anatolia. The Catalans were at that
moment joined by Berenguer de Entenza who arrived at
Gallipoli with 100 horse and 1000 foot. This leader was
descended from a family in Ribagorza which had divided
into an Aragonese and a Catalan branch, to the latter of which
he belonged. He had already gained a considerable military
reputation and was received by Andronicus with an outward
show of satisfaction. There were some inward misgivings at
this addition to the forces of an ally whom the Emperor had
begun to regard as a possible menace to himself. Roger
had not forgotten the kindness that he had received
from Entenza in his early years and was prepared to resign
his title of Megaduc and his position to the new arrival.
After some discussion Entenza agreed to accept the position,
but Andronicus, anxious not to offend Roger, conferred
upon him the title of Cæsar, a dignity which had not previously been given to any foreigner. Relations, however,
between the Greeks and the Catalans remained in a state of
tension which was brought to a head by the question of pay.
Andronicus was eventually induced to pay the arrears in
depreciated coinage which may then have been current in
his own kingdom but was regarded by the Catalans as a fraud.
A great uproar broke out as soon as they realized the manner
in which they were being cheated. Entenza threw the
insignia of his office into the sea and Roger de Flor, to pacify
the troops, was obliged to sacrifice his personal property
and his wife's jewels. The Catalans considered themselves
at liberty to reimburse themselves at the expense of the local
population, and, while Greek historians probably exaggerate

the excesses they committed, they were no doubt an oppressive
burden to the inhabitants. Andronicus, therefore, reopened
discussions with Roger in order to relieve the situation and
it was eventually agreed that the Asiatic provinces should be
held by the Catalans in feudal obligation to the Byzantine
Empire. The Catalans were to render military service when
the Emperor desired it and the Emperor should be relieved
of responsibility for their payment with the exception of a
certain annual subsidy payable at the beginning of each
year. Roger persuaded his men to accept this composition
which was advantageous to both sides. Andronicus was
relieved of financial responsibility for the Almogávares and
could keep them at a distance from Constantinople, while
Roger, as a vassal of the Empire, could exploit Anatolia to
his heart's content.

News which he received in the spring made it clear that
further operations were necessary. The Turks were besieging
Philadelphia and had also occupied the island of Chios. The
Catalans were preparing to cross the Hellespont when
the course of events was completely changed by a wholly
unexpected incident. Roger thought it was necessary
before departing to present his respects to the Prince
Michael, who made no secret of his dislike for the whole of
the Catalan force. Princess Maria, who appears to have been
deeply in love with her husband Roger and who suspected
some plot against his safety, begged him not to visit Adrianopolis where Michael was stationed with the army with which
he had been fighting against the Bulgarians. Roger declined to
listen to this advice, and went to Adrianopolis with an escort
of 1000 foot and 300 horse. He sent his wife to Constantinople
and left the army at Gallipoli under the command of Entenza
and Rocafort. Roger was received by Michael with a great
show of amiability and a series of banquets and entertain-
ments ; but on April 4, 1305, a treacherous attack was
made upon the Catalans in the course of a banquet. Roger
and all the Catalan leaders who were taking part were
assassinated and the Byzantine mercenaries attacked and
killed the escort with the exception of two or three who
escaped to Gallipoli. The loss to the expedition was irre-
parable. Roger enjoyed a respect and admiration which
no other leader could acquire ; his subordinates, Entenza and

Rocafort, were rather rivals than friends and their animosity eventually wrecked the prospects of the expedition. The tragic event has been recorded more than once in Spanish literature. The Catalan novel of chivalry, *Tirant lo Blanch*, was partly inspired by recollections of this expedition and in the last century the play by García Gutiérrez, *Venganza Catalana*, obtained a considerable success in 1865.

Michael was not content with the massacre of Adrianopolis but dispatched his Alan mercenaries to attack the Catalans in Gallipoli. They were speedily repulsed and the Almo-gávares ravaged the peninsula and exterminated the whole of the inhabitants. They now found themselves reduced to some 3500 men and confronted by the army of Michael, which was said to have amounted to 30,000 foot and 10,000 horse. The peninsula was, however, easily defensible and Entenza raised a rampart across the narrowest point, and with a respect for the laws of war which the behaviour of the Byzantines hardly justified, sent ambassadors to Constantinople to declare war upon the Empire. The ambassadors delivered their message but were assassinated on their return journey and the Catalans prepared for a desperate resistance. At that moment Don Sancho of Aragon, a natural son of Pedro III, arrived at Gallipoli with ten Sicilian galleys and was received with great satisfaction by the besieged who had been roused to fury by the news of the assassination of their ambas-sadors. They decided to send messengers to the King of Sicily, and Don Sancho undertook to enlighten him upon the situation. The Catalan fleet then proceeded to ravage the shores of Thrace and of the Hellespont and a continual stream of terror-stricken refugees arrived at Constantinople, to the surprise of Andronicus, who had hoped that the Catalans were well on the road to Sicily. In the course of these depredations Entenza with four ships met a squadron of eighteen galleys emerging from the Dardanelles and prepared for battle, expecting to be cut off from Gallipoli. The squadron, how-ever, was discovered to be Genoese, and the leader of it, one Andrea Doria, declared his friendship for the Catalans. As we have said, hostilities between Catalans and Genoese had begun from the moment of their arrival in Constantinople and the Genoese, in the hope of currying favour with Androni-cus, now detained Entenza as a prisoner and destroyed his small squadron, though at considerable loss to themselves. The disaster of Adrianopolis was thus repeated and while the Catalan forces showed themselves invincible in war they appear as mere children in fathoming the designs of a treacherous and implacable enemy. Andronicus did his best to purchase Berenguer de Entenza from his captor. The Catalans also attempted to ransom him, but the Genoese took him back to Italy with the expectation that they would gain a larger ransom at home.

Rocafort now assembled a council of war which resolved not to abandon Gallipoli and to sink the remaining vessels in order to prevent any reversal of this decision. Twelve councillors were chosen to support Rocafort in his command of the 2500 men to which they were now reduced. In front of them was a Greek force of some 10,000 men and the Catalans resolved to make a big sortie and to relieve the situation or die in the attempt. The Byzantine forces were surprised and thrown into complete confusion. No reliance can be placed upon the numbers of slain given by either Muntaner or the Greek historians, but there is no doubt that the Catalans utterly defeated a considerable force with very slight loss to themselves. After this victory they returned to their quarters in Gallipoli and the historian Muntaner, who was in general command of the camp and its arrangements, sent out spies to Adrianopolis and Constantinople to discover the intentions of the Greeks. He was informed that an enormous army was being collected to crush the Catalan forces once and for all. The Catalans again resolved not to wait behind their fortifications but to advance. They met the enemy near the town of Apros and once again the Greeks were completely defeated and the town was captured in July 1305. The inhabitants of all open towns in the neighbourhood took refuge in Constantinople, and such was the general panic that, if Muntaner can be believed, a shout of " Francs " was enough to produce a general flight in any quarter. The extraordinary victories gained by this handful of men over numbers which, however exaggerated by the historians, were certainly very much larger than their own, give the narrative of their exploits an almost fabulous character ; but it must be remembered that in the first place the Catalans introduced methods of war to which the Eastern Empire was wholly unaccustomed, and secondly that the Byzantine armies consisted of the dregs of a decadent population devoid of patriotic feeling and more anxious to escape from the enemy than to risk their lives. The real strength of the Byzantine forces depended upon their mercenaries who were already beginning to waver towards the Catalan cause, and the Greeks were without any leader who possessed any kind of military prestige. The situation then was that Andronicus was shut up in Constantinople and Michael in Adrianopolis ; Thrace was open to the incursions of the Catalans and there was no safety for the inhabitants except behind the walls of a fortified town, while the only answer which the Byzantine rulers could give to the lamentations and complaints of their subjects was the pious reflection that they must patiently bear what was doubtless a punishment from heaven for their past sins.

Rocafort now remained the leader of the Catalans. If his political insight had been one quarter as great as his military prowess he might easily have founded a separate estate in Anatolia or in Gallipoli itself with which Andronicus would have been glad to negotiate. In Gallipoli he held an excellent strategical position and could menace any part of the Byzantine Empire without difficulty. But the Catalan forces were swayed merely by military instincts and a desire for revenge, and devoted themselves to ravaging the countryside without consideration for the future. If they were not to remain as an organized community, their better plan would have been to demand a fleet and a heavy indemnity from Andronicus for the purpose of return to their own country, and the Emperor would probably have been glad to get rid of them at any price. As it was, they preferred to extend their raids further afield. The town of Rodosto, for instance, nearly half-way to Constantinople on a northern shore of the Sea of Marmora, was stormed by them and every one of the inhabitants was put to death. Some part of their forces was permanently installed in the town, and such was their confidence in their own prestige that they left less than 200 men for the defence of Gallipoli, which was entrusted to the historian Muntaner.

The Catalans were then joined by Fernando Jiménez de Arenos, who had begun the expedition with Roger de Flor,

but had left him for a time to take service under the Duke of
Athens. He now appeared with some small reinforcements
and joined the raiders on the north coast of the Sea of
Marmora. As he did not care to settle in Gallipoli near
Rocafort, with whom he was on bad terms, he attacked
Modico, or Maidos, a fortified town on the narrows of the
Dardanelles. This was captured in July 1306 after a somewhat lengthy siege and Arenos then made it his headquarters.
Rocafort and his forces usually occupied the northern end
of the peninsula while Muntaner was in command of the
central position where were established the warehouses and
stores of the company, the hospitals and the market where
booty was sold and a considerable slave trade went on.
Muntaner acted as the quartermaster-general for the army
and was also military governor of Gallipoli, where resided
a considerable number of non-combatants, old men, women
and children in some sort of relationship to the Catalans.
Rocafort and Arenos united their forces and attacked Stenia,
which was the imperial arsenal about eight miles to the north
of the Golden Horn. Making a great circuit they avoided
Constantinople itself and advanced to the shore of the Black
Sea, leaving devastation behind them, until they reached the
arsenal ; they burnt some 150 ships in course of construc-
tion or completed, seized four of their galleys which the
Greeks had captured at the time of the assassination, set
the town on fire, broke down the dykes which kept out
the sea-water, loaded their galleys with booty and sailed
home in front of Constantinople. Andronicus attempted to
open negotiations with his enemies but without success.
Their next business was an attack upon the Alan mercenaries.
These had been the chief instruments in the assassination of
Roger de Flor. The Catalans heard that they were leaving the
service of the Emperor and returning home through Bulgaria,
and resolved to catch them before they crossed the Balkans.
They were obviously a more formidable enemy than the
unwarlike Greeks, and the Catalan leaders therefore resolved
to strip Gallipoli of its defenders and leave Muntaner in charge
of the women, the children and the sick. He was, however,
given some 200 foot and about 20 horse, a force reduced
to about 140 by deserters who wished to follow the main
expedition. The Catalans appear to have caught up the

Alans somewhere in the neighbourhood of Mount Hemus, but it is impossible to follow their route with any exactitude. They defeated a force of some 9000 men and are said to have killed nearly all of them and to have captured enormous booty. The losses to themselves, though not considerable, were greater than those they had suffered in their combats with the Greeks.

Meanwhile Andronicus appears to have received news of this expedition and to have thought that the opportunity was favourable for attacking Gallipoli. A fleet of eighteen Genoese galleys had arrived at Byzantium under the command of Antonio Spinola. They were to bring back to Italy Theodore, the son of Andronicus, and his second wife Yoland Irene, whose father William V, Marquis of Monferrat, had died, Theodore thus inheriting his possessions. The King's commander agreed to join in an attack upon Gallipoli, on condition that Theodore should marry the daughter of a relative of his own. Spinola then sailed to Gallipoli and ordered Muntaner to surrender in the name of the Genoese Republic. Muntaner gained time by pointing out that Genoa and Aragon were not at war, and threatened him with the vengeance of Aragon if he persisted. Spinola none the less retired to prepare for an attack upon Gallipoli. Muntaner armed all his women and stationed them upon the rampart in squads under the command of such men as he had. He brought up supplies of food and drink that the defenders might not be obliged to leave their posts and the women showed themselves worthy wives of famous warriors. Many were wounded but refused to quit their posts and kept up such a shower of darts and stones upon the heads of the attackers that they were rapidly beaten off. Spinola disembarked with 300 chosen men and attacked in person, but Muntaner collected his own men and made a sudden sortie which threw the Genoese into confusion, in the course of which Spinola himself was killed. The Catalans pursued the enemy to their ships, who retired without delay, and Rocafort, who had heard of the attack upon Gallipoli and was hastening back by forced marches, was relieved to find that the bravery of the defenders had been successful.

In the autumn of 1306 the Catalans received some reinforcements of Turkish mercenaries. These were probably troops

employed by the Byzantine Empire, who saw greater opportunities of booty and profit with the Catalans. They do
not appear to have amounted to more than 1500 men,
who were given separate quarters to themselves, with half
the pay allotted to an *almogávar*, and were at liberty to leave
the service when they pleased. Muntaner gives them a good
character as loyal and obedient troops.

Entenza, as we have said, had been taken prisoner by
the Genoese, who took him back to their own republic, the
government of which, far from disowning this act of aggression
against Aragon, imprisoned the Catalan leader. James II
of Aragon was then approached by messengers from the East,
explaining the state of affairs in Thrace, and asking him to
procure the release of Entenza. They also suggested that he
should accept the homage of the Catalan expedition and
regard them as his vassals. James was prepared to deal
with Genoa, but he considered that the question of feudal
obligation was rather one for the King of Sicily. The Genoese
Republic agreed to release Entenza, and went so far as to
offer to indemnify him for any loss he had incurred. The
Republic was particularly anxious to secure the evacuation of
the Catalans from the East, as they were damaging the
Genoese trade. The Catalan ambassadors then proceeded to
Rome, and asked the Pope to give their undertaking the
character of a crusade. The papacy was not upon friendly
terms with the House of Aragon ; its sympathies lay rather
with the family of Anjou, and their request was, therefore,
declined. Entenza was able to recruit some 500 men at his
personal expense, with which he returned to Gallipoli.

His arrival became the occasion of a quarrel which had
serious consequences for the future of the expedition.
Entenza claimed the position of commander-in-chief, but
was reminded that the enterprise which had ended in his
imprisonment had been undertaken by him against the
opinion of the majority, and might have led to the loss of
Gallipoli. The supporters of his opponent, Rocafort, could
point to the successes obtained under his leadership, the
advantage derived from the help of Turkish mercenaries,
and the fact that he was the master of almost the whole of
Thrace. The result was the formation of two definite parties,
and the difference between them was not diminished by the

fact that Entenza was a *ricohombre* of high nobility, while Rocafort could lay no claim to any such qualification. Entenza's party was smaller than that of Rocafort, but contained the most competent and energetic members of the expedition. For some time the bands operated independently of one another, and during the winter carried out various raids in the interior of Thrace. Andronicus sent out emissaries to propose a peace, but without result. He sought for allies, and could find none. The Genoese secured a promise from the Catalans that their commerce should not be interrupted, and the Turks recovered their lost ground in Asia Minor. It only remained for the Catalans to attack the capital of Constantinople, but they were well aware that such an enterprise required greater forces than they possessed, and that it would be difficult to hold the town, even if they captured it. But Constantinople and its Emperor were in constant terror of an assault. Religious processions passed daily through the streets, and fugitives from the country increased the existing panic, while the Catalans dealt with the surrounding districts much as they pleased.

In March 1307, Fadrique of Sicily signed a compact with Don Fernando, the son of the King of Mallorca, in virtue of which Fernando was to go to the East and take command of the Catalan expedition, and govern the country in the interests of Sicily. Fernando undertook to observe an offensive and defensive alliance with Sicily, and not to marry without Fadrique's approval. The latter, on his part, was to support the expedition with money and men. Fernando appears to have arrived at Gallipoli in the summer of 1307, bearing letters to the leaders, who were asked by the King of Sicily to receive him as his own representative. Both the leaders and the rank and file welcomed the arrival of Fernando, with the exception of Rocafort, who held aloof and eventually wrecked a situation which might have put the expedition upon a permanent footing, and have more closely united the Houses of Aragon and Sicily.

The leaders had already resolved to leave Thrace and advance into Macedonia, their final objective being Salonica. Nearly two years had passed since the assassination of Roger de Flor, and the neighbouring country had been so completely devastated that it could no longer support the troops, for whom an additional supply of provisions was necessary, as their numbers had been increased by the coming of the Turks. They proposed to march along the north coast of Macedonia and, if necessary, to proceed into Thessaly. The project of a sea-voyage was abandoned, owing to the difficulty of providing and provisioning ships in sufficient force to withstand the possible danger from pirates. The expedition therefore dismantled its quarters in Gallipoli, leaving the peninsula one complete desolation, and set out in two bands, one commanded by Rocafort, while with the other were the Infante, Entenza and Arenos. It was agreed that they should always keep a day's march from one another. Muntaner undertook to convoy the women and the sick to the town of Christopolis, opposite to the island of Thasos, with the thirty-six vessels that they had at their disposal.

Such a march, through difficult country, with one flank continually exposed, was dangerous enough, but the first hostilities occurred between the two bodies. The column of Rocafort was caught up by that of Entenza, and, assuming that an attack was intended, flew to arms and charged upon them. In the resulting conflict 750 men are said to have been killed, among them Entenza himself, and only the arrival of the Infante, Fernando, put an end to the conflict. This disaster broke up Entenza's party. Arenos threw in his lot with the Emperor of Constantinople, who received him kindly, gave him a title and a princess as his wife. The Infante declined to continue with the expedition, as Rocafort had refused to recognize his powers, and went across to the island of Thasos, where he found Muntaner, who had been unable to land at Christopolis, as the Catalans were not in possession of the town. Fernando explained the situation to Muntaner, and suggested that he should accompany him home to Sicily, which Muntaner was willing to do after he had discharged his duty to the Catalans with regard to the sick and women and the supplies under his charge. When this had been done, he sailed with the Infante, leaving the island of Thasos at the end of July 1307.

Fernando and Muntaner sailed southwards until they reached the island of Euboea, and followed the Straits as far as Chalcis, which was then under the influence of the Venetians. The leading figure in the district known as

Negroponto, as the island was then called, was one Thibaut de Chepoy, who was in the service of Charles of Valois, the brother of the French King. He was one of the many people who had remained behind in the course of the crusades, and settled in one of the ports of the Levant. Charles of Valois, who had claimed the crown of Aragon and of Sicily, had also designs upon that of Byzantium, and Chepoy represented his interests in Northern Greece and in the provinces where the Republic of Venice had signed a treaty of alliance with Charles. The Infante disembarked after receiving assurances of a safe conduct, but Chepoy attacked the Catalan galleys and captured the whole of the little expedition. The Infante was taken with his chief retainers to Thebes, and the Duke of Athens, Gui II de la Roche, imprisoned him until he could learn the intentions of Charles of Valois. However, the mediation of his father, the King of Mallorca, secured his freedom, and he was eventually enabled to return to Roussillon.

Meanwhile, Rocafort's forces were advancing upon Christopolis. They eventually made their way to the peninsula of Chalcidice, and captured the town of Cassandra, the ancient Pallene, where they received a visit from Chepoy, who brought with him as prisoner Muntaner and one Palacín, whom Rocafort immediately executed as being a friend of Entenza. Muntaner, however, was well received, and his popularity among the Almogávares secured him many rich presents. Chepoy explained his anxiety to secure the help of the expedition on behalf of Charles of Valois, and Rocafort, who had refused to do homage to the King of Sicily, agreed to swear fidelity to a French prince who was hostile to the House of Aragon, and against whom probably some members of the expedition had fought in Italy. Muntaner remained for some time in Cassandra, well aware of the insecurity of his position He was able to embark at length upon a Venetian ship, on which he finally reached Messina, and informed the King of Sicily of the fate of the expedition. He also asked for permission to return to Catalonia. The King, however, made him Governor of the island of Gerbes or Jerba, where he remained until 1315. He then lived for some time in Valencia, and finally in the Balearic Islands, where he died in 1336, at about the age of seventy. He is certainly the most

attractive figure among the leaders of the expedition. He was
loyal to his leaders, self-sacrificing in the interests of the enterprise, and gave proof in his defence of Gallipoli, and upon other
occasions, of considerable military skill and powers of
organization.

The Catalans were deeply irritated by the action of Rocafort in espousing the cause of the House of Anjou, and, as
Chepoy suspected him of entertaining designs upon the
province of Thessalonica, he was able to make arrangements
with the Catalans for the deposition of their leader. Rocafort,
with his brother, was taken prisoner and handed over to the
King of Naples, Robert, who had a private quarrel with one
of them which he avenged by confining them in one of his
castles and leaving them to die of hunger. Thus the original
leaders of the expedition had all disappeared, and the last
of them was probably the worst, a man without providence
for the future or political sense, and continually irritated
with his superiors by a feeling of his own social inferiority,
a man too, whose ambitions were purely selfish, and the
complete antithesis of such a character as Muntaner.

The Catalans then chose governors among themselves,
and remained for some time in Cassandra, devastating the
province until they were induced to take service with the
Duke of Athens. After an attack upon Thessalonica they
resolved to return to Thrace, but Andronicus had barred
their way. They therefore marched upon Thessaly, descend-
ing from the mountains of Olympus in 1310. Thessaly was
then governed by John Angelo, who had married a natural
daughter of the Emperor Andronicus. He made no effort
to oppose the Catalans, but gave them a safe-conduct through
his country. The Duke of Athens, Walter de Brienne,
wished to extend his influence in Thessaly and took the
Catalans into his service; in six months they captured a
number of fortresses for the Duke, who then wanted to be
rid of them. The Catalans refused to go and the Duke
determined to drive them out. In the spring of 1311 a battle
was fought on the banks of the Cephissus; the Catalans
converted the battle-field into a marsh by diverting the river,
so that the cavalry of the enemy was unable to operate and
the Duke was utterly defeated. Thebes and Athens were then
attacked by the Catalans, who took possession of them without

difficulty, and their leader, Roger Deslaur, became Governor of the province. Some time afterwards, either because he had died or had become tired of his position, the adventurers sent an embassy to Sicily asking the King for a governor. Fadrique sent them his second son Manfred, with a Catalan knight as his guardian, Manfred being then of tender years, who was called Berenguer de Estanyol. Upon his death Fadrique sent out his other son Alfonso Fadrique, and with his arrival the expedition may be said to have ended. The Sicilian duchy of Athens, which was thus founded, lasted until the year 1387.

The political effects of this extraordinary venture were of no account, nor could any other result be expected. The expedition was begun for no other purpose than to relieve Sicily of a formidable body of unoccupied mercenaries. Aragon had no intention of founding an eastern state or of competing with the Italian republics to secure a trade monopoly. Had the Catalan mercenaries possessed a glimmer of political sense or any capacity for self-government, circumstances might have enabled them to form a separate state in Gallipoli or Anatolia, but the Almogávares and their leaders, after the murder of Roger de Flor, which made them the deadly enemies of the Byzantine Empire, had no thoughts except for war and plunder. It may, therefore, be considered that this chapter belongs more properly to the history of the Byzantine Empire than to that of Aragon ; but no Catalan writer will ever forget the fact that a few thousand warriors from his country became for six years the terror of Asia Minor, of Constantinople and of Greece, marching as and where they pleased, routing armies, destroying fleets and desolating provinces, from the Taurus Mountains to the Acropolis of Athens ; and the tale of their adventures, well-attested as it is, resembles rather the fantastic legends of some fabulous generation than the comparatively sober and pedestrian course of European history.

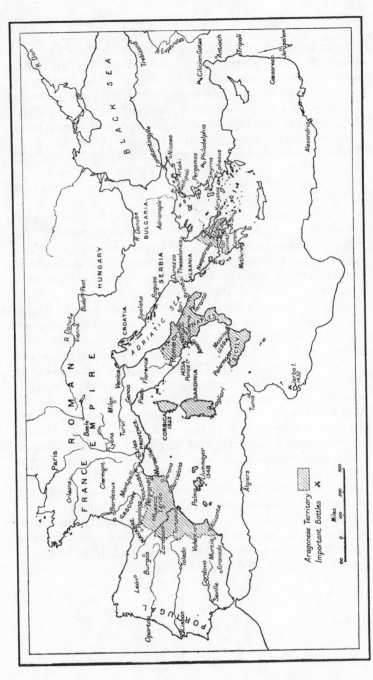

MAP 7. THE ARAGONESE EMPIRE AT ITS GREATEST EXTENT

CHAPTER XI

ALFONSO IV

His Castilian policy. Moorish invasion. War with Sardinia and Genoa.
Domestic troubles. His death.

JAMES died on November 2, 1327, in the sixty-sixth year
of his age, amid the general and genuine grief of his
subjects. His eldest son, who bore his name, was a young
man of idle and dissolute life who eventually renounced the
succession and retired to a monastery. James was therefore
succeeded by his second son Alfonso IV, whose wife Teresa de
Entenza had died only five days before his accession.
The procedure followed when a new king ascended the throne
had now become settled : the reign *de facto* was begun by
taking the usual oaths at Barcelona, after which the coronation in Aragon began the reign *de jure*. Accordingly Alfonso
spent Christmas at Barcelona, where he swore to observe
the privileges of Catalonia and received the homage of
his subjects for their fiefs. Early in 1328 he went to Zaragoza, where his coronation took place with unprecedented
splendour. Ambassadors from Castile, Navarre, Bohemia
and Granada, nobles from France and Spain, and a great
concourse of his own nobility attended a succession of
festivities, which were concluded by holding Cortes at which
the King confirmed the laws and privileges of Aragon.
Alfonso had already become involved in the disturbances
which were then harassing Castile ; Ferdinand IV had died
in 1312, leaving a son under two years of age, Alfonso XI,
who assumed the responsibilities of government in 1325.
His chief opponent was the Infante Juan Manuel, a nephew
of Alfonso X, who had applied for help to the King of Aragon.
Some Aragonese barons had been allowed to support him,
but, at the same time, the King sent ambassadors to the
court of Castile for the purpose of reconciling the contending

11   161

parties. The result was an alliance between the two Kings, which was also accepted by the King of Portugal, and the claims of the Infante Juan were set aside ; by the marriage of Alfonso of Aragon with Eleanor, the sister of the King of Castile, the alliance was further confirmed, and proposals were made for joint action against the King of Granada. Alfonso went to Valencia to supervise the preparations for this war in person, concluded a peace with the King of Tremecen, and received a grant from the Pope of the ecclesiastical tithe for two years ; but his intention of taking the field in person against the Moors was prevented by a revolt in Sardinia in 1330, and all that he could do was to send a fleet of twelve galleys against the enemy's coast and grant permission to the knightly orders within his kingdom to join the King of Castile, who won a brilliant victory over the Moors in 1330, and secured an armistice for a year ; but, before the expiration of that period, the Moors suddenly invaded Valencia, secured the support of the Moorish inhabitants in the southern part of the kingdom, and began to besiege Alicante, which was, however, relieved by Alfonso's energetic measures. In the following year, 1332, a numerous Moorish force also appeared before Elche, but this time a successful resistance was offered, and the appearance of the King obliged the Moors to beat a hasty retreat.

Alfonso, however, was not in a position to pursue this advantage, in spite of the representations of the King of Castile. The bulk of his forces were required to subdue a formidable revolt in Sardinia. The Genoese inhabitants of the island had proved very restive under the new government which had tried to restrain their previous disorderly habits, and a quarrel between certain nobles ended in a demonstration against the King's officials in Sassari. The King thereupon ordered that all Sardinian and foreign inhabitants of the town should leave it and take service under other subjects of the Aragonese Crown. Thereupon war broke out between the Genoese and Catalans in 1329, and the Count of Malaspina, who had been largely concerned in the disturbances in Sassari, took the side of the rebels. The Catalans proceeded to devastate the Genoese coasts, with the result that the two political parties in Genoa combined against their common enemy in 1331, and then began a lengthy maritime war between Genoa and Aragon, which was essentially not so much a struggle for the possession of Sardinia as one for commercial supremacy. The friction had begun with the conquest of Sicily by the Aragonese, which had given a considerable extension to Catalan trade in the Mediterranean, and the comparative equality of the two parties, in the absence of any naval genius, such as Roger de Lauria, protracted the war, which was largely confined to sudden raids upon coasts and harbours, but rarely came to any general conflict. The Genoese could pride themselves upon their success in the long struggle with Pisa, while the Catalans had behind them the consciousness of a number of naval victories, which induced them to pass a law that a captain who fled with one galley from two enemy ships should be condemned to death. In the following year, 1331, Catalan confidence was somewhat shaken by the appearance of a Genoese fleet of forty-five galleys off their coast, which burned several vessels, plundered much of the sea-board, and challenged the King of Aragon to a naval engagement. The Catalans pursued their enemy to the island of Mallorca, where they had taken shelter from a storm, but, when the Genoese admiral, Grimaldi, sailed out to meet them, the Catalans considered that discretion was the better part of valour. Lack of supplies then obliged the Genoese to retreat, but upon their way they were able to intercept a Catalan squadron sailing to Sicily. In this style the war was continued for the following year, and it was not until the end of Alfonso's reign that an armistice and a peace were concluded, which secured a pacification of the island at any rate for some time.

Some attention must be paid to internal disturbances during Alfonso's reign, which were largely due to the liberality and extravagance of his predecessors, especially James II, who had not only handed over towns and districts to his sons and to others for services received, but had also sold certain incomes and Crown rights to pay his debts. The result was that the royal income was greatly diminished at the moment when money became more than ever necessary. When the news of Alfonso's betrothal to Eleanor became known, the nobles who were apprehensive of her ambitious and self-seeking character, determined to prevent the alienation of any further parts of the kingdom, and at the Cortes of Daroca in

1328 obliged Alfonso to declare that for the next ten years he would not alienate any town, castle or other place in Aragon, Catalonia or Valencia, nor transfer any fiefs or rights of the Crown. None the less, after his marriage with Eleanor, who had been betrothed years before to his elder brother James, he gave her the town of Huesca, and other places, and to his son, Ferdinand, he gave the town of Tortosa, whose inhabitants were obliged to renounce their immediate dependence upon the Crown. Other important towns, such as Alicante, Guardamar and Albarracin, were handed over in the same way, a more dangerous transference, as they were important frontier positions. None the less, the King persuaded the barons to promise recognition of Ferdinand's possession. The only opponent was a certain Ot de Moncada, who pointed out the danger to the Crown and the illegal character of these donations. The King, however, was entirely under the influence of his wife and one of her confidantes, a fact which increased dissatisfaction among the nobility, while the various places which he had given away were not slow to express their discontent. The inhabitants of Valencia even took up arms to resist the royal officials, and sent one of their most distinguished citizens, Guillem de Vinatea, accompanied by members of the town council, to protest. The deputation pointed out that the King's action implied a separation of Valencia from Aragon, a possibility which he and his colleagues were prepared to resist to the death. The Queen is said to have told her husband in the course of the discussion that her brother, the King of Castile, would have beheaded any subject who ventured to address him in that manner, but Alfonso replied that the Aragonese were free people and not subjugated as those of Castile, and that if they regarded him as their lord, he regarded them as good vassals and companions. He then explained his willingness to revoke the various donations that he had made, but his family remained divided against itself, as the Infante Pedro was opposed to the Queen and her party, who went so far as to persecute Pedro's supporters. Apart from disputes upon these points, the kingdom was not disturbed during Alfonso's reign, more perhaps in consequence of his apathy than of his moderation. As heir to the throne he had shown much energy and bravery in the conquest of Sardinia, but after his coronation, the most brilliant event of his reign, he seems to have been overcome by an apathy which suggests the inroads of some disease, and allowed himself to be unduly dominated by female influence, which, in the case of his second wife, Eleanor of Castile, was entirely arbitrary and selfish. But he seems to have been anxious to govern as a constitutional monarch, and his title, " El Benigno," fairly represented the genuine appreciation of his subjects. He died at the age of thirty-seven, in January 1336.

CHAPTER XII

PEDRO IV

His character. He exiles his stepmother. Alliance with Castile against the Moors. Quarrel with James of Mallorca. Capture of the island. Quarrel with the nobles. Civil war. Victory of the Crown. Pedro's reprisals. Revolt of Sardinia. War with Castile. Henry of Trastamara. Invasion of Aragon. Peace concluded and broken. The battle of Nájera. War with Henry of Trastamara. Claims to Sicily. Pedro's death.

ALFONSO left five sons and two daughters by his wife, Teresa de Entenza. The first son had died in infancy, and the second, Pedro, who was born on September 5, 1319, succeeded to the throne. He was an under-sized man, said to have been prematurely born, and gained the name of " El Ceremonioso " from his insistence upon forms and ceremonies. His punctiliousness, however, did not restrain him from tyranny and murder when these courses happened to suit his purpose, and he was also known as " El del Punyalet," from the dagger which he usually wore at his belt. If he had a conscience, it was rather his accomplice than his guide ; he was a born intriguer, whose weapons were duplicity and hypocrisy ; and the strain of caution in his character which directed these vices has alone saved him from the dismal reputation of the homicidal maniac, Pedro I, who occupied the throne of Castile for the greater part of his reign. He showed dislike and suspicion of his relatives : he drove his brother-in-law out of Mallorca and probably poisoned one brother and assassinated another. Arbitrary and domineering, he early declared his principle of government, " axi volem que fos e que non sen devia altre fer " : " thus will we have it and nothing else ought to be done." He was no doubt tenacious in disaster, and a tendency to champion the cause of the poor against the rich has been urged in his favour, though it is likely that here he was merely following the policy of promoting the interests of the towns against the

166

nobles, by which other kings both of Aragon and Castile strove to secure their positions. It should, however, be said that some of his legislation shows an enlightenment beyond his age, especially that which deals with the use of torture and corporal punishment ; he had a strong sense of the importance of literature and the advantages of education ; he founded the University of Lérida and was himself an author and a parliamentary orator of skill and eloquence ; if his *Chronicle* and other works attributed to him owed probably more to his secretaries than to himself, they are evidence of his undoubted literary interest and culture.

Pedro's first business was to summon the Cortes to Zaragoza for his coronation, which was celebrated with festivities similar to those which had marked the opening of the previous reign. He placed his own crown on his own head, as an indication to the papal representatives present that he did not accept the surrender to the papacy made by Pedro II. He also took the usual oaths to observe the laws and liberties of the Aragonese. Some weeks afterwards he repeated this ceremony in Catalonia, but aroused some dissatisfaction among the Catalans by summoning them to Lérida instead of to Barcelona, and by giving the Aragonese priority in this ceremony, whereas his father had met the Catalans first. One reason for the change was Pedro's anxiety to anticipate his stepmother, Queen Eleanor, in her attempts to stir up trouble in the south of his kingdom. Shortly before Alfonso's death Eleanor had met her brother, the King of Castile, and secured a promise of help from him in case her stepson should attempt to deprive her of the donations which she had extorted from her husband. Immediately after the King's death, the King of Castile, therefore, sent a knight to his sister, professing his readiness to protect her and her sons. The said messenger, Pedro de Ejérica, conducted her to Albarracin, and a Castilian embassy met Pedro in Zaragoza, requesting him to confirm the donations made by his father to Eleanor. Pedro sent an ambiguous answer. He was prepared to treat the Queen with all respect, but not to pronounce upon the legality of the donations. Shortly afterwards, when he arrived in Valencia, he deprived the Queen of her income and outlawed her protector, Pedro de Ejérica. Remonstrances from Castile produced no effect, and, if

Alfonso of Castile had not been occupied by a war with Portugal, he might have been induced to begin hostilities against Aragon. Eleanor had a party of followers in Aragon, who seemed likely to find a leader in Pedro de Ejérica, and the King therefore thought it advisable to crush this nobleman once and for all. Pedro de Ejérica was obliged to flee into Castile, where he became the chief supporter of the exiled Eleanor, and it was not until 1338 that the intervention of the papal legates secured some measure of agreement. It was agreed that the King of Aragon should take Pedro de Ejérica again into his service and compensate him for the loss he had incurred, that the Queen should hold the domains and revenues granted her by her late husband, and that the King should allow her the right of administering justice within them. He was the more anxious to come to some arrangement as Spain was at that moment threatened by a considerable invasion from the Moors. In other parts of the kingdom peace prevailed. In Sardinia, his officer, Ramon de Cardona, had defeated the Genoese and pacified the island for the moment, while the differences between James of Mallorca and the Crown of Aragon had been temporarily settled. Pedro then married Maria, the second daughter of the King of Navarre, in the summer of 1338, and thus secured an ally on his northern frontier.

Some time previously reports had reached him that the King of Morocco, Abu-l-Hassan, who had also conquered Tremecen in Tunis, had been invited by the King of Granada to invade Spain, and was making great preparations for the enterprise. He had already sent his son across the Straits with 5000 cavalry, and captured Algeciras and Gibraltar. Apprehensions of a desperate struggle were widespread through Spain, and particularly in Aragon, as it was thought that the efforts of the invaders would be chiefly directed against Valencia, where the considerable Moorish population might be expected to support them. It was said that in Africa an army of 70,000 cavalry and an infinite number of infantry had been collected with a fleet of over a hundred galleys, some forty of which were provided by Genoa. Pedro, therefore, concluded his alliance with the King of Castile in May 1339, and hurried on his naval preparations. He was anxious to form a combined fleet to which the Kings of

Mallorca, Castile and Portugal should send contingents. When the difficulties concerning Eleanor and her sons had been settled, and the alliance with Castile had been definitely concluded, Pedro sent his fleet to join the Castilian contingent near the Straits of Gibraltar, and fortified the coasts and the main strongholds of Valencia as best he could. The son of the King of Morocco invaded Castile with an army towards the end of 1339, but was defeated and killed upon the frontier, and to avenge his death Abu-l-Hassan sent a numerous army and fleet to Spain in the early months of 1340. The Spanish navy, inferior in numbers, was out-manœuvred and completely defeated. For the next four months a continual stream of reinforcements from Africa accompanied by their women and children came over to Spain, until the King of Morocco arrived in person and began the siege of Tarifa, in company with the King of Granada. A Castilian army with Portuguese reinforcements relieved the town, and gained a brilliant victory over the Moors on October 29 on the Salado, which has been compared with the great day of Las Navas de Tolosa ; the King of Morocco was obliged to retreat to Africa without delay and all danger from that quarter was ended.

Pedro of Aragon had no part in this victory, as he was occupied by disturbances in Sardinia, and also by a quarrel with the King of Mallorca. In 1336 a peace had been concluded between Genoa and Aragon, but certain landholders had been included in the negotiations as Genoese, not as Aragonese, citizens. They proceeded to reopen intrigues with Pisa and Genoa, and war broke out again. Pedro, however, was anxious first to deal with King James III of Mallorca, for whom he cherished an implacable hatred. Alfonso III had conquered the Balearic Islands, as a consequence of the treacherous behaviour of their King James to his brother Pedro III. James, thus driven out by his nephew, was left with Montpellier and Roussillon as his sole possessions. Alfonso's brother and successor, James II, restored the islands to his uncle in 1294, who thus resumed his rule as James II of Mallorca. He had married Esclaramunda of Foix and his second son Sancho was recognized as his heir by the Cortes of Gerona in 1302. James died in 1311 ; his third son Fernando, had taken service under Fadrique of

Sicily and had been sent by him to command the Catalans in the East. After his capture by the Venetians and his release, he fought for Aragon against the Moors and returned to Sicily, when his brother-in-law, Robert of Naples, attacked Fadrique. He then married Isabella, daughter of the Count of Andria, and so claimed the Morea through his wife. While fighting in this cause he was killed in 1316, leaving an infant boy who was brought back to Aragon by the chronicler Muntaner. This child became James III of Mallorca, being adopted as heir by Sancho, who had succeeded James II in 1311 and had no children of his own. Sancho died in 1324 and James III married Constance, daughter of Alfonso IV of Aragon, and was thus the brother-in-law of Pedro IV, the Ceremonious. James had failed to show him those forms of respect which their mutual positions of feudal overlord and vassal implied, and Pedro suspected him of intriguing with the Kings of France, Castile and Naples against himself. Pedro soon found an opening for attack. James had refused to recognize the disputed French supremacy of Montpellier and, when threatened with a French attack, appealed for help to his overlord in 1341. Pedro was afraid to bring down the wrath of France upon himself, if he responded to the appeal and to weaken his feudal rights over Mallorca, if he refused it. He therefore summoned James to a Cortes to be held in Barcelona. James neither came himself, nor sent any representative, and Pedro, therefore, considered himself relieved from his duty as overlord, and called his vassal to account before him. Apart from this so-called infringement of a vassal's duty, Pedro could further complain that James had been coining and circulating money of his own in the counties of Roussillon and Cerdagne, although it was well-known that the right of coinage was a royal monopoly. The question really turned upon the feudal position of the ruler of Roussillon, and upon old custom, but Pedro found sufficient excuse for declaring James to be a refractory vassal, and for proceeding against him in the usual form. Clement VI, who had recently been appointed Pope, induced Pedro to grant James a meeting at Barcelona, at which the papal representatives were present. These efforts, however, came to nothing, and Pedro circulated a story that James intended to capture him and carry him to Mallorca

with the intention of extorting concessions. The plot was
said to have been revealed by his sister, the Queen of Mallorca.
Pedro had determined to secure the island by force, if
negotiation failed, and James realizing this fact returned to
Mallorca, and prepared for war, while in February 1343
Pedro declared, before a solemn assembly of the nobles, that
James had failed in his duty as a vassal, that his goods and
land were confiscate to the Crown of Aragon and that he was
to be considered as an enemy of the kingdom. The island
had certainly prospered under the rule of James : piracy had
been put down, the traditional privileges of the inhabitants
had been confirmed and codified in the so-called Palatine
law, which Pedro afterwards copied in his Royal Ordinances.
But James appears to have been highly unpopular with his
subjects, who were overburdened with taxes and who conceived that they would have better prospects of peace and
security, if the island formed part of the kingdom of Aragon.
One of their representatives assured Pedro that the inhabitants of Mallorca would rise in his favour as soon as the
Aragonese fleet appeared off the coast. Pedro also undertook
to confirm the privileges of the town of Mallorca, as James I
had granted them after the conquest. All officials were to
be natives of the country, any appointments that he might
make would be restricted to Catalans, the Jurats of the town
of Mallorca would have full representation upon the commercial board, and general Cortes to deal with the affairs
of the island would be held every five years. Pedro secured
the assent of his own Cortes to these proposals, recalled his
fleet from the blockade of Algeciras and appeared off Mallorca in the month of May. An army assembled by James
ran away, the Aragonese marched into the capital and
received the homage, not only of the island itself, but also of
Menorca and Iviza. Pedro then returned to Barcelona and
shortly afterwards prepared to invade Roussillon and the Cerdagne. James made repeated proposals for peace, which
were rejected, while the mediation of Pope Clement VI
was equally unsuccessful; and in March 1344 Pedro declared
that the possessions of the King of Mallorca were incorporated
for ever in those of the Aragonese Crown, and that his successors were to swear to maintain this incorporation before
their vassals or subjects could be under obligation to take the

oath of allegiance. Roussillon was speedily overrun, and James was obliged to surrender unconditionally. On the receipt of a promise of safe-conduct he appeared before Pedro in person, admitted that he had wronged his overlord, and surrendered his lands. Pedro made no proposal to return even a portion of them, and was willing only to provide the dethroned monarch with a pension, on condition that he renounced all claim to the royal title. James made several attempts to recover his position, and in 1349 sold his rights over Montpellier for a sum which enabled him to enlist an army of mercenaries. Juana, Queen of Naples, lent him a fleet and he succeeded in landing his forces in Mallorca. He was immediately attacked by the governor of the island and killed ; his troops were scattered and his son James taken prisoner. His wife Constance, sister of Pedro IV, had died in 1346 ; his only daughter had married the Marquis of Montferrat in 1358, and his son James, as will be seen, married Juana of Naples in 1362.

During the latter period of Pedro's struggles with Mallorca, the kingdom of Aragon was disturbed by a serious constitutional conflict, for the outbreak of which the King was entirely to blame. Pedro had as yet no male heir, and the immediate successor to the Crown was his brother James, whom he disliked, as he suspected him to be supporting the cause of the King of Mallorca. He declared, therefore, that he wished to nominate his daughter Constance as heir to the throne, in case he should die without male issue, and that in so doing he was merely following the common law which allowed a daughter to succeed to her father's possessions. This proposal was discussed in 1347 by a conference of twenty-two distinguished ecclesiastics and lawyers at Valencia, nineteen of whom were prepared to support the proposal that Constance should be regarded as the heiress to the throne. On the other hand, a strong party of influential people, including Arnaldo de Morera, the Vice-Chancellor of the kingdom, insisted that the custom of other kingdoms which excluded women from the succession should also be followed in Aragon, and that James I in his testament had definitely laid down the principle of male succession, which was not to be varied so long as male heirs were to be found. Pedro, however, was not to be persuaded, and on March 23

he publicly proclaimed his daughter as his successor, in case
he should have no male heir. James was at that time holding
the post of Governor-General of the kingdom, which was
usually occupied by the heir to the throne, and collected
a strong party of supporters in Valencia, whereupon Pedro
ordered him to resign this office, and to withdraw from
Valencia, forbade him to appear in any other large town, such
as Zaragoza, Barcelona or Lérida, and assigned to him as a
residence the villa of Montblanch. He dismissed the officials
whom the Infante, in virtue of his office, had appointed, and
replaced them with men devoted to himself and prepared
to work in the interests of Constance. Homage was paid
to her as the King's successor by his uncle, Pedro, by various
bishops and barons and the knights of the Royal household,
on the condition that their oaths should not be regarded as
binding should the King desire to make other arrangements
for the succession. At this moment the Queen gave birth
to a son, but the child lived only for a few hours and the
Queen herself died four days later. Pedro lost no time in
contracting a second marriage with Leonor, the daughter
of the King of Portugal ; she reached Barcelona in November
1346, the year in which his first wife, Maria of Navarre, had
died.

Meanwhile, James had gone to Fuentes, invited the barons
and knights who had gathered in Zaragoza to meet him, and
induced them to abandon all personal quarrels and to unite
in defence of the legal succession to the throne. He then led
them to Zaragoza, invited the Princes Ferdinand and John,
his stepbrothers, whom Pedro's animosity had driven into
Castile, to join him, and sent out a general call to form a
Union in the defence of the laws and privileges of the kingdom.
The formation of such a Union was, as we have seen, legalized
by the concessions which had been extorted from previous
kings. This fact induced the majority of those invited to
assemble in Zaragoza, where the Union was regularly formed,
and a seal was struck representing the King upon the throne
with his people before him pleading for justice with out-
stretched hands and with an ominous line of spears in the
background. The King was then invited to hold Cortes at
Zaragoza, and informed that the formation of the Union
was intended merely to maintain those constitutional forms

upon which the safety of the kingdom depended. Pedro then made his way from Valencia to Barcelona, but learned upon the road that the inhabitants of Valencia had followed the example of the Aragonese, and were prepared to join them. Pedro de Ejérica, whom the King had reinstated in his service on the conclusion of his quarrel with his stepmother, was governor of Valencia and succeeded in forming a royalist party by no means negligible, but not strong enough to counteract the movement in Aragon which steadily increased in numbers and represented all who held aloof as traitors to the country. Their programme was the repeal of the King's illegal proposals, the protection of all members of the Union from the oppression of the royalist party, the restoration of dismissed officials and the right of Valencia to appoint a Justicia of its own with powers equivalent to those of the Justicia of Aragon.

Pedro delayed for some time in summoning Cortes to Zaragoza, and did his best to strengthen the number of his own adherents ; but when it became clear that he was completely outnumbered, he went to Zaragoza, where he found the Princes Ferdinand and John, who were supported by 400 Castilian knights. He also found, to his considerable alarm, that the *Unidos* of Valencia had joined those of Aragon and were preparing for war, if they failed to secure their demands. Pedro opened the Cortes at the Church of San Salvador with a lengthy speech, in which he explained that important business, and in particular his war against the King of Mallorca, had prevented him from meeting the Cortes at an earlier date, that he was prepared to recognize the Union, but begged them all to demand only what he could grant and they could reasonably ask, and concluded his speech with a eulogy of Aragon, which aroused general satisfaction. He then retired to his palace, and the several Estates, expecting that he might attempt to sow discord among them, passed a resolution that no individual should communicate with him, but that all negotiations should be conducted between the King and themselves collectively. The Catalans had remained loyal to the Crown and the first demand of the Union was that certain Catalan knights who had accompanied Pedro should be excluded from the deliberations, and to this the King was obliged to agree. They then

demanded his confirmation of the privileges of the Union,
obliging the King to summon annual Cortes, and giving the
Union the power to nominate royal councillors. Pedro
objected to this, upon the ground that such privileges had
not been enforced for sixty years, and had therefore fallen
into disuse. The Estates, however, insisted and intimated
that they were prepared to elect another king. Pedro was
obliged to give way, though he declared to individuals that
he did so only under compulsion, and gave hostages as a
guarantee of the fulfilment of his promises. His chief support
at this moment was Bernardo de Cabrera, his major-domo, a
man whose unshakable fidelity was equalled only by his
sagacity and energy. He had already handed over his
county of Cabrera to his son, and was proposing to retire
from the world to a monastery, but the King, who was well
aware of his high qualities, persuaded him to return to
personal attendance upon himself. Bernardo was convinced
that the King ruled by divine right, that opposition to his
wishes was a sinful dereliction of duty, that no compact
with refractory vassals should be made, and that real peace
was only possible when the royal supremacy was undisputed.
By promises of high positions and valuable offices, he succeeded in forming a royalist party in Zaragoza itself, securing
the support of Álvaro Darín, of Lope de Luna, who had
married his aunt Violante, and of other barons not much
less influential than these two important persons. The
presence of the two princes with their Castilian following
was also a cause of dissatisfaction to many of the Aragonese.
The formation of this party was kept secret, and Pedro
proposed to return to Catalonia, where he knew he could secure
further support. His design, however, was revealed at the
final meeting of the Cortes, when he provoked a bitter quarrel
between himself and his brother James, whom he accused
of treachery to the kingdom. When the supporters of James
raised a general call to arms, the royalist party disclosed its
existence, and conducted the King back to his palace, and
the Union began to realize that the royalist party was a
serious danger to their own existence. Cabrera advised Pedro
to leave Zaragoza, but he declined to abandon the hostages
he had given to the Union. On the excuse that alarming
news from Sardinia required his whole attention, he granted

the demands of the Union, restored his brother to his office, revoked the dispositions that he had made to secure the succession of his daughter, and dissolved the Cortes at the end of October 1347. He then returned to Catalonia, delighted, as he said, to enter a country which was loyal to himself, and resolved to gather an army and attack the Union, whose hostility was not decreased by the fact that his brother James suddenly died of a mysterious disease, which was naturally attributed to poison. While convincing evidence is lacking, there is no doubt that popular sentiment accused Pedro of fratricide, and that no serious attempt has since been made to refute this accusation.

Meanwhile, war had already broken out in Valencia. The royalist party was defeated near Xátiva, but Pedro de Ejérica was able to gather an army which included some Moorish allies, and the Union of Aragon was prepared to march to the help of Valencia on hearing of their difficulties. Pedro sent his uncle, the Infante Pedro, to support the royalist party with a force of 200 knights, but before he could arrive, Ejérica was attacked by a force of 30,000 men and was defeated on December 30. The royalist cause, however, was not crushed, and he continued to gather reinforcements from the loyal towns. Pedro hurried to Murviedro, which he proposed to make his base of operations against the rebels of Valencia. The town, however, revolted, while his forces began to melt away, as they had not received their arrears of pay, and Pedro was confronted by the fact that a numerous Aragonese army was invading Valencia. Nothing remained for him but to yield. He declared Ferdinand as his successor should he leave no male issue, and gave him the post of Governor-General. He confirmed the Union of Valencia, and legalized its junction with that of Aragon, for the purpose of defending the laws, privileges and liberties of the realm, allowed the Union of Valencia to choose a Justicia with powers equivalent to those of the Justicia of Aragon, and undertook to exclude from his council Bernardo de Cabrera, and other persons obnoxious to the Union. By these means he hoped to arouse some confidence in himself, but an attempt to escape from Murviedro, which had been organized by Cabrera and Ejérica, was betrayed by some of his followers to the Jurados of the town. The population flew to arms, surrounding the palace and demanded the transference of the King to Valencia, where he was to be kept in the custody of the Union, to remove him from the influence of his own councillors. Pedro was obliged to go to Valencia in March 1348, where he was followed by his second wife Eleanor, the daughter of the King of Portugal. An uproar broke out in Valencia, in the course of the celebrations which marked the reconciliation of King and people : when Pedro appeared in person to quell the disturbance, a body of rioters who suspected him of plotting an escape, sang a couplet under his windows :

> Malhaja qui sen irá
> Encara ni encara.

" Ill to him who shall go away now or ever." The leader of the chorus was a barber named Gonzalo, to whom the King, as he relates in his *Chronicle*, gave no answer at that time. The barber received an answer at a later date. Cabrera repeatedly urged Pedro to leave Valencia, if not openly, by stealth, and return to Catalonia, where he would find adequate support. The King was convinced that this course was too dangerous, and Cabrera therefore returned to Catalonia and began to organize the royalist forces. Pedro meanwhile did his best to satisfy the demands of the Union and to distract their attention from the preparations of Cabrera in Catalonia. At that moment an unexpected ally made its appearance ; the Black Death, which had ravaged most of Europe, appeared also in Spain in the month of May 1348. The towns of Valencia and Catalonia suffered severely. The members of the Union were alarmed for their safety, and were anxious to return to Aragon, which was comparatively free from the plague. When the King desired to withdraw to Teruel, no one was willing to take the responsibility of keeping him in Valencia.

Meanwhile the King's party had been steadily growing stronger, and his supporters, Bernardo de Cabrera, Pedro de Ejérica and Lope de Luna, made continual efforts to secure adherents for his cause, and to break up the Union. It became obvious, however, that war between the two parties was inevitable, in spite of the efforts of the Justicia of Aragon, Garci-Fernández de Castro, to maintain the

12

peace. He succeeded in securing an armistice which lasted
for a couple of months, but, when the Infante Fernando
arrived at Zaragoza, the Union began hostilities against Lope
de Luna and his forces. These had entrenched themselves
at Epila, awaiting assistance from the King of Castile, who
was then besieging Tarazona. Pedro immediately hastened
to join Lope de Luna, and shortly afterwards the battle of
Epila took place. The Union was completely defeated, many
of its leaders were killed or taken prisoner, Ferdinand himself
was wounded, and the banners of the Union were captured
and preserved in Epila as trophies. 'Ferdinand, fortunately
for himself, was captured by Pedro's Castilian auxiliaries
and taken to Castile. The supremacy of the King was not
afterwards questioned, and the privileges conceded by
Alfonso III, which had given the nobility a legal right to
combine against the Crown, ceased from this moment to be
operative. Pedro was on his way to Zaragoza at the head
of his victorious army, when he was met by ambassadors
from the town, who requested him to enter it, not as a
conqueror in triumph, but as a king prepared for the work
of pacification. They were prepared to abandon any insistence
upon their rights and privileges and to throw themselves
upon the royal mercy. On the advice of his council, the
King sent a conciliatory answer. The leaders of the Union
were arrested, and thirteen of them are said to have been
executed, but it must be said that the King, in view of the
vindictiveness which his character afterwards displayed upon
many occasions, showed a moderation wholly unexpected
in the immediate emergency. Cortes were held in Zaragoza
in October to settle the constitutional question. It was
agreed that, as the Union of the kingdom of Aragon, which
had previously been set up to maintain the laws and privileges
of the kingdom, had infringed those laws and impaired the
rights of the Crown, the several Estates, desiring to offer
their due homage to the King, should now dissolve the
Union, and they were prepared to destroy the documents
which had conceded its former privileges, together with the
seal of the Union, and to regard its previous acts as illegal
and invalid. The two documents conceding the privileges
which had been granted by Alfonso III, and the confirmation
of them issued in the previous year, together with the

ordinances and books of the Union, were then publicly burned, and the seal was broken. Pedro is said to have cut one of the documents in pieces with the dagger which he habitually carried, and to have gashed his hand in the process, explaining that privileges which had cost so much blood could only be wiped out by royal blood. On the next day, at a general assembly of the Estates, in the Church of San Salvador, Pedro gave an address offering a general amnesty to all except certain leaders, undertaking to observe the laws and customs of the realm, promising that imprisonment, banishment or corporal punishment should never be inflicted without legal trial, and defining more exactly the powers of the Justicia. Discussions on this point were continued at Teruel, as the plague was raging in Zaragoza itself. Henceforward the Justicia was to act as judge between the Crown and its inferiors in case of dispute, and was also to uphold the law against officials or councillors who might attempt to infringe it. Should the interpretation of the law be in any case doubtful, the Justicia was to hold himself in readiness to deal with the point, and his decision would be final. If found incompetent or corrupt, the Justicia could be impeached by the Cortes, to whom he was ultimately responsible, and dismissed for ever from his office. It may be said, therefore, that the result of the struggle was to leave this official in a stronger position than he would probably have been able to obtain under the Union.

The King then moved to Valencia in order to crush opposition in that quarter, where the Union still maintained a considerable force. A battle was fought near the capital, in which the royalists were again victorious. Valencia threw itself upon the mercy of the King, who at first declared his intention of razing the town to the ground and sowing it with salt, but the earnest representations of his councillors dissuaded him from punishing the innocent with the guilty and inflicting great and unnecessary loss upon his own kingdom. The leaders, however, were forced to surrender their persons to the King, and in the case of the dead their property was confiscated. All the privileges of the town were revoked, and it was left to the King to decide what concessions should be made in future. Pedro's cruelty was upon this occasion unrestrained ; the bell which called the members of the

Union together was melted down and poured down the throats of some of the leaders of the nobility. The barber Gonzalo was captured and Pedro then replied to his couplet :

E qui nous rossegará
Susara e susara ?

" Who will not drag you down now and ever ? " The barber was hanged, and a continual series of executions took place, until the district was completely terrorized.

Meanwhile, disturbances had broken out in Sardinia, while relations with Castile were in a state of extreme tension, and it therefore appeared that there was occupation enough for all adventurous and unruly spirits within the kingdom of Aragon. Pedro had already secured his possession of Sardinia, but in 1347 a revolt broke out which was led by the family of Oria. The Aragonese forces in the island were completely routed and only the loyalty of the family of Arborea enabled the remnants to reach security. The expulsion of the rebellious leaders merely drove them into the arms of the Genoese, who continued to press their claims to the town of Sassari. Pedro did not grapple with the difficulty until 1351 ; he was occupied in negotiations for a third marriage, which he eventually contracted in 1349 with Leonor, a daughter of Pedro and Isabel, the rulers of Sicily. The maintenance of Aragonese or Catalan influence in Sicily and the negotiation of an alliance with Castile also diverted his attention from Sardinia until 1351, when an embassy from Venice, which was at war with Genoa, came to ask for help. Pedro made an alliance with Venice, a fact which immediately induced the Genoese to send an embassy in the hope that Pedro might be dissuaded from helping their enemies. The King, however, determined to continue his friendship with the Venetians, who were a richer and more powerful state, especially upon the sea. A Catalan fleet joined the Venetian naval forces, pursued the Genoese as far as Constantinople, and brought them to action in 1352. They gained a complete victory, but lost many of their ships through their ignorance of the coast-line, and the Genoese continued their attacks upon Sardinia and Corsica, the most prominent leader being a certain Mariano de Arborea who claimed the title of King of Sardinia. Pedro, therefore, renewed his alliance with

Venice in 1352 for a period of five years, and in the naval battle of Alghero in 1353 the allies inflicted a severe defeat upon the Genoese, who began to doubt their capacity to defend their own town, and placed themselves under the protection of the ruler of Milan. With his help, the Judge of Arborea who had quarrelled with the Catalans, was able to recover his position. He induced a number of Sardinian towns to join him, until the Aragonese were left with little more than Sassari and a few fortified places in the neighbourhood. In the summer of 1354 Pedro sailed to Sardinia with his numerous fleet ; he captured the town of Alghero after a long siege, but was unable to improve the general situation, and returned to Barcelona after nearly a year's absence. In 1356 a second attack obliged the Sardinian aspirant to sue for peace, which Pedro was the more inclined to grant, as Pope Innocent VI had secured an agreement between Genoa and Venice in which he was not himself included, while Mariano de Arborea was expecting help from Milan ; moreover, the war with Castile required Pedro's undivided attention. Disturbances again broke out, and by 1368 Mariano de Arborea was on the point of securing supremacy over the whole island when he suddenly died. His successor was an oppressive and cruel tyrant who speedily alienated his supporters. He was eventually murdered. His daughter had married a member of the family of Oria, and Pedro was obliged to allow him to occupy the greater part of the island until 1386 when he captured him and secured a treaty upon the basis of that previously concluded with the Judge of Arborea.

Relations between Aragon and Castile had been strained from the outset of the reign of Pedro I of Castile, generally and reasonably known as the Cruel. In 1352 he had concluded with Aragon the alliance of Atienza, but in spite of that fact he supported the unfounded claims of the Infante Ferdinand two years later to the Crown of Aragon. Pedro IV replied by supporting Count Henry of Trastamara and the other illegitimate sons of King Alfonso XI of Castile, who were the objects of their brother's implacable hatred. Ferdinand had ceded Alicante and Orihuela to Pedro of Castile, and Pedro IV realized that the possession of these towns was almost an invitation to invade Valencia. Both kings, however, were occupied by domestic disturbances, and the peace remained outwardly unbroken until 1356, when a war began which was carried on with great ferocity on either side, to the infinite damage of both kingdoms. A somewhat insignificant event led to the outbreak of hostilities. One Francisco de Perellós, a distinguished noble-man of the King's household, was leading a naval squadron to France in fulfilment of feudal obligations. Off Cádiz he met two Genoese merchantmen which he captured, as Genoa was then at war with Aragon, and when the King of Castile, who was present at the time, objected to such action in his waters, he was unable to obtain any redress from Aragon. He considered that Perellós had been commissioned to begin hostilities, and replied by arresting all the Catalan merchants in Seville, by confiscating their property and protesting to the King of Aragon concerning this and other alleged infringements of the peace. He also began hostilities at some parts of the Aragonese frontier. Pedro IV was anxious to avoid a war, as he was then fully occupied with the affairs of Sardinia, but, in view of what had happened, he denounced the treaty between himself and the King of Castile ; nor could the efforts of Pope Innocent VI preserve the peace between the two monarchs. The King of Aragon was obliged to remain for the moment upon the defensive. He invited the Castilian nobles who had taken refuge in France, including Henry of Trastamara, to take service under himself, made them his vassals by conferring fiefs upon them and did his best to stir up hostilities in Castile. Pedro the Cruel invaded Aragon in March 1357, and conquered Tarazona. Pedro IV took the field prepared for a pitched battle, when the papal legate intervened and arranged an armistice, during which peace was discussed. The King of Castile, however, broke the conditions of the convention, and, undeterred by the papal interdict laid upon his country by the legate, made energetic preparations for the prosecution of the war, concluded a treaty with the Genoese and began negotiations for a league with France, England and Navarre. Pedro of Aragon, in view of this urgent danger, summoned Cortes to consider the question of defence. The security of the capital was entrusted to the Justicia with full powers. An alliance was concluded with the Kings of Fez and Morocco, and also with the Infante Louis of Navarre, who was governing on behalf of his father then held prisoner in France. Louis was also joined by his brother Ferdinand, who was unwilling to trust himself any longer to the ferocity and uncertain temper of the King of Castile. War broke out again in 1358 and the King of Aragon was speedily involved in troubles. Not only was Guardamar conquered by the enemy, but party quarrels broke out in Catalonia, and not until they had been quelled by the King's uncle, the Infante Pedro, was it possible for the Aragonese to retaliate for the devastation of their territory by making an incursion into Castile. Pope Innocent worked incessantly to restore peace, and sent Cardinal Guido of Bologna to the King of Castile. He professed himself readyfor a pacification, but as he demanded the expulsion from Aragon of all the exiled Castilian nobles and the cession to himself of Guardamar, Alicante and other places, Pedro of Aragon refused conditions both disastrous and insulting to himself, and determined to continue the war in spite of the representations concerning the superior power of the enemy which the papal legate advanced. In 1359 a numerous Castilian fleet, led by the King, appeared off the coast of Valencia, joined the Genoese contingent at the mouth of the Ebro and reached Barcelona in June. The harbour was then nearly empty of ships, as the naval forces were absent, either in Sardinia or were helping King Frederick of Sicily. However, such ships as were available prepared for defence. The coast defences were reinforced, and the citizens of Barcelona marched out in a body, enraged at this threat to their coasts where their maritime power had hitherto been undisputed. The Castilian fleet was manned with picked soldiers, and its superior numbers made it confident of victory, but two separate attacks were beaten off with heavy loss ; the Catalans had mounted a " bombard " on their largest ship, probably the earliest use made of marine artillery. The King of Castile gave up the attempt and retired to the harbour of Iviza to repair his losses and attempt the conquest of the Balearic Islands. The capital of Iviza was strongly fortified and bravely defended. While the Castilians were engaged in the siege they were surprised by the appearance of Pedro of Aragon with a hastily collected fleet, who obliged them to retire with such precipitation that they abandoned all their siege engines. The failure of this enterprise merely roused the fury of the King of Castile. He made an alliance with the King of Granada, and announced a war of extermination against the Aragonese throughout his kingdom. His continual outbursts of cruelty steadily alienated the loyalty of his subjects, while Pedro of Aragon found support in many quarters, especially from the Catalans and from the Count of Trastamara, who induced many knights to take service with the Aragonese and to guard the Castilian frontier.

The year 1360 was chiefly spent in frontier raids, but in 1361 Pedro of Aragon resolved upon a greater undertaking. All preparations had been made for a pitched battle between the two kingdoms, when the indefatigable efforts of the papal legate once more induced the Kings to open negotiations which were carried on between Bernardo de Cabrera and two Castilian plenipotentiaries. In May 1361 at Tudela a peace was agreed upon on condition that all conquests should be returned by either side, and that Pedro of Aragon should undertake to give no further support to the Infante Ferdinand or to the Count of Trastamara. These and many other Castilian nobles resident in Aragon were not to approach within thirty miles of the Castilian frontier. Pedro of Aragon declared his willingness to accept these conditions and proposed a marriage between his daughter Eleanor and Alfonso, the heir to the throne of Castile. Pedro of Castile professed his willingness to consider the proposal. He had been brought to reason by a Moorish invasion in Andalucía, and as this danger was now past his treacherous instincts gained the upper hand. After concluding an agreement with the Kings of Navarre and Portugal, the Count of Foix and other Gascon nobles, he advanced upon the Aragonese frontier, under the pretext of protecting Spain from the raids of the so-called Free or White Companies, mercenary contingents under the command of leaders of more or less distinction, whose services the Aragonese had used and of whom the most famous was Bertrand du Guesclin. Pedro the Cruel crossed the Aragonese frontier and captured several fortresses. He met with little opposition, as the King of Aragon was then in Perpignan protecting Roussillon against a threatened attack from the mercenary bands, while Aragon itself was unprepared and exhausted by the previous war. The King of Castile besieged Calatayud, Pedro of Portugal attacked Daroca, Charles of Navarre threatened Tarazona, and the Counts of Foix and Armagnac with other Gascon noblemen descended from the Pyrenees to the districts of Exea. The Governor of Zaragoza and his brother, who was then major-domo, collected the prelates, barons and knights resident in Zaragoza to make such preparations as were possible for the defence of the kingdom. The King himself summoned meetings for the same purpose in Barcelona and Valencia. Meanwhile Calatayud had defended itself desperately against the enemy, but a relief force sent by Pedro was intercepted on its route and the town found itself obliged to surrender in September, under an honourable capitulation.

This siege had occupied the King of Castile during the whole of the year, but early in 1363 he resumed the attack, captured a number of fortresses, including Borja and Tarazona, and began to threaten Zaragoza itself. The King of Aragon therefore accelerated negotiations with the Count of Trastamara who, with other exiled Castilians, had retired to Provence on the conclusion of peace, and undertook to help him to conquer Castile on condition of receiving a sixth part of any conquests he might make. The King of Navarre was also detached from his alliance with Castile, and Pedro IV collected his army in the neighbourhood of Zaragoza, with the intention of fighting a decisive battle. The Castilians, however, turned southwards against the undefended province of Valencia, captured Teruel, Segorbe, Murviedro and other fortresses without resistance, and Pedro of Castile was able to take up his residence in the royal palace at the gates of Valencia, until the approach of the King of Aragon with his army obliged him to move his quarters to Murviedro. Once again the papal nuncio interfered, and with the support of King Charles of Navarre arranged a peace on condition that the King of Castile should marry Juana of Aragon and hand over the conquered towns of Calatayud, Teruel and Tarazona as her dowry, while Alfonso, the King of Aragon's son, who was still an infant, was to marry Isabella of Castile and retain the conquests in Valencia. If the King of Castile did not fulfil these conditions, Charles of Navarre who had formed a secret treaty with the King of Aragon, undertook to act against him. The Infante Ferdinand, disliking this peace, prepared to go to France. Pedro was afraid that he would be followed by his adherents and that the King of Castile would then resume the war. There is also a story of a secret treaty between the two Kings, providing for the murders both of Ferdinand and of the Count of Trastamara. The fact remains, that Pedro soothed Ferdinand's suspicions with a show of friendship, but ordered him to be arrested and to be killed if he resisted. Force became necessary, and the Infante was killed, to the general indignation of the army and the people. As he had no children his great possessions reverted to the Crown, especially the towns of Albarracín and Tortosa.

Soon afterwards the peace that had recently been concluded was again broken, the aggressor being the King of Castile who advanced and threatened the Aragonese frontier with a strong force, on the ground that Pedro IV had not fulfilled the condition which obliged him to kill or capture the Count of Trastamara. The King of Navarre made an alliance with the King of Aragon in 1364, to which the Count of Trastamara was a party, declaring their intention of prosecuting the war until they had driven their enemy out of his kingdom which was then to be divided between themselves, the northern provinces and the whole of Castile going to the King of Navarre and the southern provinces to Aragon, while the Count of Trastamara was to have the Basque provinces. While these projects were still under discussion, the King of Castile invaded Valencia by way of Murcia in the winter of 1363, captured Alicante, Elche and other places, and advanced upon Valencia itself, intending to blockade it by land and sea. Pedro sent his eldest son, the Duke of Gerona, with the young man's uncle, the Infante Pedro, to the relief of the town, but was unable himself to take the field until April 1364, as he was occupied by his negotiations with the King of Navarre. When he eventually approached the town, accompanied by the Count of Trastamara with 3000 heavily armed knights, and supported by a fleet from Barcelona, the Castilians raised the siege, and Pedro was able to enter the town on April 28. Shortly afterwards, he accused of treason and brought to trial his chief adviser, Bernardo de Cabrera, to whose energy and counsel he had hitherto been profoundly indebted. The cause and details of this business are obscure. For some unknown reason Queen Leonor had conceived a bitter hatred of the councillor ; she was supported by the Count of Trastamara, who may have learned of the compact which was to secure his death together with that of Ferdinand. Other nobles doubtless envied him the King's confidence. Pedro in any case did not wish to offend the Count of Trastamara, and the King's suspicious and uneasy disposition was readily poisoned by hints of a plot against himself. Bernardo had taken refuge with the King of Navarre, who gave him up to Pedro, and he was condemned and executed at Zaragoza in July 1364. In 1381 the King revised his opinion, declared that Bernardo's innocence was proved and conferred his estates upon his grandson. Possibly the indignation of Catalonia at the execution may have contributed to bring about this change of opinion.

After the relief of Valencia, Pedro of Castile avoided any pitched battle, but held out in Murviedro until September, when Pedro IV recaptured the town : an outbreak of sickness obliged the Castilian to return to his own kingdom. His policy appears to have been, while avoiding any general battle, to harass Aragon by continual raids ; a policy which he carried on in the following year. But in 1366 Pedro of Aragon and the Count of Trastamara succeeded in hiring the Free Companies under the leadership of Bertrand du Guesclin and other French leaders. These entered Spain early in the year, and the Count, who assumed the title of King in Calahorra, entered Castile at the head of these troops, and was everywhere received with enthusiasm. In less than a month the whole kingdom had declared for him, and Pedro the Cruel had fled to Bayonne by way of Portugal and Galicia, while the Aragonese territory was entirely cleared of the enemy forces which had all been recalled to Castile. The exiled King then allied himself to the King of England and the Black Prince, who undertook to set him on his throne again, while the King of Navarre found it convenient to change sides, and undertook to give the English a free passage through his country and to oppose Aragon. Then followed the battle of Nájera in April 1367, when Henry of Trastamara

was completely defeated and driven out of the country, and
the frontiers of Aragon again lay open to the enemy. Pedro
of Castile was too busy satisfying his passion for murder to
pay due attention to the political situation. The Prince of
Wales was disgusted both with his behaviour to his own
subjects and his refusal to fulfil his treaty obligations, and
went over to the side of the King of Aragon, who was also
rejoined by the King of Navarre. Henry of Trastamara
was therefore able to make a second attempt, supported by
the King of France and his brother, the Duke of Anjou,
who was then Governor of Languedoc. He re-entered Castile
while the Black Prince was on his way to Guyenne. His
numerous supporters in the country turned the general
hatred of Pedro to the best advantage, and he speedily
obtained possession of the greater part of the kingdom.
Pedro of Aragon thus saw a reasonable prospect of relief
from his bitterest enemy, and with characteristic duplicity,
in which respect the King of Navarre was little behind him,
began to consider what profit he could make out of the
situation. The officials of the two princes held a meeting
and agreed to support whichever of the two Castilian
Kings was prepared to fulfil their demands, but the greed
of the contracting parties prevented them from securing a
complete agreement upon all details.

In 1368 war broke out again between England and France.
Pedro of Aragon was ready to renew his friendship with the
French King, Charles V, who promised to support him against
any party in Castile which might oppose his claim to the
province of Murcia. While these negotiations were going on,
Pedro was actually forming a fresh alliance with the King
of England. The contracting parties were to lay their
demands before the Castilian Kings, and in the case of refusal,
to expel them from Castile with the help of Navarre and
Portugal, and to divide the kingdom among themselves.
These projects came to nothing, as the King of England was
occupied by the war with France, and Pedro of Aragon by
the threatened loss of Sardinia, while in March 1369 Henry
of Trastamara had defeated and killed Pedro the Cruel and
thus secured undisputed possession of the Castilian kingdom.
Pedro of Aragon was therefore ready to come to an agreement
with the new Castilian ruler, in spite of the fact that he had

given away certain properties on the Aragonese frontier to
Bertrand du Guesclin as a reward for his help. In particular
the town of Molina was in dispute. Pedro took possession
of this, and the French leader was preparing to recover it
when Henry summoned him to operate against King Ferdinand of Portugal, who declared war. Pedro of Aragon
concluded an alliance with the Kings of Portugal and Navarre
against Castile, but he could do little more than retain his
possession of the frontier towns in dispute, as he was fully
occupied with events in Sardinia, while Henry was similarly
busied with the war against Portugal until 1373.

When the Portuguese war was ended, the whole force of
Castile was turned upon Aragon, while the son of the last
King of Mallorca threatened to invade Roussillon. At the
same time, the best part of the Aragonese forces was absent
in Sardinia, and lively recollections of the sufferings endured
in the last war aroused the country to apprehension. Loud
complaints were raised over the expense and loss caused by
continual reinforcement of the troops in Sardinia, a pestilential
island generally thought to be not worth the trouble it had
caused. Pedro was glad to avail himself of the good offices
of the Duke of Anjou who was able to intervene, and to secure
an armistice until the spring of 1374, when it seemed as if
war could not be averted. The Infante, who was known as
James IV of Mallorca, had been taken prisoner when his
father was killed in his attempt to reconquer the island in
1349. Pedro had kept him in close confinement in Barcelona;
in 1362 he contrived to escape to Naples and married the
Queen Juana, but was regarded only as prince-consort and
not allowed to use the royal title. He therefore transferred
his claim to Mallorca, to his sister Isabella, the wife of the
Marquis of Montferrat, in case he should die without male
issue, and offered his services to Pedro the Cruel in his war
against Aragon. He was captured in Burgos by Henry of
Trastamara on his second invasion of Castile : Henry allowed
Juana to ransom her husband, in spite of the objections
raised by Pedro IV, who would have been glad to exterminate the Mallorcan dynasty, and when Henry began war
upon Pedro, James IV with the approval of France and the
help of Juana and the Duke of Anjou, began to collect a
force at Narbonne to conquer the counties of Roussillon and

Cerdagne. A Castilian army was collecting on the Aragonese frontier, and the son of the King of England, the Duke of Lancaster, was in Bordeaux preparing to assert the rights which he considered appertained to him as the husband of Constance, the daughter of Pedro of Castile. The Duke of Lancaster made proposals for an alliance with Aragon. Pedro was not inclined to trust him, but was none the less able to use this possibility as a means of averting war from his country. Eventually a peace with Castile was arranged at Almazan on May 10, 1374. Pedro gave back the town of Molina, but received 180,000 gulden as indemnity for war damages, and his daughter, Eleanor, was betrothed to Henry's son, John. Pedro was thus able to concentrate his forces against the Infante James, when he invaded Aragon in the following year. James was supported by the treachery of some knights in the royal household, but was none the less obliged to take refuge in Castile, where he died shortly afterwards at Soria, according to one chronicle, of poison. All claims to the kingdom of Mallorca were not entirely extinguished with his death. James's sister and heiress, Isabella, transferred her rights to the Duke of Anjou, who made an alliance with the Kings of Portugal and Castile, and prepared to enforce his claims by invasion. The Cardinal de Terouenne strove to secure a peaceful settlement, Pedro made some show of compliance, and the King of Castile was ready to listen, but misunderstandings and differences between King Henry and the Duke delayed the execution of their plans until the death of the Duke in September 1384 relieved the Aragonese ruler from anxiety on his account.

During the latter part of his reign, Pedro gained an opportunity of reuniting Sicily to his dominions. King Frederick III of Sicily died in June 1377. He had declared his only daughter, Maria, as heiress to Sicily and to the dukedoms of Athens and of Neopatria and the adjoining islands. Should she die without issue, these possessions were to pass to his legitimate son William, to whom Gozo and Malta were left, and, if he again died without legitimate children, the kingdom was to pass to the sons of his sister, Eleanor, who had married the King of Aragon. Pedro, without waiting for these possibilities, raised an immediate claim for the whole inheritance, which he based upon the will of King Frederick II, who had died in 1338. The papacy hesitated to recognize this claim, as there were precedents enough for female succession to the Crown, and Pope Urban VI even threatened to deprive Pedro of his kingdom. However, in 1378 he went to Sicily in person with a large fleet, expecting to encounter little resistance, in view of the generally deplorable condition of the country. Four of the chief barons had divided the island and were ruling on their own account, as Maria was unable to enforce her claims. Some of Pedro's councillors were in collusion with the Sicilian barons who were anxious to maintain their independence, and induced him to abandon the adventure ; he handed over his claim to his second son, Count Martin of Ejérica and Luna, reserving for himself the royal title and supremacy, while Martin was to govern as his father's representative in Sicily itself. This arrangement was carried out at Barcelona in June 1380, and shortly afterwards the dukedoms of Athens and Neopatria voluntarily submitted to the Aragonese ruler. Hitherto the support of Sicily had secured them against aggression from the Emperor of Constantinople, the Duke of Durazzo, and other local potentates. If they could no longer count upon help from Sicily, they felt that some other support was indispensable and, therefore, sent a deputation to Barcelona offering their allegiance to Pedro and asking him to confirm the liberties granted by previous rulers. Pedro granted their request, sent a fleet for their protection, with the Viscount de Rocaberti as Royal Governor and Captain-General of the two dukedoms. He was received in Athens with much enthusiasm, and, in conjunction with the Venetian Governor of Negroponte, with whom he maintained friendly relations, was able to protect his territory from all hostile aggression. Meanwhile a party struggle was raging in Sicily, the object of which was the possession of the Infante Maria. The late King had put her in the protection of Count Artal de Alagon, who proposed to marry her to Gian Galeazzo Visconti and make him King, but his opponent, the Count of Augusta, secured her person and sent her to Catalonia, where Pedro determined to marry her to his grandson, Martin, who bore the name of his father, Pedro's second son.

An incident at the close of Pedro's reign will explain the

respect which his subjects held for his sense of justice, in spite of other defects in his character. His last wife, Sibilla de Forcia, the daughter of a Catalan knight, whom he had married with much solemnity in 1380, strongly disliked his two sons, and induced him to deprive the elder, Juan, of the position of Governor General of the kingdom which was usually held by the heir to the throne. Juan had married, against his father's wishes, Violante, daughter of Duke Robert de Bar, in 1380, when Pedro hoped that he would marry Maria of Sicily. Juan's efforts to recover his father's confidence were unsuccessful. The Queen seems to have acquired a complete ascendancy over her husband, and even induced certain important towns to promise to protect her against her stepson. The Infante Juan, therefore, applied to the Justicia of Aragon, and appealed to him against the command which had illegally deprived him of his office. Domingo Cerdan, who was Justicia at the moment, immediately proclaimed his decision throughout the kingdom, and the business of the Governor General was henceforward carried on in Juan's name. The King made no attempt to interfere with the powers of the Justicia, though he declined any communication with Juan. Pedro died on January 5, 1387, at Barcelona. In the previous year he had celebrated with great splendour the fiftieth anniversary of his accession.

Pedro's wars and expeditions exhausted his dominions and brought little corresponding advantage. He certainly secured the Balearic Islands, but Sardinia was a constant drain, his interference in Sicily was profitless, and the wars with his nobles and with Castile were, from the economic point of view, disastrous. The fact that his legislation did something to improve the liberties of his subjects and that the power of the Justicia was strengthened and extended by his action was due to a line of policy which regarded the Catalan burgess as a means of defence against the Aragonese oligarch and aristocrat, a policy inconsistent with the devouring lust for power which certainly actuated Pedro upon many occasions. The more refractory of the nobles perished in the battle of Epila, and the chief obstacle to absolutism was thus weakened; but Pedro knew how far he could venture to go. A systematic dissembler, utterly untrustworthy, suspicious of everyone's motives and purposes, he none the less was able to restrain his instinctive cruelty from reckless violence, while if policy seemed to demand the commission of the most atrocious of crimes, no humanitarian feelings existed to give him pause. He was a born intriguer, without bowels of mercy, but endowed with all the prudence and caution needed for intrigue.

CHAPTER XIII

JUAN I AND MARTIN

Character of Juan. Dissatisfaction of the nobles. French invasion. Alliances by marriage. Anti-Semitic riots. The problems of Sardinia and Sicily. Martin in Sicily. Death of Juan. Foundation of the Consistori de la Gaya Sciensa. Bernat Metge. Martin accepts the crown. The Great Schism. Pedro de Luna as Benedict XIII. Operations in Sicily and Sardinia. Death of Martin.

IT is difficult to imagine a character more opposed to the restless and intriguing spirit of Pedro than that of his son, Juan I, who succeeded him. His ideal of life was peace and harmony in which he might be allowed to pursue his favourite occupations of hunting, literature and art. He would have liked to make the Aragonese court a centre of intellectual refinement and of the kind of society that troubadour patrons had gathered round them in the South of France a hundred and fifty years earlier. Statesmanship had no great interest for him, and the details of government were too often left to his Queen, Violante, the daughter of Duke Robert de Bar, a woman energetic and domineering, but in sympathy with her husband's tastes. Juan therefore maintained a court of luxury and splendour unprecedented in the annals of Aragon. Song, music and dance filled the evening hours, while the days were spent in numerous and costly hunting parties. Hence the King was known by the Aragonese as " El Cazador," and by the Catalans as " El Amador de la Gentileza." None the less, Juan began his reign by a furious persecution of his stepmother, Queen Sibila. In her was repeated the history of Leonor of Castile, but unlike her, she fell into the hands of her persecutors and was imprisoned and actually tortured by her stepson, on the charge that his attacks of ill-health were due to the practice of witchcraft on her part. After a year's imprisonment, she was set free, at the entreaty of the cardinal legate in Aragon, while some of her supporters were exiled and others executed. Juan was crowned in Zaragoza in 1388, and upon that occasion the nobility took the opportunity of expressing their dissatisfaction at his conduct. His Queen, and therefore himself, were entirely under the influence of her confidante, Carroza de Vilagut, while the King's leanings to refinement were regarded by the nobility as sheer effeminacy. At the Cortes of Monzón held in 1389, the Estates of the Realm manifested their displeasure without restraint. The Vice-Chancellor, Ramón de Francia, and the Justicia, Domingo Cerdan, speaking in the name of the deputies of Aragon and Mallorca, demanded that the royal pair should reform their court and dismiss a number of people whose life and morals were regarded as derogatory to their dignity and a bad example to others. Naturally complaints were raised that the influence of Carroza and her adherents induced the King to squander the royal revenues by giving away fiefs and incomes without consideration or restraint. Negotiations continued for some months, and when the King at length realized the threatening nature of the situation he gave way. The objectionable female party was banished from his court. He undertook to observe the laws and liberties of his realms. By keeping peace with neighbouring states he hoped to find time and opportunity to devote himself to his own favourite pursuits.

In the year 1390, however, his northern frontiers were disturbed by the Count of Armagnac, who raised a claim to the Crown of Mallorca, which he said had been transferred to him by Isabel, wife of the Marquis of Montferrat, a short time after the death of Louis of Anjou, an earlier claimant. The Count gathered an army largely composed of the wandering mercenaries who were the plague of the South of France, crossed the frontier and overran much of the country in the neighbourhood of Gerona. He was defeated by Bernard de Cabrera in a battle near Navata, and when Juan was able to conclude his quarrel with the nobles and collect an army, the French retired precipitately across the Pyrenees. They continued their ravages in Roussillon until the Count was called to Italy in 1391 to help his brother-in-law, Charles Visconti, against Galeazzo Visconti who had driven him out of the town of Milan. The Count then abandoned his claims to Mallorca ; Isabel of Mallorca also disappears from history shortly afterwards, and with her the conflicting claims to the sovereignty of the Balearic Islands came to an end.

In 1391 Juan married his daughter, Violante, to Louis of Anjou, who styled himself King of Jerusalem and of Sicily, and was the son of the Count of Anjou, who claimed the crown of Mallorca. To Maria of Sicily he married his nephew, Martin, the Count of Ejérica, an alliance already proposed by his father, and then prepared to deal with the position in Sicily and with the revolt which had broken out in Sardinia. His preparations were disturbed by a general attack upon the Jews which broke out in various parts of the kingdom and especially in Barcelona. In that town the Aljama or Jewish quarter was entirely destroyed ; a massacre went on for several days and the few Jews who saved their lives were obliged to make a nominal profession of Christianity. Similar scenes occurred in Gerona, Tarragona, Valencia and other towns. The causes of the outbreak appear to have been those common in all ages for outbursts of anti-Semitism : complaints of debtors against extortionate interest, envy of Jewish wealth and commercial success, sentiments further inspired by religious fanaticism. When this uproar had subsided Juan was able to return his attention to Sicily and Sardinia. Pedro IV had secured a convention towards the end of his life, which he hoped would guarantee a permanent pacification of Sardinia. This had been broken in 1387, and subsequently renewed ; but Juan's pacific policy gave the numerous unruly elements in the island every opportunity for asserting themselves. In 1391 Brancaleo de Oria with his wife, Leonora de Arborea, gathered a large body of Sardinian adherents, drove the Aragonese and Catalans out of their possessions, and induced even the town of Sassari to revolt ; it seemed likely that Aragon would lose entire control of the island in a short time. The position of affairs in Sicily was no less confused. Juan certainly had the assent of the Avignon Pope, Clement VII, to a marriage between Maria and Martin, but the Great Schism was now in full progress, and the approval of Avignon was not sufficient to secure the loyalty of the barons of the island, many of whom aspired to independence. As soon as the news arrived that the

father of Martin, the Duke of Montblanch, proposed to place
his son and daughter-in-law in possession of the island, and
was making preparations for that purpose, a league was
formed to oppose the Duke, in case he should attempt to
act without their general consent, and this refractory body
naturally declared for Pope Boniface IX, whom the Aragonese
regarded as a schismatic. However, in 1392, when his
preparations were nearly complete, the Duke sent two barons
to Sicily with promises and representations which secured a
number of adherents to his cause, while many came over to
him in fear of the power of Aragon. The majority of the
Sicilians, however, were prepared to offer resistance and to
make their loyalty to Boniface their excuse. When the
Duke appeared in Sicilian waters with a fleet of a hundred
sail and a large force of well-trained infantry, the
numerous barons and knights of the Sicilian party were
unable to oppose his landing. In March 1392 he seized the
harbour of Trapani, captured Palermo some months later
and imprisoned numerous leaders of the opposition. Some
barons, however, continued to hold out in their castles, the
chief among them being Artel de Alagon, the nephew of the
Governor of the same name who died in 1388, and Pope
Boniface excommunicated the Catalans as enemies to the
Catholic faith. The result was a general rising in 1393, and
only by the help of reinforcements sent by Juan was the
Duke able to maintain his footing in the island. Meanwhile,
the duchies of Athens and Neopatria had been seized by the
Lord of Corinth, Nerio Acciajuoli, a Florentine. He was
attacked by the Venetians and the struggle was ended by
the Turks who made themselves masters of the duchies by
1394. The Catalan rule in Greece thus came to an end, and
while his possession of Sardinia and of Sicily was still doubtful, Juan died in May 1395, killed, according to the usual
account, by a fall from his horse while hunting. The papal
difficulty was further increased by the death of Pope Clement
in Avignon, and the election of a Spaniard, Pedro de Luna,
Cardinal of Aragon, who took the name of Benedict XIII,
and to whom the Aragonese naturally continued their
recognition.

It will thus be seen that Juan was not the right king for
Aragon in these desperate and troublesome times. Few of his

contemporaries had much sympathy with his leanings to art and refinement, and he was freely charged with leading an idle and dissolute life, and leaving the business of government to his women. To him is said to be due the foundation in Barcelona of an institution in imitation of that which had been begun in Toulouse as early as 1323. In that year a number of citizens had gathered together and had formed the *Sobregaya Companhia dels Set Trobadors de Tolosa* with the object of reviving the dying spirit of troubadour poetry ; it is probable that this movement arose from informal meetings of poets held in earlier years. This committee, the *Consistori de la Gaya Sciensa,* elected a chancellor and seven judges, or *mantenedors,* and offered an annual prize for the best poem produced among contemporary poets, the famous Golden Violet, and as the second prize, a wild rose in silver, while other prizes of a similar kind were afterwards given for particular forms of poetry. Hence the name *Jochs Florals,* or floral games, that was afterwards given to these assemblies. A series of rules was drawn up ; the *Leys d'amors,* an Ars Poetica, was produced, and a new if temporary impulse was given to lyric poetry, which soon made itself felt beyond the Pyrenees. A number of theoretical works appeared, of which the most famous are those by Ramon Vidal de Bezaudun. This movement was precisely of the kind to attract the attention of King Juan. He is said to have sent an embassy in 1388 to Charles VI of France, asking him to commission a few members of the Academy of Toulouse to found a similar institution in Barcelona. For this story there is no evidence, and in any case Juan had two men in his own kingdom who were perfectly competent to perform the work, Jayme March and Luis de Averso, who were commissioned by him to found an academy in Barcelona on the model of the institution in Toulouse. Every year in March a poetical contest was to be held in honour of the Virgin Mary, and a prize for the best poem was to be given. Funds for the Academy were provided, and its privileges and wealth were increased by Juan's successor, Martin I, but subsequent political confusion ended its activities for a time, and it was not until the reign of Ferdinand I in 1412 that the Catalan Poetical Academy resumed its work.

Juan's sudden death brought into being a work of out-

standing importance in the Catalan literature of this period,
the *Sompni* or " Dream " of Bernat Metge. Bernat, who was
the King's secretary, was suspected of having plotted against
the King's person and was imprisoned in 1395 ; he wrote his
book while he was in captivity to clear his name. His Dream
occurs in his prison, the King Juan appearing to him in person, accompanied by Orpheus and Tiresias ; the King
explains the cause of his death and asserts that he has been
saved by his devotion to the doctrine of the Immaculate
Conception, and orders Bernat to relate the vision to the
Queen and to his friends ; Orpheus then tells the story of
his life ; Tiresias explains the cause of his blindness and
inveighs against women, whereupon Bernat takes up the
defence of the weaker sex. The book is full of reminiscences
of other authors ; the account of hell given by Orpheus is
entirely Virgilian, and Bernat draws upon Cicero, Cassiodorus,
Thomas Aquinas and Ramon Lull, but the argument is
connected in strict logical form and presented in admirable
style ; the invective and satire of Tiresias is amusing in its
vigour and the scene of jealousy which he describes must
surely have been drawn from life. Bernat Metge, who
also translated Boccaccio's story of Griselda, deserves more
fame than he has obtained.

As soon as the unexpected death of Juan was known,
the Catalan Estates of the Realm met in Barcelona and
decided to nominate Martin, the Duke of Montblanch, as
King. They sent deputies to Sicily to offer him the crown,
with a fleet to support him in his war against the refractory
nobles of the island. This war delayed his arrival in Spain,
and the opportunity was seized by another pretender to the
crown, in the person of Count Mateu de Foix, who claimed
it through his wife, Juana, the daughter of the deceased Juan.
The Count gathered an army to support his claims, and his
attitude caused much alarm in Catalonia where he had a
numerous body of supporters and considerable estates,
including large possessions in the neighbourhood of Vich,
Martorell and other places, while his possessions in Foix
and Béarn provided considerable resources on which he could
draw. He also secured the support of the Count of Armagnac,
who could command the services of several Free Companies
of mercenaries who were then wandering about southern

France, while the Duke of Berry, the uncle of the French King, and other French nobles promised to help him ; in a short time he was able to invade Catalonia with a formidable army, and began the siege of Barbastro. The town, however, offered a desperate resistance. Queen Maria had returned in the absence of her husband, and had taken over the duties of the government, and her vigorous measures, together with the outbreak of disease in the Count's army, and the interruption of his supplies, obliged him eventually to give up the enterprise and return to France by way of Navarre. Shortly afterwards, King Martin left Sicily after handing the government to his son of the same name, and in March 1397 he went to Avignon in the hope of composing the Great Schism which was then dividing the Church.

Clement VII had been succeeded by Pedro de Luna, the Cardinal of Aragon, who took the title of Benedict XIII and was elected in September 1394. The occasion was thought to be an opportunity for ending the Schism, and the cardinal electors drew up a form of oath, binding any one whom they might elect to resign the papacy if he should be called upon by a majority of the cardinals so to do in the interests of the Church. Pedro de Luna declared his willingness to abdicate as readily as to take off his hat. He was well-known as a man of exceptional ability, the worthy representative of an old Aragonese family. He was profoundly learned in canon law, of which he had been a professor in the University of Montpellier, while his personal reputation was blameless. His cleverness, however, was liable to degenerate into craft and subtlety ; he had a genius for managing complicated affairs and, in fact, most of the qualities of a great ecclesiastical statesman. Few could defeat him in argument and if he is compared with Boniface IX at Rome, an avaricious materialist, the preference of Aragon cannot be blamed. He was elected in consequence of his expressed determination to bring the Schism to an end, but the cardinal electors soon discovered that the only conclusion which he would contemplate was one which pleased himself. The first two or three years after his election were filled with negotiations upon this point ; Benedict established himself in Avignon and cleverly refuted every argument urged in favour of his abdication. Quarrels broke out between the University of

Paris and the University of Toulouse upon legal and canonical points of argument. The University of Paris urged the King of France to make Benedict abdicate by force, and at the end of 1396 embassies were sent to Germany, England and Spain to secure their co-operation with this policy. It was when matters had reached this pitch that Martin attempted to interfere, but he was unable to change Benedict's determination, and continued his voyage to Barcelona.

Upon his arrival, he declared the Count of Foix to be a rebel and traitor, confiscated his estates in Catalonia and, when he attempted to renew the attack in 1398, obliged him to beat a hasty retreat. The Count died a few months later. His French possessions passed to his wife, and his sister, Isabella, who was married to a Gascon lord, was compassionately granted most of the fiefs in Aragon which her brother had held. Meanwhile, the King was obliged to send further reinforcements to Sicily, where his son eventually subdued the turbulent nobles of the island, and himself went to Zaragoza for his coronation, which took place in April 1399 with great splendour. At the same time, the domestic peace of the kingdom was disturbed by private quarrels between two noble families, represented by Pedro Ximenes de Urrea and Antonio de Luna. The discord thus engendered spread over a considerable part of the country. The towns were drawn into the dispute. The Justicia was unable to compose the quarrel and, as the King's presence was required in Valencia, he was obliged to appoint a Governor General of the kingdom, a dignity conferred upon Count Alfonso de Denia. For a considerable period the authorities were unable to secure complete domestic peace and order, partly in consequence of the fact that the King's attention was distracted by the papal question at Avignon and by further disturbances in Sardinia and Sicily.

As regards Avignon, Benedict had been informed by the French King that the Schism must be healed by February 1398, otherwise the King would himself remove the cause of it. Benedict declined to yield; the French Church therefore withdrew its allegiance from him in July of that year, and Benedict was cut off from all means of raising money from the ecclesiastical revenues of France ; most of his cardinals left him, and Marshal Bouciquot was commissioned to remove him from Avignon by force. Benedict held out in the palace of Avignon, apparently deserted by every possible supporter. He summoned the King of Aragon, who held the position of Gonfalonier of the Church, to help him, but Martin was not inclined to begin a war with France, as he had other pressing matters upon his hands. He contented himself by sending an embassy to the King of France, urging a reconciliation with the Pope, and finally Charles VI agreed to withdraw his troops from Avignon, provided that Benedict undertook to abdicate in case Boniface at Rome abdicated or died, and not to leave Avignon without the King's permission. For the next four years Benedict remained a virtual prisoner in his palace. A gradual reaction in his favour took place. The French clergy discovered that they were better off under the Pope than they were under the King, who demanded large contributions from the Church to meet the expenses in which the schism has involved him. Benedict escaped from Avignon in March 1403 and took up his position in Château Renard, a few miles from the town, where he could rely upon the protection of Louis of Anjou, whose claims upon Naples he had supported. The Duke of Orléans had also urged the King to release him, and an embassy from Aragon had made similar representations. Benedict determined to return to Avignon, which he garrisoned with Aragonese soldiers and provisioned for a siege in case of emergency, and by the end of May the obedience of France was restored to him. The question was reopened when Boniface IX died in October 1404, but Benedict maintained his position, as will be seen, until 1415.

In 1400 Martin was obliged to send another armament to Sicily, where a revolt had been supported by King Ladislas of Naples. Martin the younger, however, succeeded in crushing the revolt to such purpose that it was possible to turn attention to the problem of Sardinia. Here again the Aragonese were helped by the outbreak of domestic feuds. Brancaleone de Oria, with the help of the Genoese, had succeeded in conquering much of the island, but had so enraged the inhabitants that they turned for aid to the Viscount Aimerich of Narbonne, who had married Beatrice of Arborea, the sister of Leonora, and had already claimed the inheritance of the last Judge of Arborea. Martin of Sicily arrived in

November 1408, determined not to leave the island until its conquest was complete ; and on June 30, 1409, he won a decisive victory at San Luri. Many of the Sardinian nobles who had hitherto been independent submitted, and Martin appeared to have every prospect of fulfilling his determination, when he suddenly died on July 24. The general grief was increased by the fact that he left behind him only an illegitimate son, Fadrique, while the King of Aragon himself was in weak health. Negotiations, therefore, began for the nomination of a successor to the crown, but before these were completed the King of Aragon died on the last day of May 1410, leaving no directions in his will except that the inheritance should pass to his rightful heir. With him ended the dynasty of the Counts of Barcelona, which for nearly three centuries had provided the kingdom of Aragon with a succession of competent and energetic rulers, for the most part equal to the difficult times in which they had to govern.

CHAPTER XIV

THE " COMPROMISE " OF CASPE

Six claimants to the throne. Electors choose Ferdinand of Castile. He secures the crown. Attempts to end the Great Schism. Quarrels concerning finance. Premature death of Ferdinand.

ON the death of King Martin there was no direct heir to the throne, and six claimants came forward. The first was James, the Count of Urgel, who based his claim upon his own rights and those of his wife, Isabel. He was the great-grandson of Alfonso IV, and his wife was the daughter of Pedro IV by his fourth wife, Sibila. Secondly, there was Alfonso, the Duke of Gandía. He was the son of Pedro, the Count of Ribagorza, and therefore grandson of James II. He died in the course of the discussions on the succession, and his son, also named Alfonso, took his place. The third claimant was Luis, Duke of Calabria, the son of Violante of Anjou, the daughter of King Juan. Fourthly was Ferdinand, the Infante of Castile, the son of Eleanor, who had married Juan of Castile, and was therefore the grandson of Pedro IV. The fifth claimant was Fadrique, the Count of Luna, an illegitimate son of the Infante Martin. Lastly, there was Juan, the Count of Prades, the brother of the first Alfonso, who was Duke of Gandía, and who came forward upon the death of the Duke, considering that his rights were better than those of his nephew.[1] It was to be expected that with a vacant throne and so many claimants disturbances would break out, and the Catalans entrusted the government to twelve commissioners who succeeded in maintaining order, but Aragon was disturbed by the family quarrels of the Luna and Urrea parties, which were further exasperated by the attempt of James, the Count of Urgel, to secure recognition as Governor General of the kingdom. In Valencia things were

[1] See footnote, p. 205.

204

even worse. The claims of the Count were there espoused by the party led by the family of Vilaregut, who were opposed by the Centellas. Sardinia now seized the opportunity to try to secure independence, while Sicily was divided between the causes of Queen Blanca, the widow of the Infante Martin, and the supporters of Bernardo de Cabrera. It soon became obvious that only two candidates need be seriously considered. James, the Count of Urgel, was a handsome and attractive young man, whose personal charm and liberality in gifts and promises had secured him a large body of supporters. He could rely upon the support of Catalonia almost as a whole and of many localities in the other two kingdoms. He seriously damaged his prospects by his attempt to seize the position of Governor General, which was usually held by the immediate heir to the throne, and aroused so much discontent in Aragon and in Zaragoza that he actually improved the chance of his chief rival Ferdinand. Ferdinand was the son of Leonor, the daughter of Pedro IV, who had married Juan, the son of the Count of Trastamara. His elder brother, Henry III, became King of Castile, and, on his death in 1406, left an heir named Juan, barely two years of age, whom he recommended on his death-bed to his brother's care. Ferdinand undertook the responsibility, and performed it honourably. He refused to listen to any suggestions that he might himself occupy the throne, and secured the coronation of Juan II under the regency of himself and the widowed Queen. Apart from domestic disturbances in Castile, the

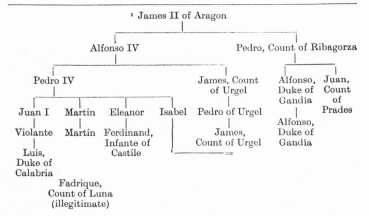

country was also involved in a dangerous struggle with the Moors of Granada. Ferdinand successfully dealt with these difficulties, and his defeat of the Moors and the capture of their chief fortress gave him the title " El de Antequera." While he thus restrained any ambitions he may have had to rule Castile, on the death of his uncle he had no hesitation in claiming the crown of Aragon, though there were not wanting critics who pointed out that Juan II of Castile had a better right to the crown, as being in a more direct line of descent. Ferdinand was strongly supported in Aragon, as he made no aggressive claims and professed to rely upon justice and right, and in sending ambassadors to Aragon to advance his claim he was careful not to cross the frontier in person. Of the two contending parties in Aragon, that led by Antonio de Luna declared for the Count of Urgel, but the party of Urrea which supported Ferdinand also secured the co-operation of the Archbishop of Zaragoza, and his influence brought over most of the influential men in the kingdom to the side of Ferdinand. Two opposed policies were thus represented : the party of the Count of Urgel stood for separatism, while the supporters of Ferdinand looked for a movement towards peninsular union with the help and friendship of Castile.

The Count of Urgel then proceeded to ruin his prospects by murdering the Archbishop, in the hope of breaking up the opposition party. The Archbishop was attacked and killed on a journey by the adherents of Antonio de Luna, but their attempt to seize Zaragoza was frustrated in time, and the general horror aroused by this treachery contributed to strengthen the cause of Ferdinand. Thus it was possible to gather an assembly representative of Aragon in September 1411, at Alcañiz, while the Catalan representatives had previously assembled in Tortosa. It was more difficult to secure any agreement in Valencia. The famous churchman and orator, Vicente Ferrer, whose influence in Valencia was considerable, espoused the cause of Ferdinand, and, after the contending parties had fought a battle at Murviedro in January 1412, in which the Count's party was utterly defeated, some measure of agreement was secured. Pope Benedict was indefatigable in his attempts to bring the representatives of the three kingdoms together, and, after lengthy negotiations, it was decided that each kingdom should nominate three persons who were to meet and decide upon the respective claims now before the country. The claimants were allowed to be represented by their proctors or lawyers to make out their case, and every precaution was taken to preserve the commission from outside interference. The Aragonese representatives were Domingo Ram, the Bishop of Huesca, Francisco de Aranda, a Carthusian monk, and Berenguer de Bardají, one of the most distinguished lawyers of his time. Catalonia was represented by Pedro Zagarriga, the Archbishop of Tarragona, Guillermo de Vallseca, a lawyer of high repute, and Bernardo de Gualbes, learned both in canon and civil law. The Valencian representatives were Bonifacio Ferrer, the head of the Carthusian Order, the Dominican, Vicente Ferrer, who enjoyed a wide reputation even beyond Spain for piety and eloquence, and Ginés Rabasa, a lawyer. These nine electors met in Caspe, situated on the Ebro and belonging to the Knights of St. John. After deliberating for thirty days and hearing evidence, on June 28, 1412, they announced that they had decided in favour of Ferdinand of Castile as the nearest relative of the deceased King, an announcement made by Vincente Ferrer as the climax of a long and eloquent sermon. It was not to be expected that any choice would produce universal satisfaction, and chroniclers vary considerably in their accounts of the feeling with which the announcement was received. But it became plain that the three kingdoms as a whole were prepared to support Ferdinand, and it was to be hoped that the Count of Urgel would accept the decision of the commission.

Ferdinand I, therefore, made his way to Zaragoza, where he agreed to observe the liberties of the kingdom. He had previously visited Catalonia and received the homage of Valencia. The election had a good effect upon outlying portions of the Aragonese dominions. In Sicily, for instance, Ferdinand confirmed the position of Queen Blanca as regent of the island with a council of advisers to help her. Bernardo de Cabrera, who had been persecuting the Queen with offers of marriage and opposition to her government, was arrested and brought to Barcelona. In Sardinia, the Viscount of Narbonne had attempted, in conjunction with the Genoese, to conquer the whole of the island, and had already secured a considerable part of it, when the announcement of Ferdinand's election made him realize that he would be opposed not merely by Aragon but that Ferdinand could also rely upon support from Castile. He and his allies immediately sent an embassy to Aragon, and concluded a five years' truce. In the Balearic Islands Ferdinand had been previously recognized, and his supremacy over the Aragonese dominions thus appeared to be undisputed.

It was, however, impossible to satisfy the disappointed ambitions of the Count of Urgel. Ferdinand had excused his absence from the Cortes, had given him an honourable place at court and had promised large sums of money towards the payment of his debts, but the continual complaints of his mother and the incitement of his friend, Antonio de Luna, induced him to make plans for the overthrow of Ferdinand. He opened communications with the Duke of Clarence, son of Henry IV of England, who was at Bordeaux, and, on gaining promises of help from him and from other French nobles, he collected an army and invaded Aragon in the spring of 1413. Antonio de Luna ravaged the neighbourhood of Jaca, while the Count himself operated in the neighbourhood of Lérida, in the hope of winning support in Catalonia. The Duke of Clarence, however, was hurriedly recalled to England by the death of his father, and the help that he had promised was not forthcoming, while other nobles began to consider the imprudence of attacking so powerful an adversary as the King of Aragon. Ferdinand had already taken adequate measures for the security of the country. He had garrisoned the vulnerable spots, and when the Count's intentions became plain he collected a force from the nobles of the realm, which was strengthened by a body of Castilian knights who were supporting him in Zaragoza. The Count and Luna were besieged in Balaguer and held out for more than two months, vainly hoping that English reinforcements would relieve them, while Ferdinand's forces battered the town with every type of artillery then known. Eventually the rebels were forced to surrender, and threw themselves upon the King's mercy. In November 1413 Ferdinand commuted the death penalty which the Count had incurred as a traitor to the kingdom to one of imprisonment for life with the confiscation of his property. The King then returned to

Zaragoza, his position now being secure, for the coronation ceremonies which were carried out with unexampled splendour in February 1414.

Two matters occupied the King's attention immediately after his coronation. The first of these was the question of the papacy. The Council of Pisa held in 1409 had in vain attempted to heal the breach in the unity of the Church caused by the Great Schism. The Council had declared the deposition of the existing Popes, Benedict XIII and Gregory XII, and had elected Alexander V in their place ; but this solution was by no means generally accepted. The Emperor Sigismund had summoned a General Council to deal with this pressing problem. As early as October 1413 he had invited representatives of all Christendom to meet at Constance in November of 1414 for a general Church Council, and invitations were issued to King Ferdinand and to Pope Benedict XIII, who had been active in Aragon, as we have seen, in conducting negotiations for the election to the throne. It was obviously necessary for Ferdinand to decide whether he should support the Spanish Pope or not. For that reason, a meeting between himself and Benedict was arranged at Morella. Fifty days spent in argument failed to induce Benedict to resign his position. Ferdinand was convinced that no other remedy was possible, and withdrew his support from Benedict, who then retired to the seaside settlement of Peñíscola, where he proceeded to issue a series of arguments showing that he was the only genuine Pope, and that it was impossible to dispute the legitimacy of his election. A second meeting at Perpignan, at which the Emperor Sigismund was present and did his best to persuade Benedict to resign, proved equally fruitless. Ferdinand proclaimed that he should be disregarded, and that none of his subjects should refer to Benedict, or Pedro de Luna as Ferdinand styled him, in ecclesiastical matters, but should refer these to the General Council. This example was followed by the other rulers in the Spanish peninsula, and, whatever may be thought of Ferdinand's action, it cannot be denied that no other policy seemed possible if the unity of the Church was to be restored.

Differences also arose between the King and his subjects upon financial matters. The royal incomes had been considerably diminished by the negligence of earlier rulers,

14

and the unwillingness of subjects to contribute. Ferdinand
was a prince of liberal views, who was anxious to give
petitioners even more than they asked. It is also probable
that his administrative experience in Castile had accustomed
him to a greater freedom of action than he could hope to
exercise when dealing with the Cortes of Aragon or Catalonia.
Especially was this restriction obvious in the financial sphere,
and the necessity of bargaining for concessions from his
subjects was continually irksome to him. His view was that
his predecessors had been forced to barter the rights of the
Crown in order to gain the necessary supplies for carrying
on the Crown business, and he proposed to restore the Crown
to its former position and so to avoid the necessity of continually harassing his subjects with small demands. His
conflict with the municipality of Barcelona will show the
kind of difficulty which he had to encounter and the character
of the opposition with which he had to deal. On returning
to Barcelona, after concluding his negotiations with Benedict,
it became necessary to supply the royal household with
meat and other provisions, and it appeared that the purchases,
even when made by the King, were subject to a tax from
which the clergy and the nobility were free. This the King
refused to pay. An uproar followed. It was asserted that
he was infringing the ancient rights of the town. The Council
of the Hundred was called together and the King summoned
the President. one Juan Fivaller, to an interview. He
pointed out the injustice of demanding a tribute from the
King which was not required of the most inferior clergy, and,
when he was reminded of his oath to observe the ancient
customs of the town, he replied that that oath obliged him
no less to maintain the ancient rights of the throne, and in
particular the royal revenues. Fivaller then urged him not
to attack the Catalans upon a question of privilege, however
small, which might be regarded as a breach of the convention
between the King and themselves. Ferdinand paid the
amount required, and left Barcelona the next day, declining
any further communications with the inhabitants, who sent
messengers after him begging him not to leave their country,
and asserting their readiness to render him any services in
their power. This combination of intense attachment to
every article specified in the ancient privileges of their town,

the proposal to abrogate any of which aroused universal resentment, together with the apparently inconsistent protestation of loyalty to the King and desire to profit commercially by the presence of his court, is characteristic of the people with whom Ferdinand had to deal, and was no doubt intensely exasperating to any ruler of absolutist tendencies.

Ferdinand went as far as Igualada, about a day's journey from Barcelona, where his health was so impaired that he could travel no further, and in April 1416, he died after a reign of only four years, at the age of thirty-seven, according to the majority of the annalists. He had barely had time to compose the disturbances which the interregnum had brought about or to learn the peculiar character of the people with whom he had to deal, and to this fact no doubt are due the adverse opinions upon his character which have been passed by some historians. None the less, his death was a misfortune to the country. The titles of " El Justo " and " El Honesto " which have been given to him, were not undeserved. His personal life was blameless, and he left behind him none of the illegitimate progeny so often attached to the names of his predecessors. Simple in his habits and an indefatigable worker, he seems to have been endowed with that gift of sympathy which enabled him to estimate the grievances and the characters of contending parties. There is no evidence to support the suggestion that his abandonment of Benedict XIII was an act of bad faith towards one who had secured his election to the throne nor that he had bribed any of the other electors for the same purpose. On the contrary, his efforts to secure the unity of the Church can only be regarded as laudable, even if they were based upon a misconception of the future powers of the papacy in Europe, upon which subject his contemporaries were no more enlightened than himself.

CHAPTER XV

ALFONSO V

Attempts to conclude the Great Schism. Expedition to Sardinia and Sicily. Attack on Corsica. Affairs in Naples. Alliance with Juana II., Alfonso at war with Juana. Returns to Aragon. War with Castile. Álvaro de Luna. Five years' armistice. Juana captures Naples. Alfonso returns to Italy. Alliances with Northern cities. Death of Juana. Claimants to the kingdom of Naples. Alfonso defeated by the Genoese. Alliance with Milan. René of Anjou in possession of Naples. Alfonso captures the town. Discontent in Aragon. Intrigues of the King of Navarre Defeat of Aragon at Olmedo. Alfonso in possession of Naples. Carlos de Viana. Death of Alfonso.

ERDINAND was succeeded by his eldest son, Alfonso V, the date of whose birth is disputed, but who seems to have been twenty-two years of age, and nearly a year previously had married Maria of Castile, the eldest daughter of Henry III, and the sister of John III, the King of Castile. After celebrating his father's funeral at Poblet, he met the Catalan Cortes in Barcelona, gave the usual promises to observe the constitution and proceeded to continue his father's policy for dealing with the pressing question of the unity of the Church. A general Church Assembly was summoned to Barcelona, where he advised his prelates to attend the Council of Constance which had deposed Pope John XXIII in 1415 and was to provide for the election of a pope who should represent a united church. The majority of the clergy were on the side of Benedict and declined to admit that the papacy was vacant. The King, however, refused to accede to their views, and sent his own ambassadors to the Council of Constance, who were instructed to state that the King had sent them to co-operate in the work of extirpating heresy, ending the Schism, reforming the Church and electing a supreme pontiff. They also asked that the ecclesiastical revenues of Sardinia and of Sicily might be placed at the King's disposal, in view of the expenses

to which he had been put by his action in supporting the
General Council. In 1417 the Council of Constance elected
Cardinal Odo Colonna, who took the title of Pope Martin V.
Alfonso recognized him as such, and thus confirmed the
sentence of the Council declaring Benedict XIII to be a
schismatic. The new Pope gave Alfonso the pecuniary
concessions which he demanded, and asked him to exile
Benedict from Peñíscola by way of return. This Alfonso
declined to do. His policy aroused much discontent in the
kingdom, and the Catalan Estates met at Molins in 1418
where they were joined by those of Zaragoza and Valencia,
and sent a deputation to the King, requesting him to remove
all Castilians from his household and following and to change
his policy in accordance with their desires. Alfonso informed
them that the only Castilians in his service were a few old
servants of his father whom he certainly did not propose to
dismiss, while as regards his general policy he was prepared to
take advice but to act in accordance with his own judgment.
When the deputation followed him to Valencia, he received
the Catalan members apart and reminded them that they had
no constitutional right to combine with the representatives
of other towns and certainly not with those of other orders,
and, having thus shelved the dispute for the moment, he
turned the energies of his subjects in another direction by
preparing for an expedition to Sardinia and to Sicily, in both
of which islands the prevailing disorder demanded his
presence. He left the government in charge of Queen Maria,
who was supported by a council, and took with him those of
the nobility who were likely to embarrass the government
in his absence. He proposed to recover the maritime
supremacy which his predecessors had lost and to crush
the Genoese who were harassing Catalan traders both in
the Levant and nearer home. In 1420 he appeared off
Sardinia with a considerable fleet and speedily subjugated
the refractory elements in the island. He then proceeded to
Naples where Queen Juana required his help against the
Duke of Anjou and Genoa. She proposed to endow him with
her right of succession and to give him a footing in Calabria
without delay.

After his conquest of Sardinia Alfonso determined to
exercise the rights which had given Corsica also to the

Aragonese Crown. The island had been in the possession of the Genoese ever since 1360, but, like Sardinia, was disturbed by the quarrels of party factions, of whose dissensions the King hoped to take immediate advantage. He began by attacking the fortified town of Calvi in 1420, which speedily surrendered, but an assault upon San Bonifacio, which was followed by a siege, remained unsuccessful. The Genoese were able, after desperate efforts, to throw reinforcements into the fortress, upon the possession of which depended that of the whole island and the safety of their communications also. Alfonso, therefore, gave up the attempt in the following year, and sailed for Sicily to deal with affairs in that island and in Naples.

King Robert of Naples had left his possessions in 1343 to his granddaughter, Juana I, who was then sixteen years of age, since which time the affairs of the kingdom had been brought to the uttermost confusion by the clash of contending parties and interests. From these disturbances emerged about the beginning of the fifteenth century the figure of Ladislaus, the son of Duke Charles of Durazzo, an enterprising and ambitious ruler, who seemed likely to control the reactionary and contending parties within his kingdom. He, however, died in 1413. His sister and heiress, Juana II, was generally recognized as Queen, and married Jacopo de Borbon, Count of La Marche, as her second husband, who took the title of Duke of Calabria and the position of Prince Consort. With this he was dissatisfied, and attempted to assume the title and powers of a king, when a general rising of the people who were dissatisfied with his aggressive attitude obliged him to take refuge in his own country, where he ended his career as a Franciscan monk at Besançon. Juana strengthened her position by an understanding with Pope Martin V, who was induced to crown her as Queen in 1419, and, as she had succeeded in reconciling the two powerful leaders, the Grand Constable, Sforza de Tennebello, and the Grand Seneschal, Juan Caraccioli, in whose hands the ordinary business of the kingdom lay, her possession of it seemed to be assured. There was, however, another claimant to the throne of Naples, namely Louis III of Anjou, whose grandfather had been adopted by Juana I in 1382, as her heir, and whose father, Louis II, had made vain attempts to exercise

the rights of inheritance thus acquired ; in 1420 Louis III
(who had claimed the throne of Aragon and been rejected by
the Parliament of Caspe) secured the ear of Pope Martin V,
who was inclined to support his claims. In 1419 the Pope
had named Sforza as Gonfalonier of the Church, in other
words Commander-in-Chief of the papal forces, with the
idea of reconquering, with his support, the papal possessions
held by Braccio di Monteone, the lord of Perugia. He also
expected the support of Naples in his enterprise, but Caraccioli, who hated his rival Sforza, induced the Queen to
refuse her assistance. The Pope was therefore secretly
inclined to favour the claims of the Duke of Anjou, while
Sforza made no concealment of his support. He marched
against the capital in the Duke's name, while risings, incited
by the partisans of Anjou, broke out in other parts of the
country. Sforza is perhaps the most famous of the Italian
condottieri, and, at this time, becomes one of the chief figures
in Italian history. He was one of those professional soldiers
who organized his own countrymen into a military force to
replace the lawless bands of mercenaries who had ravaged
Italy after the system of citizen militia had declined. Of
these foreign captains, the last and the best-known was the
famous Englishman, Sir John Hawkwood, who died at
Florence in 1394 ; but, when native companies were formed,
the soldiers of which were united by other ties than the mere
hope of plunder, discipline became stricter, and the laws of
warfare were better observed, in fact so well observed that
commanders spent their energies in attempts to outmanœuvre
an opponent, and pitched battles and slaughter were avoided.
The first leader who initiated this change was Alberigo da
Barbiano, and under his command Sforza had received his
early training. His real name was Muzio Attendolo ; Sforza
was a nickname, derived from his violent attitude when
Alberigo attempted to interfere in a dispute concerning the
division of some booty. Born in 1369, he served under
Alberigo, formed a band of his own and fought for Florence
against Pisa. He served Pope John XXIII until they
quarrelled, when he took the side of Ladislaus of Naples, and
had hitherto remained in the service of that country.

Juana, thus suddenly threatened by a formidable enemy,
sent her minister, Antonio Caraffa, to the Pope, who soon

discovered the true inclinations of the papacy. He visited
Alfonso of Aragon, and told him that the Queen would adopt
him as son and heir, on condition of securing his assistance
at the earliest possible moment. Alfonso and his councillors
hesitated for some time. They apparently knew that Juana's
political principles were as unstable as her morality, and that
her subjects were no more reliable than herself. The Pope
also strove to dissuade Alfonso from the enterprise, but, as
he refused to break off his relations with the Genoese, the
King of Aragon determined to make the attempt. He went
to Palermo, and, when the negotiations with Juana had been
satisfactorily settled, he sent a formal defiance to Louis of
Anjou, declaring war upon him, not only as the adopted
son of the Queen, but also as possessing a definite claim to
Naples by his descent from King Manfred. Early in July
1421 he appeared off Naples with his fleet. The troops of
Anjou, who were besieging the town, immediately retired,
and Alfonso was received with great joy by the inhabitants.
Pope Martin did his utmost to raise further support for the
Duke of Anjou, sending ambassadors to the rulers of Milan,
Florence and other Italian towns ; but in October Alfonso
won a brilliant naval victory off Pisa over the Genoese, who
were obliged to place themselves under the supremacy of
the Duke of Milan. Alfonso also appointed Braccio di
Monteone to the position of Grand Constable, or Commander-
in-Chief to his armies, and, as Monteone was regarded as the
best of the Italian generals next to Sforza, it was hoped that
the Aragonese would be as successful on land as they had been
by sea. In the following year, Louis, who had lost a number
of important positions, was obliged to conclude an armistice,
which the Pope himself negotiated, as he was afraid that
Alfonso would restore his favour and support to the Aragonese
Pope, Pedro de Luna, and for this reason he was inclined to
recognize the adoption of the King and to confirm his rights
to the Crown of Naples.

However, at this time a series of differences between
Alfonso and Juana began. Alfonso had taken possession of
the towns which he had captured from the Duke of Anjou,
and Juana suspected that he meant to reduce her to a position
of complete inferiority, a suggestion which was made to the
Queen by her Seneschal, Caraccioli, whose influence over her

was considerable. The Duke of Milan also began an intrigue against Alfonso, and suggested to the Pope that a league might be formed for driving the Aragonese out of Italy altogether. The Pope, whose preference for Louis of Anjou remained unshaken, gave serious consideration to this idea, and did his best to allay any suspicions that might be aroused in the mind of Alfonso. Alfonso has been criticized for his failure to push his advantage with greater energy, but the fact was that he was anxious to return to Spain, where domestic affairs urgently required his presence ; the ambition of his brother, Enrique, to marry Catalina, the Infanta of Castile, and the opposition of the third brother, Juan, to this project, brought discord into the kingdom. Alfonso found it impossible to allay the suspicions of the Queen, and when an attempt was made upon his own person, he determined to take Juana prisoner. She anticipated him by taking refuge in Castello di Capuana where Alfonso besieged her. Sforza came to her relief with an army, defeated the Aragonese and secured possession of the town. He also captured the greater part of Naples, and shut up the Aragonese in Castello Nuovo, until the arrival of a Catalan fleet in June 1423 relieved the situation. Sforza showed incredible bravery, but a series of attacks in different quarters distracted his attention, and he was obliged to retire with the Queen and some of the leading citizens to Aversa, leaving Alfonso once more in possession of the whole of Naples. Juana then, at the Pope's advice, revoked her act of adoption, on the ground that Alfonso had shown himself ungrateful and untrustworthy, and replaced him by Duke Louis of Anjou, on whom she conferred the dukedom of Calabria, as her son and heir. The Duke, reinforced by the Duke of Milan, and in conjunction with Sforza, advanced upon Naples and defeated the Aragonese, but Alfonso was unable to continue the struggle for the moment. His presence in his own kingdom was imperatively necessary, and he entrusted the defence of his possessions in Naples to his brother, Pedro, with as large a force as he could afford to leave behind.

The relations between Aragon and Castile provided the urgency for Alfonso's recall. Castile had been governed by Enrique III and, after his death, by his widow, Catalina, and his brother, Fernando, in comparative peace, until the death of the Queen in 1418 brought about a period of dissension and disorder. The King's brothers, Enrique and Juan, the Infantes of Aragon, were at the same time vassals of Castile by hereditary right. Each of them formed parties of their own and attempted to secure ascendancy over King Juan II, who was only fourteen years of age, though they were themselves, in respect both of age and experience, totally unqualified to conduct the affairs of any kingdom. In 1420 Enrique secured possession of the King's person in Tordesillas, and attempted to negotiate a marriage with his sister, Catalina, in the hope of consolidating his own position ; but the King escaped, enlisted the help of the Infante Juan and other nobles, began war against Enrique, and in 1422 obliged him to surrender his person at Madrid. Alfonso had attempted to compose the quarrel, but it was obvious in 1423 that his personal interference was required if his brother were to be released from virtual imprisonment. On his homeward voyage he attacked the important town of Marseilles, the most valuable possession of his opponent, Louis of Anjou. The defences of the harbour were forced by a brilliant operation conducted by the Catalan admiral, and the chain which formed its chief defence was carried away as a trophy. The town was sacked and reduced for the most part to ashes, but Alfonso made no attempt to occupy it, and continued his voyage to Barcelona which he reached early in December. He then began negotiations with the King of Castile, which were to go on for another twelve months.

Alfonso's attempts to secure a meeting with the King of Castile came to nothing owing to the opposition of Juan's councillors, and in particular of Álvaro de Luna, and Alfonso began to consider that an invasion of Castile was the only means of securing a personal interview with the King. Charles III of Navarre intervened, but, in spite of his pacific representations, Alfonso declared in 1425 at Zaragoza that he intended to invade Castile, to put an end to the tyranny of Álvaro de Luna and release the King from his domination, which was the cause of civil disturbances throughout the country. He was approaching the Castilian frontier when his brother, Juan, who had recently become King of Navarre, on the death of his step-brother, Charles, again intervened between the two kings and persuaded them to submit their quarrel to his decision. He induced them to agree that the Infante Enrique should be set at liberty, recover his previous possessions and swear allegiance to the King of Castile as a feudal vassal. The opposition between the parties of Álvaro and the Infante of Aragon none the less continued. Álvaro's opponents secured his banishment from the court, but his domination over the King enabled him to return in no long time, while the interference of Alfonso on his brother's behalf induced the supporters of Álvaro to believe that he was himself forming an opposition party in Castile. King Juan was therefore induced by Álvaro to enter into relations with Count Fadrique de Luna, who had been an unsuccessful claimant to the Crown of Aragon. Alfonso had vainly attempted to satisfy his disappointment by kind treatment and marks of high respect. His party was also supported by the Archbishop of Zaragoza, Alfonso de Argüello, and some leading citizens in the town. The King of Aragon, however, took adequate precautions to prevent any outbreak in his own kingdom. The Count was carefully watched while elaborating his plans, and the citizens and the Archbishop were arrested. The Archbishop died shortly afterwards in prison, and rumours were speedily circulated that he had met with a violent end. The King, in conjunction with his brother, Juan, then marched against Castile in June 1429 at the head of a strong army, declaring once again that his relationship with the King of Castile obliged him to insist upon an interview for the purpose of convincing him of the true interests of his kingdom and the ruinous influence of some of his advisers.

The King of Castile vainly attempted to decline this undesirable offer of assistance, and sent Álvaro with a force to oppose the advance of his cousins. The armies were already in battle array, and the Cardinal de Foix was vainly preaching peace, when another pacificator appeared, in the person of Queen Maria of Aragon. She immediately ordered her tent to be pitched exactly between the two armies and, after a lengthy interview, induced the Castilian barons to declare that no attempt would be made to occupy territory belonging to the King of Navarre nor to damage the interests of the Infante Enrique, and when this had been settled the armies were induced to withdraw. Juan of Castile, however, shortly

afterwards arrived with reinforcements, and was so dissatisfied with this convention that he immediately occupied the
possessions of the Infante Enrique whom he accused of
conspiracy with the enemies of Castile, and drove him to
take refuge in Aragon. Queen Maria, his sister, with great
trouble persuaded him to declare his readiness to stop his
military operations, if Alfonso would promise to abandon his
support of his brothers and not to attempt to defend them in
their Castilian possessions. The King of Aragon declined to
accept this condition, and Juan's forces advanced, but the
Aragonese declined a pitched battle, his supplies failed him and
he therefore retreated to prepare for a campaign in the following year. In the meantime, he attempted to arouse dissension
between Alfonso and his subjects by issuing a proclamation
to the Estates of the three realms of Aragon, declaring that he
had taken up arms only in defence of his just cause, whereas
the Aragonese King was prosecuting unjustified claims and
wrongfully interfering in the domestic concerns of a foreign
country. This propaganda produced no effect. The Estates
granted the necessary sums for military preparations and the
Count de Luna found himself in a short time deprived of all
his possessions on his return to Castile in the spring of 1430.
The outbreak of hostilities was for some time delayed, partly
owing to the fact that the papal legate succeeded in arranging
a short armistice between the contending parties, and also
because the Kings of Aragon and Navarre discovered that
their subjects were getting tired of the war and were unwilling
to provide the necessary reinforcements. Alfonso was also
anxious to re-establish his tottering power in Italy. He and
his brother, therefore, sent ambassadors to the King of
Castile, who was also ready to make peace, as he proposed
to attack the Moors in Granada, and in July 1430 an armistice
for five years was concluded. It was agreed that those who
had abandoned their country to join the hostile party should
not be allowed to return, and that the Infantes of Aragon,
Enrique and Pedro, should withdraw from Castile. Other
points in dispute were to be settled by a court of fourteen
judges appointed by either side. Such a peace was obviously
not likely to be of long duration so long as the ambitions of
the Infante Enrique remained unsatisfied. But Alfonso
considered that the peace and security of his dominions in

Spain were sufficiently assured to enable him to return to the conduct of affairs in Italy.

In this year was also concluded the great papal schism. In 1429 the Cardinal de Foix induced Gil Muñoz, who had succeeded Benedict XIII in Peñíscola with the title of Clement VIII, to abandon his shadowy claim to papal authority and to accept the Bishopric of Mallorca. In 1430 Alfonso agreed to recognize Martin V as Pope.

Queen Juana and Duke Louis had combined with Pope Martin V to drive the Aragonese out of Italy, while the Duke of Milan, who saw an opportunity of becoming the dominant power in the peninsula, promised his support, and induced the Genoese to equip a fleet for the same purpose. The party had lost their famous leader, Sforza, who had been drowned in the River Pescara early in 1424 while attacking Braccio, who was then besieging Aquila, but his position and responsibilities were taken over by his son, whose reputation was already almost equal to that of his father, and upon whom his father's possessions in Naples were conferred. Juana first conquered Gaeta. A formidable party, supporting herself and Louis, rose in the town, and forced the Aragonese to capitulate, on terms which allowed them a free departure. The island of Procida was captured, and the allies then began the siege of Naples, and Alfonso's Italian general, Jacopo Caldora, handed over the town in April, on a promise of security for the property of the inhabitants and a considerable grant of money for arrears of pay. Many Aragonese and Catalans were captured by this unexpected advance of the enemy, and the remainder retreated with the Infante Pedro to the fortresses of Castello dell' Oro and Castello Nuovo. By the end of June little more than these two fortresses were left to Alfonso. Braccio had been completely defeated and killed at Aquila, most of the towns had submitted to the Queen and the competence and liberality of the Duke had won the favour of the Neapolitans. Alfonso was, therefore, particularly anxious to secure allies in Italy itself. He concluded an alliance with the Doge of Venice, Tomasso Campofregoso, and his supporters, who had been driven out of Genoa by the Duke of Milan. The Duke, who was hard pressed by Florence and Venice and feared an Aragonese attack after the conclusion of the differences with

Castile, invited Alfonso to an alliance which was concluded in 1426. The King undertook to exclude from his territories exiles from Genoa, to support the Duke's dominion over that town, and allow him to enlist troops in ·his own territories. The Duke undertook to hand over the Genoese possessions in Corsica, and hoped to secure the consent of Genoa to that arrangement. He had, however, entirely overestimated his power in that town, while the war in Upper Italy so far occupied his forces that Alfonso could expect no help from him. Alfonso, therefore, postponed his attempt upon Naples until more favourable prospects in the Neapolitan kingdom seemed probable. Within a short time the fickleness and selfishness of the Neapolitan lords, who hoped by intrigue to gain individual advantages, brought about a change in the situation. In September 1430 am- bassadors appeared in Valencia from the Prince of Tarentum, inviting the King to undertake the conquest of Naples in the name of several other barons. Jacopo Caldora, who was regarded as the most competent of the Italian generals, declared himself ready to return to the Aragonese service, if the past were forgotten, and even Pope Martin V, who had hitherto been an energetic supporter of Duke Louis, was beginning to waver. The Pope died in 1431, and his successor, Eugenius IV, was not favourably disposed to the claims of Aragon, but Alfonso none the less considered that the situation justified preparation for his enterprise. In 1432 he renewed an early alliance with Portugal, began to collect an enormous fleet in his harbours, for the ostensible purpose of conquering the island of Gerba from Tunis, and then returned to Sicily to await the most favourable moment.

The Queen of Naples had already quarrelled with Duke Louis, whose powers she had restricted to the government of Calabria, while she allowed the Grand Seneschal Caraccioli to conduct the government of the country as he pleased. He thus brought down upon himself the hatred of many nobles and eventually of the Queen, with whose approval he was finally assassinated. The removal of their bitterest enemy allowed Alfonso's friends at court to make their influence felt, and to suggest that, instead of handing over the govern- ment to the Duke, negotiations should be resumed with the King of Aragon, who was then in Zaragoza. Shortly after-

wards a convention was concluded, by which Juana revoked
her adoption of the Duke and reaffirmed her adoption of the
King, who undertook to drive his opponent out of Calabria,
to hand over such parts of Neapolitan territory as he still
possessed, and not to enter the Neapolitan kingdom without
permission ; but a very short experience convinced him that
the Queen was only using him as a means of defeating the
claims of Louis, and that most of his so-called adherents
were more inclined to support the Queen than himself. The
Pope was also busy forming a union between Florence,
Venice, the Duke of Milan and the German Emperor to drive
the Aragonese out of Italy, and Alfonso therefore retired to
Sicily after concluding an armistice for ten years.

For the moment Alfonso's cause was threatened with
complete destruction, and Juana induced Duke Louis and
the Prince of Tarentum, Jacopo Caldora, to pursue the war
with such energy that they besieged Alfonso in his own
capital ; but the situation was changed in 1434 by the death
of the Duke, who appears to have been a very popular
character, while in the following year Queen Juana also died,
and Alfonso was thus relieved of his most powerful enemy.
The kingdom of Naples was thus left vacant, and three
claimants came forward. The Pope, Eugenius IV, regarded
the country as a fief of the apostolic chair, and sent an army
to support his claims. The next claimant was Duke René
of Anjou, the brother of Louis III and a son of Violante of
Aragon, whom Juana had named as her heir and successor.
At that moment he happened to be a prisoner in the hands
of the Duke of Burgundy, and was thus not an immediate
cause of anxiety to Alfonso, most of whose supporters were
derived from the enemies of the Anjou party. The Prince
of Tarentum and the Duke of Sessa were brought over to
his side by promises and gifts, and with their support Alfonso
landed at Gaeta and began to besiege the town in May 1435.
Francesco Spinola, a Genoese, was in command of the town,
and, when provisions began to fail, drove out all the women
and children, whom Alfonso received in his camp, and
provided them with food and transport elsewhere, in spite
of the protestations of his troops, who urged that they should
have been sent back to the city. This act of generosity
enabled the town to hold out until a Genoese fleet arrived for

its relief. Alfonso decided to intercept it at sea, and in the
ensuing battle off the island of Ponza he suffered a complete
defeat. He was himself taken prisoner with his brothers, Juan
and Enrique, and with other Italian and Spanish nobles, while
most of his ships were either captured or burned. The Pope
and the Venetian party greeted this victory with mixed feelings, as they feared the ambitions of the Duke of Milan and
the possibility that he might disturb the whole of Italy. The
Genoese commander conducted Alfonso to Milan, instead of
handing him over to the Genoese authorities, and the Duke
treated him rather as a friend and an ally than as a prisoner.
In a short time Alfonso succeeded in persuading the Duke that
the true interests of Milan were best served by an alliance
between themselves directed against René of Anjou. To put a
Frenchman upon the throne of Naples would sooner or later
open the doors for the extension of French dominion throughout the Italian peninsula, and the territories of the Duke would
be the first to suffer. On the other hand, if he himself were
established at Naples, France would have no footing in the
country, and he would be prepared to join the Duke in
resistance to any form of French aggression. The Duke was
speedily persuaded by these arguments to set the King and
his knights at liberty and to open an offensive and defensive
alliance without delay, notwithstanding the protestations
offered by Genoa.

When Alfonso returned to Naples, he found that his brother,
Pedro, had secured possession of Gaeta. The party of Anjou
was led by the wife of René, Isabella of Lorraine, an energetic
and capable woman, whom the Pope, Eugenius IV, was
prepared to support, while a revolt on the part of the Genoese
and of the Florentines who had joined them attracted the
energies of the Aragonese allies elsewhere. Alfonso, however,
relying upon his own resources, began and carried on the war
for some three years. He fought as much with diplomacy
as with military force, securing allies by threats and by
favours, and introducing dissension among his adversaries by
the same means. The Church Council of Bâle and the election
of an opposition Pope gave him an opportunity of dealing
with Eugenius IV, and he was well aware that the Italian
barons and princes were only bound to himself by self-
interest. In 1438 René of Anjou secured his freedom by

ransom, and arrived at Naples. He succeeded in collecting an army of some 8,000 or 10,000 men, but his ransom had apparently exhausted his pecuniary resources, and, when his allies found that their connection with him brought more honour than profit, they gradually fell away. By the end of a year, Alfonso was able to blockade the capital by land and sea. The Infante, Don Pedro, was killed by a chance shot in the course of the siege, to the great grief of his brother. The reluctance of his allies to make a vigorous attack so late in the season, and the badness of the weather, obliged him to postpone the undertaking until the following year. Alfonso continued his intrigues together with his military operations. He informed the Pope, Eugenius, that he should support the nominee of the Council of Bâle, who had taken the name of Felix V, if Eugenius did not see his way to invest him with the kingdom of Naples. At the end of 1441, he succeeded in capturing the town of Puzzolo, and this victory enabled him to resume the siege of Naples. The defenders offered a vigorous resistance and professed unwavering loyalty to Duke René ; and Alfonso began to doubt the possibility of success, when two prisoners informed his son Ferdinand that there was a way into the town through an open drain, which happened to be dry at that season of the year. On June 1, 1442, 300 well-armed men entered the town by this means, captured one of the main gates and let in the army. The town was captured after some hours' fighting, and sacked. René escaped to Florence, and Alfonso made his triumphal entry into the capital after clearing the surrounding country of the bands of Sforza and Caldora. His only enemy in Italy was thus the Pope, who threatened to issue a declaration that he was in unlawful possession of Naples, Sicily, Corsica and Sardinia, while Alfonso declared that he would support the Council of Bâle, and that Felix V would invest him if Eugenius declined to do so. Eugenius, therefore, determined to give way, and, after a great expenditure of diplomacy, it was agreed that the King of Aragon should recognize him as the genuine Pope, should withdraw his Church representatives from the Council of Bâle and should send a contingent to the papal fleet intended for action against the Turks. The Pope was prepared to recognize Alfonso as the King of Naples, to invest him with that position and to declare him free of

15

other obligations to the Holy See. In 1444 Alfonso received an embassy from Genoa, asking him for friendship and protection. The King of Bosnia also recognized his authority, but the Duke of Milan began to fear that the Aragonese monarch would consider himself master of Italy, and found an excuse for dissolving the alliance which had hitherto been effective.

Meanwhile, Alfonso's lengthy absence had caused considerable dissatisfaction in the kingdom of Aragon, which was left under the government of Maria, the Queen, supported by Juan, the King of Navarre, a restless and ambitious character, who was more anxious to stir up intrigues in Castile with the hope of interfering in her politics to his own advantage than to secure the peace and prosperity of his own dominions, and thus to support Alfonso in his foreign enterprise. In 1442 Juan lost his wife, Blanca, who left him a son and two daughters. The daughter who bore her mother's name, Blanca, had married Enrique, the eldest son of the King of Castile. The other daughter, Juana, married Gaston, Count of Foix. The son, who was twenty-one years of age at the time of his mother's death, was Carlos, the Prince of Viana, who was to play his part in the history of Aragon at a later date. His mother had appointed him her heir to the Estates of Navarre and Nemours, as she was entitled to do under the contracts of her marriage. The Prince did not, however, assume the royal title, but was content to act as the heir and viceroy of his father, who continued to style himself King of Navarre. Juan considered that the death of his wife provided him with a further opportunity of strengthening his influence in Castile, and married Juana Enríquez, the daughter of the King of Castile. Similarly, Enrique, the Infanta of Aragon, whose wife, Catalina, the sister of the King of Castile, had recently died, proceeded to marry a sister of the Count of Benavente. Thus these two princes hoped to form a party of Castilian nobles, sufficiently powerful to overthrow Álvaro de Luna, and their ambitions in this direction were one of the causes of the civil war in Castile. Meanwhile, the Aragonese states remained peaceful, though the prolonged absence of the King aroused irritation and discontent in all classes. Embassies were sent, urging him to return, and were put off with promises which the condition of affairs in Italy prevented the King from fulfilling. The Aragonese were naturally affronted, and considered that the King regarded them as a colony and was anxious to move the seat of Aragonese government to Naples. In 1445 the Justicia of Aragon, Ferrer de Lanuza, went to Naples in person to urge the return of the King, a request supported by the King of Navarre, who hoped that Alfonso's return would enable him to enlist the influence of Aragon on the side of his anti-Castilian party. Alfonso's interest in the affairs of Castile had somewhat diminished with the death of Catalina ; he appears, however, to have been convinced by the Justicia's arguments, when, at that moment, he received the news of the battle of Olmedo. This important conflict was fought by the King of Navarre, the Infante Enrique and their respective supporters, against the King of Castile, his son, Prince of Asturias, and the Constable, Álvaro de Luna. The King of Navarre thus found himself fighting against his own son-in-law. The Aragonese were completely defeated ; the Infante Enrique died of his wounds on the following day, while the King of Navarre succeeded in saving his life with the loss of his possessions and his influence in Castile. For the next two or three years he spent his time in plots and intrigues to recover his lost ground. He attempted to use the Aragonese as the instruments of his vengeance, and to persuade his subjects of Navarre that their national honour was at stake. Neither country was willing to support him, and their respective Cortes openly declared their anxiety to live in peace and harmony with Castile. From this moment appears to begin the resentment which Juan began to feel for his son, Carlos de Viana, a resentment productive of serious consequences in later years. Juan continued to enlist such reinforcements as he could collect in Navarre and Aragon for the purpose of making war upon the King of Castile, in the conviction that Alfonso would support his cause if he could only be persuaded to return home. Alfonso preferred Italy to Aragon ; in his beloved Naples he could pursue his political designs unhampered by the mistrust of interfering Cortes, and could enjoy Italian art and culture in its purest forms. Thus these intrigues went on from 1446 to 1448, King Juan attempting to drag the King of Aragon into war with Castile, the Aragonese striving to avoid any struggle of the kind, and hoping that the return of their ruler would avert the troubles which seemed to be threatening the Crown. In 1448 the King of Navarre succeeded in inducing Alfonso to agree to a breach with Castile, and to an alliance with the discontented factions in that country. Another struggle thus began, which did not, however, produce any consequences of immediate moment, as the only interests at stake were the personal ambitions of the King of Navarre.

Alfonso made his triumphal entry into Naples in February 1443. He thus appeared to have reached the crown of his ambition, in the pursuit of which he had certainly displayed unusual energy and perseverance ; the victory had been won by his refusal to accept defeat, to be deterred by adverse circumstances or by unfavourable times and seasons, and his own invincible assurance of success had repeatedly inspired his troops to victory. In the hour of triumph, he also distinguished himself by moderation, liberality and kindness, and these qualities, together with his known respect for the Church, secured for him the general admiration of his subjects. It might have been possible for him to spend some time in peaceful enjoyment of the dominions he had won, but his own restless energy and the unstable conditions of Italian politics involved him in new adventures. Negotiations between himself and the Pope ended in an agreement by which he recognized Eugenius IV as the one and only true head of the Church, and in return was invested by the Pope with the kingdom of Naples, under the same conditions as those under which Charles I of Anjou had held it. His son, Ferdinand, whom he had already appointed Duke of Calabria, was recognized as his legitimate successor. He had, however, promised to support the Pope in an attempt to recover the territory of Ancona from Francesco Sforza, and was, therefore, obliged to take over the command of an army which had been assembled in the papal states for this purpose. Florence and Venice, alarmed by this enterprise, united in support of Sforza. Alfonso continued the war during the year, but Sforza won a victory which secured for him a favourable peace, and enabled him to retain most of the territory in dispute. Shortly afterwards, Alfonso concluded the Peace of Genoa, promising to withdraw his support from the enemies of the Genoese, and restoring the commercial privileges which they had enjoyed under previous kings of Naples. The ambitions of the Duke of Milan soon disturbed the peace, and a war broke out between the Duke and Sforza, in which Florence and Venice were involved. The Duke, however, died in 1447, appointing Alfonso as his heir. The Aragonese troops were able, for a moment, to take possession of Milan, but the general dissatisfaction of the other towns in the district, the claims of Sforza and the hostility of the Venetians, convinced Alfonso that it would be impossible to maintain his hold of the country, and Sforza became the leader, and afterwards the Duke, of the Milanese. In 1448 Alfonso invaded Tuscany, but vigorous resistance prevented him from capturing more than a few castles, and before Piombino his progress was definitely checked. The war was ended in 1450, by the mediation of Pope Nicholas V, who had succeeded Eugenius and was anxious to secure a general peace. Their commercial privileges were returned to the Florentines, who undertook to pay an annual tribute to the Aragonese monarch. At the same time, a similar peace was concluded with Venice, and it appeared that quieter prospects for the country were in sight. These were disturbed by dislike of Sforza's actions as Duke of Milan, and by commercial quarrels between Florence and Venice ; nor could the intervention of Frederick III, the newly-crowned Emperor, in 1452 relieve the prevailing tension. In March of that year, he came to Rome for his coronation ; the Venetians seized the opportunity to attack the Duke, and Ferdinand of Calabria was ordered by his father to advance against the Florentines with a formidable army. Little result was achieved, as the bravery of the Florentines and the competence of their leader, Malatesta, defeated the efforts of the Aragonese.

Even the surprising fact of the conquest of Constantinople by the Turks in 1453 did not induce Alfonso to accept the general opinion that Christians had better abandon their private quarrels and combine against the Unbeliever. Nor was he moved by the destruction of the Catalan states in Attica and Bœotia, which were overrun by the Turks, and appealed in vain to Aragon for help. Further complications began with the arrival of René of Anjou, whom Sforza had induced to intervene ; he arrived in Italy in 1454, with 3000 horse, and left his son, Jean, behind him to continue operations after his return. Meanwhile the Pope, Nicholas V, had been working to secure a general peace with the hope of taking measures to confront the Turkish danger. Venice and Milan were induced to agree, and Alfonso, in 1455, also consented to a peace, in spite of the annoyance which he felt at the fact that he had not been consulted at the outset of negotiations. He made it a definite condition that the town of Genoa should not be included in the agreement. Once again points of difference had arisen, and Alfonso felt that he could not trust either the Genoese or their doge, Campo Fregoso. The successor of Nicholas V, Calixtus III, invited him to take the cross, but Alfonso refused to entertain this possibility, and even employed a crusade fleet which the Archbishop of Tarragona had collected, as the papal legate in Spain, for the purpose of devastating the territory of his enemies. The Genoese found no support in Italy, and turned for help to France. Charles VII sent them Duke Jean of Anjou as their Governor, with the idea of recovering the kingdom of Naples, should opportunities occur for that purpose. Alfonso was aroused to greater efforts by this development, and had almost completed his preparations for besieging Genoa by land and sea when he unexpectedly died in 1458, an event which seemed to bring the prospect of peace somewhat nearer to the Italian peninsula.

During Alfonso's absence, Juan II of Navarre continued his attempts to embroil his country and Aragon with Castile, the King of which country invaded Navarre in 1451 and besieged the town of Estella. Carlos, the Prince of Viana, who ruled Navarre, but had not assumed the royal title, which his father Juan retained, was in no position to offer resistance ; he sought an interview with the invader and explained that neither he nor the people of Navarre desired war with Castile and that they should not be held accountable for the machinations of Juan. The Castilian leaders accepted this explanation and retired after concluding a treaty of peace with the Prince of Viana. His father, enraged at the failure of his plans, sent his wife, Juana Enríquez, to Navarre with authority to supervise the Prince's methods of government. The inevitable result was a succession of quarrels

and the formation of two national parties, led respectively
by the families of Agramont who supported the Queen, and
Beaumont who declared for Carlos. In the following year
was fought the battle of Ayvar between stepfather and son,
in which the Prince of Viana was defeated and taken prisoner ;
the intervention of Aragon enabled him to regain his freedom
in 1453, but there was no prospect of securing peace for
Navarre. In the previous year the Queen had given birth to
a son, Ferdinand, who, though the son of Castile's bitterest
enemy, was eventually destined to marry a daughter of the
Castilian royal house and to unite the kingdoms of Aragon
and Castile in permanent union. For the moment, Queen
Juana was more than ever estranged from the Prince of
Viana, whom she regarded as depriving her own son of the
right of succession. The matter was further complicated
by the action of Enrique, the Prince of the Asturias, who had
married Blanca, the sister of Carlos, Prince of Viana ;
Enrique, who hated profoundly his father-in-law and all his
connections, repudiated his wife on a charge of witchcraft
and married Juana of Portugal, whose imprudence brought
trouble upon him, when he became Enrique IV in 1454.
Blanca joined her brother, Carlos, and incurred her father's
wrath in consequence. The change of rulers in Castile became
the occasion of a fresh treaty between that kingdom and
Aragon, and Queen Maria of Aragon made every effort to
arrange a peace between Navarre and Castile and to compose
the domestic quarrels of the Navarrese. No conditions, however, could appease the animosity of Juan. In December 1455,
he made a treaty with the Count of Foix, under the terms of
which the Count was to invade and subjugate Navarre,
while Juan undertook to disinherit Carlos and Blanca and to
transfer their rights to the Count ; the fact that the Count
had married Juan's second daughter, Leonor, was the only
available excuse for so monstrous a pact, under which Juan
proposed to dispose of an inheritance and of rights which he
had never possessed. Meanwhile Alfonso, who had begun
at length to appreciate the character of his brother's policy,
informed him that his persecution must stop, or he would
himself espouse the cause of the Prince of Viana and remove
Juan from his participation in the government of Aragon.
Carlos was more than willing to leave his case in the hands of

Alfonso and went to meet him in Italy, where he was kindly
received by the King of Aragon, who found that the young
Prince shared his own interest in art and literature. In spite
of the malignancy of Juan, the covetousness of the Count
of Foix and the interference of the King of France, Alfonso
might have ended the dispute, had not the negotiations been
cut short by his death.

Alfonso's exploits were apparently inspired by the ambition
to form an empire which should dominate the Western
Mediterranean. For a brief moment his hopes were realized ;
his policy brought him a wide reputation for himself, but
aroused little enthusiasm among his subjects, who objected
to a transference of the centre of power from Aragon to
Naples. His continuous absence from his kingdom, and the
dissatisfaction which it caused, enabled the turbulent and
disorderly elements to combine, with the results which were
more perceptible in the following reign. On the other hand,
it may be argued that the absence of so restless and adventurous a character was in some sense a positive advantage.
Alfonso's energies confined within the narrow bounds of a
constitutional monarchy might have caused more trouble in
Aragon than his continual absence afterwards produced.
He enjoyed a high reputation in Europe ; when Frederick
III came to Rome for coronation as Emperor in 1452, he
paid a special visit to Alfonso who received him with great
magnificence. He maintained a brilliant court at Naples
which was distinguished as a centre of literature and learning.
He himself is said to have read Livy and Cicero as his favourite
authors, and to have translated Seneca's Letters into Spanish ;
translations of Aristotle's *Natural History* and Xenophon's
Cyropædia were made at his command. Poets and scholars
were his constant visitors, a fact which no doubt largely
contributed to strengthen the influence of Italian learning upon the literature of Spain. Two classes of literature
were developed at his court : that produced by Italian
humanists such as Eneas Silvio Piccolomini and Spaniards
or Catalans who followed their lead, of whom the royal
historiographer Pedro Miguel Carbonell is the best-known
figure : he belongs also to the other school, that of poetry
in both courtly and popular lyric, examples of which were
collected in the Cancionero de Stúñiga, a collection similar

to the more famous Cancionero de Baena and reflecting the life both of camp and court under Alfonso's rule. Torrellas, a Catalan who had been tutor to the Prince of Viana, Carvajal, the first Spanish poet who wrote in Italian, and Lope de Stúñiga, the enemy of Álvaro de Luna, were the outstanding personalities. This body of court poetry shows the rapid development of the Spanish vernacular of Aragon side by side with the Catalan language.

CHAPTER XVI

JUAN II. UNION OF ARAGON WITH CASTILE

Settlement of Alfonso's possessions. Carlos de Viana imprisoned by Juan Catalan enthusiasm for Carlos. Agreement between Carlos and Juan Death of Carlos. Indignation of Catalonia. Civil war. Catalan separatism. Pedro of Portugal. His defeat by Ferdinand of Aragon. René of Anjou invited to Catalonia. War with France. Ferdinand marries Isabella of Castile. End of the Catalan revolt. Peace with France. Death of Juan.

ALFONSO left his Italian possessions to his illegitimate son, Ferdinand, while the Aragonese territories went to his brother, who ascended the throne as Juan II when he was already sixty-two years of age. Juan was recognized by the Cortes of Aragon and Barcelona as their ruler in the latter half of 1458, and Italian affairs immediately claimed his attention. Pope Calixtus was unwilling to recognize Ferdinand, Alfonso's son, as the King of Naples, while the local barons were divided into parties, some preferring Carlos de Viana, others Juan II himself, others the son of René of Anjou, while Ferdinand was not without supporters. Juan was not prepared to support his stepson, Carlos de Viana, whom he profoundly disliked, nor was he any more inclined to the son of René of Anjou, and his own supporters were too few to enable him to prosecute his own claim. He therefore gave his support to his nephew, Ferdinand. Pope Calixtus died in that year, but his successor, Pius II, invested Ferdinand as King of Naples, in spite of the opposition of Jean of Anjou, the son of René, who continued to assert his claims until 1463, when he was definitely defeated and returned to Provence. Juan II was thus relieved of anxiety with regard to Naples, but the same could not be said of Sicily, where his hated son, Carlos, had taken up his residence. It seemed likely that the Sicilians would offer the crown to Carlos de Viana out of loyalty to their

234

memory of his mother, and these expectations were realized. Carlos was living a retired life, devoted to literary study, in which he was disturbed by a deputation urging him to accept the crown of Sicily. Carlos declined, and the only obvious reason for his refusal seems to have been his desire for a reconciliation with his father, and for a period of repose in some spot removed from the political disturbances of the epoch. Juan was chiefly anxious to get his son out of Sicily, as he did not wish to deal with the possible revolt of the inhabitants in favour of Carlos. The Prince eventually went to Mallorca, and, after lengthy negotiations, a convention was concluded in 1460, under which Carlos submitted himself and his possessions in Navarre to the King's authority, and received his pardon.

It was generally expected that at the Cortes which were shortly afterwards held in Fraga and Lérida, in which Juan declared that Sardinia and Sicily were for ever to be united with the Crown of Aragon, he would declare his son as his successor and request the Cortes to acknowledge him as such. This longstanding custom secured the existence of a viceroy in case of need, and was thus an additional guarantee for the peace and security of the kingdom. Juan, however, declined to make any announcement of the kind. From the Admiral of Castile, Fadrique, the father of his second wife, Juana, he received information that Carlos was beginning secret negotiations with the King of Castile for a marriage with his sister, Isabella, and for the support of Castile in pushing his own claims. The Queen, who profoundly hated her stepson, induced her husband to summon him to Lérida, and imprison him. This unexpected treatment of a prince whose popularity was general aroused great dissatisfaction in the several Estates of the Realm which had come together for the recent Cortes. The accusation that Carlos had been plotting against his father's crown and life found not the smallest credence, and both Catalan and Aragonese deputations requested the King to set his son at liberty. When this request was declined, the Catalans displayed the utmost dissatisfaction. They regarded themselves as pledged to secure the liberation of the Infante, as he had been illegally arrested upon their territory. The Council of Barcelona summoned a general meeting of the citizens, and called the whole country to arms. A fleet was equipped, and a formidable army prepared for operations against the evil advisers of the king. Juan hastily made his way to Zaragoza. He found that Aragon was no less disturbed than the other parts of his kingdom, while the King of Castile was threatening a descent upon his frontier ; and in March 1461 he therefore gave way. Carlos was released and handed over to the Catalans, who conducted him with great delight to Barcelona, into which town he made a triumphal entry amid unbounded enthusiasm. The Queen, who had been appointed Governor-General of the Principality, then began negotiations between Carlos and the King, and at length a convention was concluded at Villafranca. The Prince was to be recognized as successor to the Crown, and to be permanent Governor of Catalonia, while a general amnesty was to be granted to all his supporters. The King found himself obliged to agree to these conditions, however disadvantageous to himself.

The conclusion of this arrangement was immediately followed by the death of the Prince, and by the no less immediate explanation of that event as due to poisoning by the hand of his stepmother. Juana, an energetic and determined character, immediately went to Barcelona with her son, Ferdinand, then ten years of age, and attempted to calm the prevailing agitation by explanations and assurances, but her efforts were in vain. It was generally believed that poison had been administered to the Prince during his imprisonment. He had, as a matter of fact, been in feeble health from the time of his release. Lamentations were general, and popular indignation expressed itself in a desire for independence. The Queen was obliged to leave Barcelona in 1462, having done nothing to relieve the prevailing tension. It was commonly felt that, if no independent ruler could be found, Catalonia would be well advised to form a republic upon the model of the Italian states. The Catalans considered that their rights had been infringed, and welcomed the preaching of the Dominican, Juan Gualbes, who related that the Prince's tomb had already begun to work miracles, a clear proof that revolt against the King and his evil Queen would be regarded by heaven as a righteous act. The Archbishop of Tarragona and other Catalan nobles attempted to stem the tide, but the spirit of revolt swept over the whole country, and King

Juan realized that his own crown was at stake. His first precaution was to secure the friendship of Louis XI of France, whose support was as indispensable as his hostility would have been dangerous. Through the good offices of his son-in-law, the Count of Foix, a treaty was concluded in 1462 between France and Aragon, Louis promising to send a force to help in the subjugation of the Catalan rebels, while Juan pledged Roussillon and Cerdagne as guarantees for the costs of the expedition. A peace was also concluded with Castile and Portugal. But these facts did not turn the Catalans into a more pacific frame of mind. Under the leadership of the Count of Pallars they attacked Gerona, and succeeded in conquering that town, but were unable to get possession of the castle in which the Queen had taken refuge with her son, Ferdinand. The approach of the Count of Foix and the French auxiliary troops obliged them to raise the siege. The King then captured the town of Balaguer and began operations against Tárrega ; actions which aroused the Catalans to the highest pitch of exasperation. They publicly declared that the King, as well as the Queen, their councillors and servants, were enemies of the country, and issued a general proclamation that everybody above the age of fourteen years should take up arms against the King.

At the same time, many who had supported the formation of a republic began to doubt their capacity to hold their ground without foreign support. A deputation of ten resolved to approach the King of Castile, who was more closely connected with their former dynasty than was the King of Aragon, and to offer him the position of their ruler on the ground that Juan had forfeited that position by making an alliance with foreign princes and introducing foreign troops into the country. Enrique IV of Castile accepted the proposal at the instance of a majority of his councillors, received the oath of allegiance through deputies and sent a force of 2500 cavalry to help. The city of Barcelona had been already closely besieged, but the courage of the inhabitants was raised by the advent of these reinforcements, and proposals for peace were rejected, whether emanating from the King or from the Pope. Winter put an end to the siege, but Tarragona and other places made a voluntary surrender to Juan, while the war with Castile, which had already broken out upon the frontier, was interrupted by an armistice in the following spring. Louis XI succeeded in negotiating a permanent peace between Castile and Aragon, who agreed to accept his decision upon their differences. In April 1463, he declared his decision that Catalonia should submit to the King of Aragon, and that the King of Castile should withdraw his troops and refrain from sending any further support to the Catalans. Enrique himself advised the deputies of Barcelona to come to some arrangement with their lawful ruler. That stubborn race, however, in spite of the fact that their land had been devastated, were unwilling to ask favours of the King, even though he was ready to grant them. They proceeded to offer their country to the Infante Pedro of Portugal, whom they hoped would find supporters in other parts of the Aragonese dominions, as he had some claim to the succession through his mother, Isabella, the elder daughter of the last Count of Urgel.

Pedro, who bore the title of Constable of Portugal, was the grandson of James the Unfortunate, whose claims to the throne had been set aside by the Parliament of Caspe and whose eldest daughter, Isabella, had married the Infante of Portugal, Pedro, Duke of Coimbra, the second son of Juan I of Portugal. Pedro, therefore, arrived at Barcelona in January 1464, received the homage of the citizens, and proceeded to style himself King of Aragon and Sicily. He had no money and no troops, and his cousin, the King of Portugal, declined to give him any support. He was, therefore, confined to Barcelona, while King Juan continued his operations against the rebels and captured Lérida in July. Juan, however, showed no particular energy in prosecuting this success, and appears to have preferred to wait for dissension among the ranks of his enemies, as happened in 1465, when one of their allies, Juan of Beamonte, the most powerful personality in Navarre, deserted the rebels and made his peace with Aragon. At the same time King Juan was involved in the confusion of Castilian politics. Enrique of Castile was dissatisfied with his convention with Aragon, and quarrelled with the Archbishop of Toledo and the Marquis of Villena who had been responsible for its conclusion. They, therefore, joined the Admiral of Castile and other barons who were opposed to the King, and Juan of Aragon had given them his support as early as 1464, promising to join in the defence of the Catholic faith, to co-operate in the conquest of Granada and to secure the succession to the Castilian throne to Enrique's brother or sister, Alfonso and Isabella, to the exclusion of his putative daughter, Juana. Civil war, therefore, broke out in Castile with greater intensity in 1465, when the rebels proclaimed Alfonso as King. In February of that year, the Infante Ferdinand of Aragon, who was then thirteen years of age, was placed by his father at the head of an army, and gained a brilliant victory over Pedro of Portugal at Prats del Rey or Calaf, between which two villages the battle took place. The Catalan forces were completely defeated, and a number of their chief leaders were taken prisoner. Certain fortresses continued to hold out, Cervera and Amposta in particular. But in 1466, Pedro suddenly died, and the important town of Tortosa then submitted to the King of Aragon. A number of leaders in Barcelona were inclined to follow this example, but were overweighted by those who desired once again to choose their own monarch, and who were supported by Count Gaston of Foix, the husband of Leonora, the sister of Prince Carlos of Viana, who had advanced into Navarre. It was also pointed out by the malcontents that King Juan's attention was largely occupied by the state of affairs in Castile. Their choice fell upon Duke René of Anjou, who could claim the Crown of Aragon as the brother of Duke Louis of Calabria. The Duke had come forward as a claimant after the death of Martin, and the fact that the Aragonese King had deprived him of the possession of Naples was sufficient to account for his hostility. René was an important and influential personage. By marriage he was in possession of the Duchy of Lorraine, and his son, Jean, was one of the foremost generals of his time. Thus Juan of Aragon found himself confronted by a fresh war at the age of seventy, and at a moment when he was almost blinded by an attack of cataract. He attempted to secure the alliance of the Kings of Naples and of England and that of the Pope against the House of Anjou, without success ; nor was an application to the Dukes of Savoy and Milan any more fruitful. But the Aragonese nobles were prepared to support him, and his Queen, Juana, undertook the conduct of affairs with the help of their son, who had been already recognized as his successor, and whom he shortly afterwards appointed King of Sicily and co-regent.

The Duke of Lorraine, Jean, came to Catalonia in 1467. King Louis of France, who saw an opportunity of interfering to his own advantage, had given him a free passage through his country. The Duke began the siege of Gerona, but the approach of Ferdinand with a numerous army obliged him to retire. As soon as his allies had sent him adequate reinforcements, he offered battle and Ferdinand was defeated after a desperate conflict. Gerona was once more besieged, when the Aragonese King recovered his sight, thanks to the skill of a Jewish doctor, Crexcas Abiatir, and was able to take the field in person. Meanwhile, Ferdinand took a step which eventually led to the political union of Spain. Enrique's brother, Alfonso, had died in July 1468; his supporters had proclaimed his sister, Isabella, as Queen-regent, and her right to the succession was recognized by the great majority of the kingdom. She was, moreover, inclined to favour the project of King Juan, who proposed that her marriage with his son should bring about the union of Aragon and Castile. Enrique had proposed a marriage with the King of Portugal, but this and other proposals were declined by Isabella. Negotiations were carried on by the Archbishop of Toledo, with such success that, on March 5, Ferdinand and Juan respectively gave their assent to the conditions under which the marriage was to take place. The heir to the Crown of Aragon undertook to observe all the laws, customs and freedoms of the Castilian realm and of particular localities within it, to take up his residence in Castile, to alienate none of the Crown property without the consent of his consort and to appoint only Castilians to his council. Isabella was to make appointments upon her own responsibility, to sign all public documents and to have the deciding voice in questions of peace and war. The marriage was celebrated in October 1469 at Valladolid under difficulties related in detail by the chronicler Alfonso of Palencia, but it brought no immediate support to the King of Aragon in his struggle with his rebellious subjects, as the weakness and irresolution of Enrique IV and the restless ambition of the Marquis of Villena provided every opportunity for the continuance of disturbances in Castile.

A further prospect of danger was opened by the action of Louis XI, who sent ambassadors to Castile to negotiate a marriage between his brother, Charles, the Duke of Berry, and Enrique's daughter, Juana, while Duke Jean of Lorraine succeeded in capturing Gerona, Besalú and Ampurias at a time when Juan of Aragon was called to Navarre by a series of petty struggles, and by the fact that the Count of Foix was threatening Tudela. The Count was obliged to withdraw, and Juan concluded a convention with him for the purpose of ending the Navarrese quarrels and devoting his sole attention to the affairs of Aragon. This agreement was concluded in May 1471. Under it, Juan was recognized as King by the inhabitants of Navarre, on promising to respect the laws and freedoms of their country, while, after his death, and he was then of advanced age, the nobles swore to accept the Infanta Leonor, the wife of the Count of Foix, as their Queen. She was also to occupy the position of Governor-General forthwith, and only to relinquish her functions as such when the King of Navarre should be actually present. A general amnesty for all past wrongs and outrages was proclaimed. The situation in Catalonia was further relieved by the death of the Duke of Lorraine, which occurred in Barcelona in 1470. The more obstinate party among the Catalans continued to struggle for some time, with the help of the French and Italian forces that the Duke had brought into the country, but in the course of 1471 Gerona, the Ampurdan and other important districts were reconquered, and a considerable number of barons and knights returned to their obedience. The inhabitants of Barcelona none the less continued to hold out, and refused to receive Cardinal Borgia, whom Pope Sixtus IV had sent to Spain to negotiate a peace. But eventually starvation appeared in the town, quarrels broke out among the citizens and the mercenary troops, and the courage of the defenders steadily sank. Juan summoned the leaders to a conference in October 1472, promised them far milder treatment in the case of a surrender than they had any reason to expect, but threatened that, if surrender was not offered immediately, the town and its inhabitants would be treated with the utmost severity. The leaders of Barcelona, therefore, opened negotiations, asserting that they had acted merely from fidelity to the Infante

16

Carlos, asking that they and all Catalans should be regarded as legal and faithful vassals, that there should be an amnesty for all past wrongs, and that the laws and privileges of the capital and the country should be once more recognized. The foreign troops were allowed to depart, together with any one else who declined to submit, while the remainder were given ample time to renew their oath of obedience to the King. On October 17, 1472, these negotiations were brought to an end, and the King made his entry into the town on the next day. Thus was ended a conflict which had momentarily ruined the prosperity of Barcelona, and which a little common sense and statesmanship might easily have avoided. The most striking feature of the struggle is the unswerving support which the nobles of Aragon and Valencia gave to their King, whose own energy and determination were able to bring the struggle to a conclusion.

Juan was now seventy-five years of age, but, none the less, after restoring peace in Catalonia, he proposed to revenge himself on Louis XI, who had overrun the counties of Roussillon and the Cerdagne and was largely responsible for a war which had ravaged parts of Catalonia for four years, not to speak of disturbances in Navarre. The inhabitants of the two countries offered the strongest objection to a foreign rule, and the towns of Perpignan and Elne arranged with the King to attack the French garrisons on the same day. Such of their numbers as managed to escape to the castles were immediately besieged by Juan's army. A numerous French force speedily approached, and Juan was himself besieged in Perpignan for three months, until reinforcements from Aragon and Catalonia and the approach of an army under the King of Sicily obliged the enemy to retire. Louis of France began negotiations in 1473, which were apparently only a mask to conceal fresh preparations on his part for renewing the attack. He detained the Aragonese ambassadors in France, in spite of the safe-conduct that had been assured to them, and advanced into Roussillon in the summer of 1474, capturing all the important towns, and pushing forward even beyond the Pyrenees. The danger was increased by the disturbed state of Castile, even after the death of Enrique IV in December 1474, as the new sovereigns, Ferdinand and Isabella, were not immediately able to secure a general pacification. Enrique had declared Juana in his will as his heiress and successor, and had once more expressed his desire for a marriage between her and King Affonso of Portugal. The Portuguese King was thus induced by the representations of a number of Castilian nobles to come forward as a claimant to the crown, and to invade Castile, where he was proclaimed as King, with his betrothed Juana. King Ferdinand was thus obliged to remain constantly in Castile, and a local quarrel among the barons of Aragon prevented King Juan from defending Perpignan, which fell into the hands of the French in March 1475. An armistice was concluded from April to September, after which Louis entered into an alliance with King Affonso, and renewed his attacks upon Catalonia. However, Affonso was decisively defeated by Ferdinand at Toro in 1476. A French army which had entered the Basque provinces to support him was driven back. A guerrilla warfare continued for some time upon the Catalonian frontier, but a final peace was concluded in October 1478, under which Juan was obliged to leave the counties of Roussillon and Cerdagne in the hands of his enemy until he could raise sufficient money to redeem them. He retired to Barcelona, and early in 1479 he died in the eighty-second year of his age. Navarre became once more an independent kingdom, but Aragon was united with Castile, so that, for the first time, the Spanish peninsula may be regarded as a political whole.

It was a union fraught with many difficult problems. Aragon and Castile stood, as it were, back to back. The interests of Aragon were foreign and Mediterranean ; the problems of Castile were domestic and Atlantic. It had seemed, in fact, more likely and more reasonable that Portugal rather than Aragon should be united with Castile, and the marriage of their respective rulers was the only immediate bond of union between the two states. These rulers began their complicated tasks with considerable advantages to help them ; they were a united and affectionate couple, enjoying high popularity among their subjects ; they were inspired by lofty ideals of statesmanship and endowed with full determination to pursue them. It is doubtful if any other combination could have rescued Castile from its condition of dreadful anarchy and have restored the prestige of monarchy in so short a time, or have conciliated interests so diverse and local prejudices so deeply rooted as those which divided their respective states. Had their successors continued their policy of gradual extension of the monarchical power, it is possible that political union might in the course of time have led to real national unanimity. But there were too many distracting possibilities before the ambitions of Spanish rulers ; relations with France and the Netherland possessions, commitments in Italy and Africa, the government of the New World beyond the Atlantic, the religious struggles and European entanglements in which Charles V involved the country ; in the embarrassment of alternative policies the interests of domestic statesmanship were too often neglected. Here our narrative comes to an end ; henceforward the history of Aragon and Catalonia cannot be separated from that of the Spanish peninsula as a whole.

CHAPTER XVII

SOCIAL AND POLITICAL CONDITIONS DURING THE THIRTEENTH AND FOURTEENTH CENTURIES

The nobility and clergy. Serfs and villeins. Jews and Mudéjares. Results of the struggle between the Crown and the nobility. Administration. Relations with the Papacy. Social conditions in Catalonia. Serfs and overlords. Municipal development. Barcelona. Separatist tendencies. Finance. The Army and Navy. Commerce.

AS regards Aragon, no great changes are to be noted in the relations between the different classes and the State. The distinction among the nobility which has been previously explained remained unaltered, with the exception that the Cortes of 1451 abolished the old custom whereby the King was able to create *infanzones* who might be of plebeian origin. The *ricoshombres* were able to receive lands and honours from the King as before, on condition of dividing them among their subordinate vassals and fulfilling their obligations to military service. Towns or fortresses that might thus have been entrusted to them as *honores* could be reclaimed by the King at any moment. The nobility could not build castles without the royal permission. They might go on service outside the realm to other princes, but upon condition that their action was in no way prejudicial to the interests of the King. No great change was made in the privileges of the clergy, who were exempt from taxation, were allowed to conduct their own courts for purely ecclesiastical cases, but were not to use their churches or monasteries as asylums for criminals. The increasing importance of the towns implied an increase in the influence of the middle class. Some town councils were inclined to aim at the extortion of privileges from the Crown, analogous to those enjoyed by the nobility, whereas others, more particularly in the south, preferred to conduct their affairs without continual reference to the Crown. The class of serfs or villeins was but little affected by these changes. The burden upon them was rather increased than lightened, and the social struggles which took place in Catalonia do not appear to have brought any relief to the class of serfs in Aragon. The nobility were certainly forbidden by such laws as that of 1247 to oppress the population of estates entrusted to them as *honores*, but there were a number of customary rights which contradicted this prohibition and allowed the overlord to punish his vassals, and, if necessary, " to kill them by hunger, or by thirst, or by imprisonment," and, in the case of an oppressive or tyrannical overlord, the villein had no opportunity of appealing to another or to a higher court of justice. In this and other respects the social organisation of the province of Aragon was more rigorously feudal than that of Catalonia or of any other part of the Peninsula.

No great change took place in the position of the Jews, who were persecuted and oppressed both by popular opinion and by the law. They were allowed to lend money on usury when no other means of getting a livelihood were open to them, were obliged to pay the Church dues and occasionally to attend exhortations from Dominican preachers. Sporadic outbursts of anti-Semitism took place, and the Jews, where they could, emigrated to Africa. In 1412 Vicente Ferrer, the famous preacher, is said to have persuaded a large number of Jews to accept baptism, after which they formed the class known as Marranos. About the same time, Pope Benedict XIII convened a council at Tortosa for public discussion with the Rabbis, the end of which was that the Jews were forbidden to read the Talmud or other anti-Christian writings. Thus the Jewish communities rapidly diminished in Aragon. At the same time we hear of meetings of rich Jews at the end of the thirteenth century, and in the early years of the fourteenth. In 1354 representatives of all the Aljamas in the kingdom of Aragon met together and drew up a memorandum which provided that their communities should elect five deputies with full powers to negotiate with the King on matters of importance to the Jewish communities. The *mudéjares* enjoyed better conditions of life. They were certainly obliged to observe special dress regulations and to pay heavy dues to their

overlords, but they had their own magistrates, their own
places of worship, and were allowed to continue their
religious observances, notwithstanding the objections raised
by various Popes. Both the Crown and their overlords were
very sensible of the fact that much of the wealth of the country
was due to the assiduous work of the *mudéjares*, while, for
a considerable portion of this period, religious indifference
rather than proselytizing zeal was the prevailing state of
mind. Thus both the kings and the nobles are found conceding considerable privileges to this Moorish population.
Pedro III allowed them to buy and sell as they pleased, and
to change their habitations when they wished. Alfonso III
brought criminal cases in which they were concerned under
Christian jurisdiction, which often treated the Moors more
leniently than their own courts would have done. Thus the
Moorish populations are both important in number and
comparatively prosperous during this period, both in Aragon
and Valencia. During the fifteenth century, heavy restrictions were laid upon them ; both their liberty of movement
and their religious freedom were curtailed, and it was no
longer possible for them to emigrate to the kingdom of
Granada as they had been in the habit of doing. We find
mudéjares serving in the Army, and apparently proving
themselves loyal troops.

The chief characteristic of the constitutional history of this
period is the struggle between the King and the nobles, and
this was fought out in Aragon with greater vigour and with
more definite results than in the neighbouring kingdom of
Castile. The general policy of the nobility was to confirm
and increase their ancient privileges and to regard the State
as an organization worked by a number of aristocrats for
their own benefit. The King, on the other hand, was anxious
to centralize his power and to secure that every class in the
kingdom obtained due measure of justice. We have seen
that in the Cortes of Exea in 1265 the nobles succeeded in
establishing the Justicia as an arbitrator between their own
class and the King. This official was appointed by the King
with the special function of dealing with lawsuits among
nobles. We have also seen the nobles securing the General
Privilege from Pedro III, when the Justicia becomes a judge
of all lawsuits at court and is subjected to the influence of

that powerful party which wished to abolish the legislation
of James I and to return to the old confusion of custom law.
The privileges which the nobility then extorted brought
about the struggles which filled the reign of Alfonso III, and
the granting of the new privilege called the Privilege of the
Union, by which the King undertook not to proceed against
any member of the Union without the consent of the Cortes
and of the Justicia. The Cortes of Aragon were to meet every
year in Zaragoza, when the King was to accept the advice
of a number of councillors representing the interests of the
nobility. If he contravened the Privilege, members of the
Union could refuse obedience without incurring the charge
of treachery. The state of affairs was summed up by
Alfonso III in the saying that Aragon had as many kings as
there were *ricoshombres*. James II succeeded in disregarding
some of these conditions, but the aristocratic party reasserted
its power under Pedro IV, when it declared the rights of the
Union to depose the King, if he punished nobles without the
approval of the Justicia and the Council. The kingdom was
divided into districts governed by the nominees of the Union,
which not only defied the Crown but oppressed those who
did not agree with its principles, in particular the democratic
townships of the south, and any other royalist parties. This
struggle was definitely decided in favour of the Crown by the
victory of Epila, after which Pedro IV, at the Cortes of
Zaragoza in 1448, abolished the Privilege, while preserving
the essential liberties of Aragon, and returning in general to
the position as it had existed under James II. After this
event, the Crown is certainly predominant, and when civil
struggles broke out in the reign of Juan II, they were by no
means of the bitter character which had marked previous
civil wars, nor was the predominant position of the Crown
called in question. Thus it may be said that, after Pedro IV,
the Crown becomes the centre of the political organization.
The functions of the Justicia are reduced to those of a court
of appeal, with subordinate judicial authorities. The Cortes
of 1348 certainly made the Justicia a life appointment and
irresponsible to the Crown, with powers as previously
explained (see chap. viii). On the other hand, we find the
Crown obliging a new appointment to sign documents
confirming his liability to dismissal. Pedro IV also arranged

that the Cortes should meet every two years, and not annually, as the Privilege of the Union had declared. Catalonia and Valencia retained their own Cortes, and when these bodies were not sitting they were represented by juntas or committees, known in Aragon as the Diputación-General and in Catalonia as the Generalitat, which were intended to watch legislative and financial practice. Pedro's successors made few changes in the constitution, as he had left it, which was thus based upon royal absolutism, though this did not imply the suppression of a very large number of local privileges and customs. Such an event as the Compromise of Caspe was enough to show that, notwithstanding the disturbed spirit of the age, Aragonese society had developed a political sense which realized the necessity of a centralized monarchy.

We find during this period a gradual development of administrative and financial organization ; a hierarchy of court officials for collecting taxes and tributes worked side by side with the judicial authorities. A distinction is made between the King's private property and income and the revenue of the kingdom as a whole, the latter being placed under the charge of a particular officer, whose business was to secure the payment of the various tributes due to the Crown. It cannot be said that the system worked successfully. The evils of financial administration apparent in almost every country in Europe were no less obvious in Aragon. Public offices were bought and sold, taxes were farmed out or exploited and embezzled by their collectors, while punishment was difficult or impossible, as practically the whole of the upper classes of society were more or less tainted with guilt. The Army and Navy underwent but little change in organization, but seem to have been generally able to raise a force when it was wanted. The custom of engaging mercenary companies seems to have grown, especially during the wars between Pedro IV and Pedro I of Castile, and was also suggested by the employment of the *almogávares* in Italy and in the East. The maintenance of popular order, and the work of policing the country-side, was left to the municipalities and to the nobles, who were supposed to check robbery and murder under pain of death if they did not perform this duty.

The relations of the Aragonese Crown and the Papacy during this period were largely influenced by two events : the extension of the Aragonese dominion in Italy and Sicily, and the part which the country played in the Great Schism. The most famous of the opposition Popes, Pedro de Luna, known as Benedict XIII, was, as has been said, himself an Aragonese, and established himself for a considerable period upon Aragonese territory. He was a man of considerable influence in the Church before he was elected to the Papacy. He had induced Juan I of Aragon to recognize Clement VII, the Pope then resident in Avignon. His energy in the cause of clerical reform displayed in the National Council at Valencia in 1388 largely contributed to secure his election as Pope on the death of Clement VII in 1394, one of his warmest supporters being San Vicente Ferrer. Under the name of Benedict XIII he was distinguished both by his piety, which led him to found numerous convents and churches, and also by his zeal in the cause of education. He was a generous benefactor to the University of Salamanca, and the University of St. Andrew in Scotland owes its foundation to him. His legitimacy as Pope was recognized by both Castile and Aragon until the election of Ferdinand of Antequera. Ferdinand was anxious to bring the Schism to an end, and, under the influence of the Emperor of Germany, attempted to induce Benedict to resign. This he refused to do, and retired to Peñíscola with a few cardinals among his supporters in 1416. Then followed the General Council, which appointed Martin V as the sole legal Pope, and called upon the supporters of Benedict XIII to withdraw their allegiance to him. However, he maintained his position until 1424 when he died, as was supposed, in consequence of a dose of poison administered by a friar. His party of cardinals declined to submit to Martin V, and appointed the Canon of Barcelona as the new Pope, Gil Muñoz, who eventually resigned in 1429 at the Council of Tortosa, when the Schism came to an end. His brief term of office involved Alfonso V in quarrels with Pope Martin V, and Alfonso then definitely established the rule known as *Pase regio*, which laid down that papal bulls should have the King's approval before circulation in the country. The abuses connected with papal appointments were a strong argument in favour of this principle. James II had granted to the Pope the right of appointing bishops. Cathedral chapters had objected, but the principle had been followed during the period of the Schism. Private influence and nepotism had produced several bad appointments ; Clement V sent a young cousin of his to the see of Zaragoza, 'and Benedict XIII himself made an equally unsatisfactory choice for the Archbishopric of Toledo. The Popes, on the other hand, were anxious to assert the rights of vassalage which had been acknowledged by Pedro II. Pope Martin IV thus excommunicated Pedro III and deprived him of his lands and sovereignty as a contumacious and rebellious son of the Church, declaring that any Catholic prince who could take them might occupy the possessions of Aragon. Upon the whole, the Aragonese kings maintained that authority in ecclesiastical affairs that had been a tradition of the Crown since Visigothic times, and were prepared to intervene in ecclesiastical disputes, and to settle them in their own interests, whenever necessary.

The social history of Catalonia during this period underwent considerable changes in consequence of the revolution of the serfs and the rise to power of certain municipalities, the chief of which was, of course, Barcelona. The period is marked by the diminishing influence and power of the nobility, who were overshadowed by new political and economic influences. The power of the various baronial lords in the north of Catalonia had been gradually absorbed by the Count of Barcelona and afterwards by the centralizing policy of the Aragonese monarchs. The chief point of interest, therefore, became the question of the relations between overlords and their vassals or serfs, especially with regard to questions of tribute and jurisdiction. The greater part of the territory was, from this point of view, in the hands of the nobles, who asserted feudal rights over the population there settled. Estimates made in the middle of the fourteenth century showed that some two-thirds of Catalan territory were thus removed from the direct jurisdiction of the Crown and were under the management of nobles, knights or ecclesiastical communities, and the process of alienation and appropriation by the Crown of these rights, if it proceeded regularly, was slow and lengthy. The serf population (*payeses de remensa*) was heavily burdened with obligations of tribute and service.

The complicated system of customs, dues and rights of passage, the obligation to hand over particular portions of the produce of the soil and to perform forced labour upon the roads and fortifications had become both a heavy burden and a continual source of irritation, while the extraordinary difference between local customs in these respects made any uniformity of practice impossible. In some cases the peasant's wife was obliged to act as nurse to the children of the overlord. If the peasant killed a pig, he was obliged to hand over the best part of it to the overlord, without whose permission he could not sell his crop nor, if he died, could his family bury him, without surrendering some part of his personal possessions. Petty impositions of this kind in some cases numbered as many as twenty-five or thirty possibilities, in addition to the ordinary rent or tribute that was due from the occupant of the soil. In short, the Catalan appears to have been much worse off than the Castilian peasant. Some attempts had been made to secure a right of manumission, or to allow him to redeem some of these obligations by monetary payments, and such kings as Pedro III, Juan I and Martin the Humane had done their best to alleviate the peasants' unhappy lot, but their efforts had been frustrated by the shortsightedness of the nobles and the general spirit of conservatism. They had, however, shown the peasant that there were prospects of better things, and his discontent was inflamed by the famines and plagues which ravaged Catalan territory during the middle of the fourteenth century. Maria, the wife of Alfonso V, espoused the cause of the peasant class with particular zeal, and arranged for the collection of a tribute which was to indemnify the overlords for any loss they might suffer from the liberation of the peasant class. The collection of this money and the measures suggested aroused a considerable ferment among the lower orders, who began to combine for purposes of revolt, when they had paid the money and saw no immediate result. Trouble began in 1462 when peasants are found combining to attack their overlords, besiege their castles, sack their houses and plunder them upon the highway. Queen Juana attempted to use this movement for political purposes against the General Council of Barcelona and the citizen party. The peasant class thus came under the protection of the Crown in some quarters, while others preferred to turn for help to the municipalities. War broke out in 1462, though hostilities were interrupted by the French invasion in that year. A temporary pacification was followed by another outbreak in 1475, which was particularly directed against the exactions of the Church. A large number of the peasants withheld their payments and continued in a state of revolt until the death of Juan II, and the social problem was not settled until the time of Ferdinand the Catholic.

The losers in all this conflict were the nobility. From the time of Alfonso V it was impossible to depend upon the payment of tribute from the class of serfs, while the old counties which had been the chief bulwark against the encroachment of the royal power had entirely disappeared by the time of Martin. The nobles themselves, with singular shortsightedness, made their position worse by private quarrels and struggles with the municipalities. The lower orders of nobility, knights and so-called *hombres de paraje*, who formed a kind of country aristocracy, were thus enabled to obtain considerable influence, for they regarded the high nobility as their natural enemies and were inclined to support the Crown. It is true that a check to the decay of the power of the feudal nobles could be found in the tendency of the Crown to sell or to alienate royal property for the purpose of raising money, such sales carrying with them considerable rights of jurisdiction ; but, upon the whole, it may be said that the power of the nobles steadily declined as that of the Crown, the lower classes and the towns increased.

It was during this period that the towns attained to the height of their power. They also followed the example of the nobility and bought rights of jurisdiction from the Crown, extending their authority by the use of various ancient privileges. It was possible for a municipality, for instance, to extend to a neighbouring village the right of *carreratge*, which meant that the village was considered as one of the streets of the town which took it under its protection. The Kings naturally objected to this process, if it implied the withdrawal of the tributes due to them. But in general the Crown helped the municipalities both to free their towns from the authority of the nobles and to increase their privileges and, had the municipalities been able to avoid the continual plague of internal feuds and dissensions which occasionally brought one corporation into armed conflict with another, their influence would have reached very much further. From the thirteenth century onwards a certain uniformity of development in town life can be observed. The foundation of municipal government was the assembly of the citizens, and, when this became too unwieldy, the administration was carried on by a council of some kind ; a *curia*, *cort* or *senado*, composed of the leading men, the *jurados* or *pro-hombres*, from whose meetings the plebeian element was excluded, and who were often appointed without plebeian concurrence. This tendency to aristocratic government was checked in the fourteenth century, when we find the common people securing rights of representation upon the councils. At the same time the General Assembly by no means disappears in every case. The town might thus become the centre of a district including minor towns and villages, under the administration of a royal official who exercised jurisdiction on the part of the Crown without infringing the administrative rights of the municipality as such. Towards the end of the fourteenth century the municipality was able, in some cases, to secure possession of this royal office, and the Kings were naturally anxious to form strong municipalities upon the frontiers of feudal territories which they suspected of aspirations to independence. The nobles attempted to counteract this influence by forming municipalities or allowing them to grow under their own influence and control. In such cases we find the overlord retaining the rights of justice, with control of the salt works, mills and water-courses, etc., claiming a certain proportion of the cattle or produce of the soil, and the right to appoint certain leading officials, while the population controlled the common property of the corporation, through the General Council, which was usually formed of a certain number of councillors and four leading men (*consules*) who were all of the middle classes. It naturally depended upon the energy of the municipality, or the political power of the overlord, how far this kind of constitution would persist in subjection or would manifest its right to independence.

Barcelona may be regarded as the type of Catalan munici-

pality in the highest state of development. As a municipality,
indeed, it passed the norms of the Peninsula, and developed a
vitality like that of the Italian city-states. It was their
nearest equivalent outside Italy, and so their rival in Mediterranean commerce and thalassocracy. From them it differed
by the greater driving force it obtained from its hinterland of
sovereign states, and also by the disturbance continental
politics could offer to its maritime adventures. During the
fourteenth and fifteenth centuries the organization of local
government did not greatly change from the type established
under James I, except that the powers of the municipality
were recognized by successive monarchs, in particular Pedro
III and James II. The government of the town was carried
on by a body of councillors (*concelleres*), and by a muncipal
council (*consello*). The councillors varied in number from
128 to 177, and contained representatives of every class of
population, their business being to maintain public order,
administer the municipal finances and guard the town
privileges, the last-mentioned duty being carried out with the
most jealous care, which occasionally brought them into
conflict with the royal authority. The administrative and
judicial powers of the town extended far beyond its actual
limits ; the right of *carreratge*, together with other privileges,
had given Barcelona control of a whole series of townships
along the coast-line, and in the fifteenth century Barcelona
was generally regarded as the capital of Catalonia, maintaining
a number of subordinate officials in the various towns under
its control. Such a situation naturally led to occasional
differences with the Cortes or Diputació-General of Catalonia,
and Barcelona at times attempted to make life difficult
for other towns by imposing a commercial embargo, as
happened in one instance with Valencia. On the other hand,
her influence was also exerted in the cause of peace, and we
find her intervening in quarrels between municipalities or
internal quarrels within her township. The subordinate
officials who managed these wide interests were appointed
by the Council. Such were the *Batlle*, or chief magistrate,
the *Claver*, who supervised the financial department, the
Mestre Portolà, who was in charge of the harbour, the *Consul
del Segell*, who stamped the textile and other fabrics which the
town produced, as a guarantee of their good quality. Typical

also of the commercial life was the class known as *Homes Honrats*, the distinguished citizens and the rich and powerful merchants who had risen above their fellows, and enjoyed the same reputation and the same rights as members of the nobility under other circumstances. Enough has been already said concerning the struggles of the municipality with the Crown and the nobles. On the whole, the Catalans were inclined to be suspicious of the Kings of Aragon, and the accession of Ferdinand I and the House of Castile was regarded as the admission of a foreigner, who for that very reason was objectionable, apart from his absolutist and centralizing ideas. On the other hand it must be said that the Catalans were generally inclined to support the international policy of the Aragonese Kings and their enterprises overseas, which they naturally regarded as a means of extending their own commercial interests. They certainly grumbled at the long absence in Italy of Alfonso V and the expense of his wars, but were in agreement with the general policy of the undertaking. The chief points upon which they came into conflict with the Aragonese monarchy were those which aroused some suspicion of an infringement of their privileges : Ferdinand I had trouble over the question of a tax payment ; Pedro IV and Alfonso V were regarded as acting without due regard for the privileges of the town, and this general spirit of independence rose to the point of rebellion, as we have seen, in the wars between the Prince of Viana and Juan II. A Catalan party then appears, formed for the most part of nobles and middle class, showing a distinct movement in favour of separatism, inclining at one time to a union with France, and when this project came to an end, suggesting a republican organization upon the model of the Italian states. The struggle between the Catalans and Juan II was certainly brought about by the King's behaviour to the Prince of Viana, but its continuance was due to the clash of two opposite theories ; monarchical absolutism on the one hand, and municipal freedom upon the other. The victory of the Crown did not imply the disappearance of the traditional rights of Catalonia. In fact the privileges of Barcelona itself were somewhat increased ; but the Crown had, none the less, asserted its superiority, and this fact in the long run implied the overthrow of the particularist point of view, upon which the assertions of the municipality were founded.

Catalonia had Cortes of its own, which usually met independently of the Cortes of Aragon. Their most important function was that of voting taxation. They insisted that redress should precede supply, and on more than one occasion were dismissed without granting the supplies required by the King. There was also a General Assembly of the Cortes of the whole Catalan-Aragonese kingdom, including Catalonia, Aragon, Valencia, Mallorca, Roussillon and the Cerdagne. In 1383 it was agreed that the King should make his opening speech at this meeting in Catalan, and that the Infante should reply in Aragonese in the name of the Cortes. There was also a body known as the General Deputation or Generalitat, which varied in number from time to time, and which was composed of individuals representing each class in their respective Cortes. Their business was to watch over the maintenance of the privileges, in case the King or his officials should infringe them by any course of action, and to take the oaths of fidelity from the Viceroy, Governor or other high functionary who might from time to time be installed. They were also responsible for the naval defences of the coast and for supplying arms to the military forces, if these were mobilized. They might also in extraordinary cases call a meeting of the Cortes or consult with the leading individuals upon any line of policy to be followed. Naturally these conflicting authorities produced a considerable amount of legislation, and judicial powers were in such variance as to amount almost to confusion. The large towns had judicial rights of their own, as had also the nobles upon their own territories, notwithstanding the fact that the King was regarded as the ordinary fount of justice. Attempts were made to reduce these anomalies to some form of order by the promulgation of legal codes, but individual corporations and townships had their own legal codes which were also published. We have, for instance, the constitutions and customs of Lérida, of Gerona, of Tortosa, side by side with the ordinances of the royal household, published in the time of Pedro IV. The general tendency of legislation was to go back to the tradition of the Roman jurists, but it was obviously necessary for a litigant who left his own territory to make careful enquiry

17

into the laws and customs prevailing in any other area in which he had business.

State finances during this period cannot be regarded as other than badly organized ; while taxation was increased, the Kings were constantly involved in pecuniary difficulties which they attempted to relieve by the sale of rights and the alienation of royal territories when they could not secure special grants from the Cortes. The Deputation of Catalonia was more orderly in its proceedings and could count upon a regular income derived from import and export duties, from taxes payable by various classes of the population in the nature of *taille* or *gabelle*, and from the tax known as the *botlla*, a leaden seal placed upon textile and other wares exposed for sale. Naturally a number of officials were maintained to secure the due imposition and collection of these moneys, which were paid to the bank or *taula* at Barcelona, and were then available for naval and military expenses, for the payment of judges and for grants to the monarchy. The municipalities naturally had their own financial arrangements, side by side with this general fund, one of the chief expenses of which was the defence of the Catalan territories. This was the special business of the Deputation, which had the right of enlisting and paying troops, providing arms and munitions and supplying them to the King in case of need. The backbone of the Catalan army at this time was the troops raised by the townships (*somatents*). The nobles certainly maintained their own bands of followers whom we find in conflict with the lower orders, in the rising of the serfs and in the struggles with Juan I, but they were overshadowed in importance by the municipal troops. The municipalities occasionally forbade their citizens to enlist in the royal army, for fear of impairing their own military strength. The Barcelonese troops were organized in companies upon a basis of trade guilds, led by captains of their own choice, with a commander-in-chief known as *coronel*. Of greater importance was the Catalan navy, the development of which was continually stimulated, not only by foreign wars, but by the necessity of maintaining a defence against the continual aggressions of piracy. The Navy consisted of three classes of vessels : royal ships built or hired and maintained at the expense of the King, ships belonging to

the *Generalitat,* maintained by the corporation for coast
defence and paid from the particular funds which they
controlled, and the municipal vessels of Barcelona which
the township had the right of maintaining by a privilege
more than once confirmed. Some feudal lords also had
vessels of their own, and occasionally used them for piratical
purposes. These forces when concentrated might amount
to a very considerable fleet. Important as were the occasional
expeditions overseas, the ever-present necessity was the
defence of the coasts against pirates and corsairs, both
Christian and Muslim in origin. The latter were chiefly
concentrated in Algiers, but others were continually lurking
in the Balearic Islands or in the neighbourhood of the coast-
line. A system of coast-guards and means of communication
between them were developed, by which news of a sudden
descent could be immediately passed to the nearest municipality. In spite of these precautions and of occasional
punitive expeditions, piracy seems to have been a profitable
business. So many prisoners were taken by the Moors that
a particular organization, the Order of Mercy, was brought
into existence to provide for their ransom.

The remarkable successes of the Catalans in naval warfare,
especially in the great days of Roger de Lauria, were due not
only to a long tradition of seamanship, but to careful preparation and strict discipline. The famous compilation of
maritime law and custom, the *Consulat del Mar,* contains a
collection of ordinances on the subject of warships, which
explains the organization of the crew for offence and defence.
Each ship had its *comitre* or captain, its *condestable,* who
commanded the fighting troops on board, its *senescal* or
purser with whom was associated a *cominal* or quarter-
master ; pilot, chaplain and surgeon were also carried. Of
tactics not much is known ; the Catalans attached great
importance to the efficiency of their crossbowmen, whose
skill was notorious over the Mediterranean and who appear
to have laid the foundations of several important naval
victories, as, for instance, that gained over the French in the
Bay of Rosas in 1285 ; their better found and better handled
vessels had little difficulty in ramming and sinking an enemy's
ship, when the crossbow had thrown the crew into confusion.
When Pedro of Castile attacked the port of Barcelona in

1359, one of the guardships is said to have discharged a
" bombard " which severely damaged one of the invading
vessels ; but it does not appear that cannon of any kind
were a regular part of naval armament at that time. It
was possibly this unwonted invasion which induced the
magistrates of Barcelona to organize a standing force of city
crossbowmen who could be embarked, if occasion required,
and to institute public shooting competitions with prizes
upon certain days in the year. Discipline was severe, and the
captain of a ship who fled from two enemy vessels was liable
to the death penalty for cowardice.

Aragon and Valencia were able to export some agricultural
produce, and to this Catalonia added manufactured goods,
especially textiles of various kinds, the production of which
had grown considerably during the thirteenth and fourteenth
centuries. Catalan merchant ships went to all the chief
Mediterranean ports and also to those of Northern Europe ;
Catalans were established in Bruges in 1389, and were the first
people to provide maps of the Danish coast and of the Baltic ;
manuals of seamanship and navigation were also produced.
Their relations with Germany were regular and far-reaching ;
German merchants were resident in Barcelona ; in 1502 a
Catalan–German vocabulary was printed in Perpignan. In
all important towns the kingdom of Aragon had its consuls
who were not merely commercial agents, but were also bound
to protect the interests and the property of their compatriots.
Barcelona encouraged home manufactures by protective
duties against foreign wares of similar character ; the
importation of grain was encouraged and a heavy export
duty retained what was produced in the country for home
consumption, as Barcelona had a considerable industrial
population to feed. New industries were encouraged and
foreign experts were introduced to start them. As the
city grew wealthier, it spent much money upon the improvement of its harbour, an example followed by Valencia which
became a formidable commercial rival to Barcelona. Communications inland were also much improved throughout
the kingdom of Aragon ; roads were laid down or remade,
bridges were built, and towards the close of the thirteenth
century a postal or messenger service was begun.

CHAPTER XVIII

LITERATURE AND LEARNING

Universities. Italian influence. Ramón Lull. Francesc Eximeniç. The
chroniclers. Poetry and Provençal influence. Translations. The Consistori de la Gaya Sciensa. Ausias March. Jordi de Sant Jordi. Influence
of Dante and Petrarch. French influence. Decadence.

DURING the twelfth and thirteenth centuries a steadily
increasing interest in literature and learning can be
clearly seen. There were universities at Gerona,
Barcelona, Tarragona, Vich, Tortosa, and especially at
Lérida, which last was refounded by James II in 1300 and
produced such men as St. Vincent Ferrer and Pope Calixtus
III. The majority of these institutions were under municipal
government, a fact indicative of the general interest felt in
education. There were also schools and colleges, such as the
Lullian foundations at Barcelona and Mallorca, the College
of the Assumption at Lérida, where a chair of Provençal was
instituted, and the episcopal school at Vich, which enjoyed a
high reputation and was visited by Gerbert, afterwards Pope
Sylvester II. The encouragement of literature and learning
had become a tradition in the Aragonese court ; Martin, the
last of the Barcelona dynasty, delivered a speech in 1406 at
Perpignan before the Estates of Catalonia, praising the
national capacities and achievements, in which he quoted
Horace, Ovid, Livy, Cæsar, Sallust, Lucan and other later
Latin writers in a manner which showed a close acquaintance
with their works. A powerful stimulus was given by the influence of Italy ; young Catalans, like young Spaniards,
studied humane letters in Padua, law in Bologna, medicine in
Salerno, and brought back a knowledge not only of ancient
literature, but of Dante, Boccaccio and Petrarch. The number
of translations made in the fourteenth century is further
evidence of literary interest ; the *Consolatio Philosophiæ* of

Boethius, the tragedies of Seneca, the works of Valerius Maximus were translated in the fourteenth century, and Antonio Canals, who also translated some of Seneca's prose, became the forerunner of others who worked in this field after 1400.

The great and dominating figure in the thought and literature of this period is Ramón Lull, who was born about 1235. His father had taken a prominent part in the conquest of Mallorca and James had given him a valuable estate in the island. It was thus natural that the young Ramón should enter the royal service ; the luxury and profligacy of court life absorbed his energies until his conversion ; the story is well known of the lady whom he pursued with his attentions, until she showed him a fearful ulcer devouring her breast, a shock which turned his thoughts towards religion. He studied at Rome and Paris, learned Arabic to fit himself for missionary work among the infidels, founded the missionary seminary of Miramar in Mallorca, travelled over the greater part of the Mediterranean and Western Europe and poured forth a continual stream of works, philosophical, theological, scientific, mystical, poetical, meeting a martyr's death in the pursuit of his missionary work in 1315, when more than eighty years of age. All knowledge was his province, for all could be regarded as part of theology, the mistress of the sciences ; but he was eminently practical and for him the contemplative life had no overpowering attraction ; whether as poet, philosopher or scientist, one purpose was ever before him, the conversion of unbelievers to Christianity. He is known to have written four hundred and eighty-six treatises and has been credited with many more. Two points only need concern us here ; Ramón Lull, though living in the period of the crusades, declined to believe that conversion could be accomplished only by fire and sword ; the crusade should be supported or replaced by the mission and the spiritual weapons of the missionary could be effective only when he knew the language of the people whom he wished to convert. This principle guided his vast schemes for the conversion of Islam and for missionary activity in Asia ; his college at Miramar was the first institution of the kind for the study of Oriental languages ; it was possibly due to his influence that the Council of Vienne, at which he was present in 1311, resolved to create chairs of Oriental languages at the Universities of Paris, Louvain and Salamanca. If little came of his endeavours in this direction, the new principle which he had asserted gained an increasing number of adherents after his death. His misgivings concerning the popular methods of conversion are expressed in his " Desconort que Mestre Ramón Lull feu en sa vellesa, com viu que lo papa ne los altres senyors del mon no volgueren metre orde en convertir los infaels, segons que éll los requerí moltes e diverses vegades."

Quant pris a consirar del mon son estament,
Com son pauchs christians e molts li descresent,
Adonchs en mon coratage haych tal conçebiment
Que anés a prelats e a reys exament
E a religioses, ab tal ordenament
Que s'en seguís passatje e tal preycament,
Que ab ferre e fust e ab ver ergument
Se des a nostra fe tan gran exalçament,
Que.ls infaels venguessen a ver convertiment.
Et eu hay ço tractat trenta anys, e verament
No.n hay res obtengut, perqu'eu n'estaig dolent
Tant, que.n plore sovén e.n suy en languiment.

[The lament which Master Ramón Lull made in his old age, as he saw that the Pope and the other secular lords would not arrange for the conversion of the infidels, as he urged them many and divers times.

When I began to consider the state of the world, how few are the Christians and how many the unbelievers, then in my heart I conceived the idea of going to prelates, also to kings and religious, showing them that they should advance and preach in such wise that with fire and sword and true argument our faith should be so high exalted that the infidels would come to true conversion. And in this way I have been busy for thirty years and indeed I have achieved nought, for which reason I am so grieved that I often weep and am in despondency.]

The second point concerns Lull's influence upon literature. It may be said at once that his extraordinary mastery of Catalan prose first showed the possibilities of the language as a means of expression. He did for the Catalan what Dante did for the Italian language. James the Conqueror had opened the way, but it was Lull who showed subsequent writers how splendid an instrument they had at hand. Of his prose writings, the best known and the most characteristic is his mystical religious romance, *Blanquerna*, possibly suggested by some of the *contes dévots* which he must have heard in France. The story begins with the marriage of Evast, gallant and wealthy, and Aloma, beautiful and virtuous, and the eventful birth of their son, Blanquerna, who decides, when he is of age, to consecrate himself to a life of religion and cannot be shaken in his resolution even by the attractions of a beautiful maiden, Cana, whom he persuades to follow his own example. Cana becomes the abbess of a monastery and Blanquerna attains a similar dignity, after a series of adventures in which his faith and constancy are tried ; he meets, for instance, the inevitable knight in a forest, carrying off a captured maiden who implores his help ; Blanquerna is unarmed, but shows that spiritual are more powerful than worldly weapons ; he preaches the knight into a state of collapse and conducts the maiden to her home, resisting all the temptations that naturally attack him in the course of the journey. Strengthened by these and similar trials, he rises from the stage of hermit to that of abbot, when a picture of his daily life is given which must be that of Lull himself in his monastery of Miramar. " At midnight he rose, opened his window and after contemplating the starry heaven, betook himself to prayer and meditation and then entered the church to say matins with his deacon. At dawn he said mass and talked with the deacon upon the things of God. The deacon then went to work in the garden, while Blanquerna read his Bible, meditated, said terce, sext and nones in due course, when the deacon prepared certain herbs and vegetables, while Blanquerna went to the garden and occupied his brief leisure in the cultivation of the ground, after which he went alone to the church to give thanks to God. He went early to rest to gain strength for the exercises of the night ; on waking washed his face and hands and said vespers with the deacon, afterwards remaining alone, preparing himself by meditation for prayer. When night had come, he went up to the terrace and remained there in profound meditation, his mind uplifted and his eyes fixed upon the heaven and the stars, considering the greatness of God and the aberrations of mankind." An account of the mission school of Miramar follows shortly afterwards. Blanquerna then appears as a bishop and an archbishop and is finally elected Pope, in which position he does his utmost to encourage missionary work. He is attended by a court fool, under whose form Lull describes himself and is thus enabled to speak his mind upon subjects which move him deeply. Eventually Blanquerna resigns his office to enter a hermitage and devote himself to prayer, and in this connection were produced the *Book of the Lover and the Beloved* and the *Art of Contemplation*, in which Lull's mystical teaching reaches its height. " Digues, foll, ¿ que es aquest món? Respos : Presó dels amadors, servidors de mon amat. ¿ E qui.ls met en presó? Respos : Consciencia, amor, temor, renunciament e contriccio e companyia d'auol gent : e es treball sens guaardó, hon es puniment. ¿ E qui.ls deliura? Misericordia, pietat, justicia. ¿ E on los conloga? En la eternal benenança, on de vertaders amadors es alegra companyia, loant degudament sens fi, benehint e gloriejant l'amat, al qual sia donada tots temps laor, honor e gloria per tot lo mon."

" Say, O fool, what is this world? He answered, it is the prison of the lovers, servants of my Beloved. And who puts them in prison? He answered, conscience, love, fear, contrition and the companionship of evil men ; and it is toil without reward, wherein is punishment. And who delivers them? Mercy, pity and justice. And where are they placed? In the eternal blessedness, where is a joyous company of true lovers, duly praising, blessing and glorifying the Beloved without end, to whom be ever given praise, honour and glory throughout all the world."

Such is the conclusion of the three hundred and sixty-five sentences of moral mysticism, one to serve for each day in the year, which make up the *Libre de Amic e Amat*. *Blanquerna* became a popular work and was translated into Latin, Arabic and Castilian ; it is difficult to say that any work is characteristic of a writer whose interests covered the whole field of human knowledge ; but its limpidity of style and diction show what heights Catalan prose could attain in the hands of a master. Ramón Lull left a school behind him ; in 1369 Pedro the Ceremonious licensed one Berenguer de Fluvià to lecture in Barcelona upon the Lullian system and doctrine.

Teachers were similarly authorised by Juan I, Martin, Alfonso IV and Ferdinand ; Ximenes encouraged the study of his works at the University of Alcalá and his doctrine was expounded at Paris and Bologna.

If Ramón Lull had not existed, his place would have been taken as an encyclopædist, if not as a stylist by Francesc Eximeniç (Ximenes), who lived from about 1340 to 1409. His mind as compared with the generalizing tendencies of Lull's, was more analytic and critical : next to Lull, he is the most voluminous of Catalan authors. He wrote in a delightfully clear and unemphatic style, with a quaint originality of thought apparent in the numerous moral fables strewn throughout his works. His most monumental work is *El Crestià o del Regimen dels Princeps y de la cosa Publica*, an encyclopædia of Christian moral philosophy, which can take its place beside such great compilations as the *Speculum Historiale* of Vincent de Beauvais or the *Tesoro* of Brunetto Latini (of which latter a Catalan translation was made). Posterity regards the thirteen books of this work with awe, and prefers to read the *Libre de les Dones*, in which Eximeniç dealt with the virtues and failings of women (a subject treated at a later date by Jaume Roig), and attempted to counteract Boccaccio's *Corvaccio*, which scandalous work appeared about 1355.

Catalonia has been fortunate in its chroniclers. James the Conqueror, Desclot, Muntaner and Pedro IV, " els quatre Evangelis de la Historia de Catalunya," will bear comparison with Villehardouin, Joinville, Froissart or any similar company of contemporary historiographers in Western Europe. Of James's *Chronicle* mention has been already made ; he set an example which encouraged secular writers to use their own vernacular, and the Latin *Chronicle* of the monk ceases to monopolize the field of historical writing. It has been stated that Catalan is exceptional among Romance literatures, in that its beginnings are in prose and not in verse ; but the field of poetry was occupied by troubadour productions ; the Provençal examples were continually imitated by writers south of the Pyrenees, and community of language was so close that it is sometimes difficult to say where Catalan begins and Provençal ends. The four annalists were either themselves observers of the facts which they record or were able to consult eye-witnesses and do not attempt to go far beyond the range of their own experience ; they do not belong to the school of writers which considered that any contribution to the history of the Spanish peninsula must begin with the creation of the world and be rather panoramic than detailed. Nor were they restrained by those limitations which inhibited the freedom of other chroniclers ; two of them were rulers who could say what they liked ; Desclot records the failures as well as the virtues of the Crown ; Muntaner is inspired by a romantic loyalty towards Catalonia, its language and its royal house, and is certainly biased by his preference for his patron, James II of Mallorca, the younger brother of Pedro III ; he attempts to maintain the reputation of James by omitting incidents which did not redound to his credit ; but if he suppresses truth, he does not usually supply its place with fiction. Thus these writers are not mere annalists, recording the yearly sequence of notable events ; nor do they pretend to be scientific historians ; the thread of their narratives is provided by their own experiences, which are told with some pretensions to literary style, more intimate and less sophisticated in manner and matter than the work of the professional historian.

All that is known of Bernat Desclot is gathered from his *Chronicle* itself, and so impersonal is his narrative that little can be said of him. He seems to have been a nobleman in the household of Pedro III and to have been in personal attendance upon this King during his momentous struggle against Philip III of France. He had access to state documents and made careful use of them, as Amari has shown in his *Guerra dal Vespro Siciliano*, confirming the credence accorded to Desclot by Zurita, the first of historians to recognize the value of his *Chronicle*. Desclot's object was to write an account of the reign of Pedro III ; the early part of his work, as introductory to this subject, deals with the early history of the Counts of Barcelona and the connection of Aragon with Provence : here he introduced stories and traditions which had won their way to the fabulous, and the historical part of the *Chronicle* begins with his account of James the Conqueror. His rapid narrative of events, his insertion of speeches and the curt sobriety of his manner recall the style of Xenophon's *Anabasis*. Far more readable, if not always so reliable, is Ramón Muntaner who stands high above every Spanish chronicler of his age.   He was born in the same year as Dante, 1265, at Peralada in the County of Ampurias ; in 1285 his estate was ravaged by a French invasion, and about 1300 he joined the famous admiral, Roger de Flor, and began the long and adventurous career which saw thirty-two battles by land and sea, until he settled in Valencia where he died in 1336.   On May 15, 1325, he was moved by a vision to begin his famous *Chronicle.*

"Un dia stant yo en una mia alqueria per nom Xiluella qui es en la horta de Valencia, e durmint en mon llit, a mi vench en visio un prohom vell, vestit de blanch, qui.m dix : Muntaner, lleva sus e pensa de fer un libre de les grans marauelles que has vistes que Deus ha feytes en les guerres hon tu es estat ; com a Deus plau, que per tu sia manifestat.   E vull que sapies que per quatre coses asenyaladement t'a Deus allongada la vida, e t'a portat en bon estament, e portara a bona fi.   De les quales quatre coses es la una : primerament com tu has tengudes moltes senyories, axi en mar, com en terra, hon pogres haver mes de mal feyt, que no lo has.   La segona cosa es, perço com james no has volgut guardar a nengun qui en ton poder fos ne sia vengut mal per mal ; ans molts homens de grans affers son venguts en ton poder, qui t'avien molt de mal feyt, qui cuydauen esser morts, com venien en ta ma, e tu lauors feyes ne gracies a Deus nostre senyor de la merce qui.t feya, e lla hon ells se tenien per pus morts e pus perduts, tu.ls reties a nostre senyor ver Deus propriament, e.ls deslliuraues de la tua preso, e.ls trameties en llur terra saluament e segura, vestits e aparellats, segons que a cascu pertanyia.   La terço raho es, que a Deus plau que recomptes aquestes auentures e maruelles ; car altre no es huy al mon viu, qui ho pogues axi ab veritat dir.   E la quarta ; perço que qual que sia Rey d'Arago que s'esforç de be affer e dir, entenent les gracies de Deus que ha feytes en aquests affers que tu recomptaras a ells e a les sues gents : . . . e que vejan e conegan, que a la dretura ajuda tostems nostre senyor ; e qui a dretura quarreja e va, Deus lo exalça e li dona victoria."

"One day when I was on a farm of mine which is called Xiluella, which is in the garden of Valencia (i.e. the district irrigated by the Moors), and asleep in my bed, there came to me in a vision an old man dressed in white who said to me : Muntaner, rise and prepare to make a book of the great marvels which you have seen that God has wrought in the wars in which you have been ; for it pleases God that these things should be manifested by you.   And

I would have you know that for four reasons in particular God has prolonged your life and has kept you in good estate and will bring you to a good end. Of these four things this is the first; that whereas you have held many high positions both by sea and land, where you could have done evil, you have not done it. The second reason is that you have never wished to keep anyone who was in your power nor have requited evil with evil; on the contrary, many of high rank have fallen into your power who had done you much evil, and who thought themselves dead when they came into your hands, and you offered praise and thanks to God our Lord for the mercy which he showed you, and then, when they considered themselves as dead and lost, you duly restored them to our Lord the true God and delivered them from your bondage, and sent them to their land safe and sound, clothed and equipped, as was each one's due. The third reason is, that it has pleased God that you should relate those adventures and marvels, for there is none other living in the world who could do this with such truth. And the fourth reason; that whatever kings of Aragon may strive to speak and do right, they may learn the grace that God has granted in those matters which you will relate to them and to their people . . . and may see and know that our Lord ever helps the right, and that if a man follow the right path, God exalts him and gives him victory."

Muntaner's estimate of his own character is not lacking in exactitude, whatever may be thought of his modesty. His share in the Catalan expedition to the East showed him as a man of affairs, competent and energetic, with the power of securing the confidence and respect of those about him. He was a patriot with a great admiration for the Kings of Aragon whose reign he relates, and a belief that Catalonia was the best of countries, and he possessed an unusual power of descriptive writing. The spirit of medievalism can be learned better from Muntaner than from any other chronicler of his age; Froissart and his school tell us of feasts, jousts and processions, the pomp of chivalry and the exploits of knighthood; but Muntaner goes behind this outward show and enables us to understand how men thought and why they acted as they did in his restless and hazardous times.

The fourth *Chronicle* is generally known as that of Pedro IV, the Ceremonious. The actual work was composed by Bernat Dezcoll, of whom little is known except that he was a councillor under Juan I and died in Mallorca between 1388 and 1391, and there were other collaborators selected from the court historians whom Pedro kept in his employment ; the King provided the material and, as one of his letters shows, directed the space and attention which was to be given to particular transactions and exercised an editorial control over the work, which forms a kind of continuation to Muntaner's *Chronicle*. It begins with a brief account of James II and Alfonso IV, the grandfather and father of Pedro, and continues the history of his own reign to 1380, seven years before his death. The style is clear, cold and unemotional, relieved at times by the rhetoric of which Pedro was fond ; the reputation of the work for accuracy and reliability is better than might have been expected, and the character of its editor is more clearly reflected in the omissions made in his narrative than in its positive statements. In fact, the record of the movements of troops is detailed with the elaborate accuracy of a diarist. Pedro seems to have had a genuine interest in history. He paid a hundred florins to Nicolau Capellà for making a Catalan translation of the *Croniques de Aragon e de Sicilia ;* he commissioned the Inquisitor of Mallorca, Jaíme Domenech, to translate parts of the *Speculum Historiale* of Vincent de Beauvais. His *Libre de les Ordinacions de la real casa de Arago* was a code compiled upon the model of the *Leyes Palatinas* of James III of Mallorca, and the minute regulations there laid down for the conduct of court ceremonial gave Pedro his customary title ; he also devoted much time and money to alchemy and astrology.

Prose preceded poetry in the development of Catalan literature, for the reason, as has been already pointed out, that the Provençal troubadour lyric dominated the field of poetry for some two hundred years. Similarity of language, political connections and the tastes of Aragonese princes and of their courts combined to secure for Provençal almost an official status as the language of regular poetry. Decadence became apparent about the middle of the thirteenth century. Cerveri de Gerona may be regarded as the last representative of the Provençal school, and the numerous Catalanisms in his work show how far the poetical tongue had been modified by the vernacular. One characteristic clearly marks the Catalan troubadours of the classical period, their objection

to the *trobar clus*, the obscure, involved and complicated
style expressing sublimated thought in tortuous stanza
schemes and far-fetched rhymes. It was a style which
appealed only to the cultivated and aristocratic class, and
prided itself upon having no message for the people ; a
style not without resemblance to the gongorism which
infected Spanish literature in later years. Catalan poets
preferred the *trobar plan* or *leugier*, the style of clarity and
simplicity. Ramón Lull, pre-eminent as a prose writer,
was one of the first to show the possibilities of native Catalan
poetry. It was inevitable that both the form and expression
of his poetry should show strong traces of Provençal influence,
but this is overshadowed by the intensity of his purpose.
His poetry is didactic, and, if certain poems are little more
than rhymed and metrical prose, there are many occasions
upon which his moral fervour and burning enthusiasm
raise him to the height of true poetical inspiration. Such
are the *Plant de nostra Dona Sancta Maria* or the *Cant de
Ramon*. Other court poets of the period clung more closely
to the form and spirit of the classical troubadour poetry.
Lorenz Mallol shows the beginnings of Petrarchism, and his
Escondit suggests both the influence of Bertran de Born and
of Petrarch's fifteenth *Canzone*. Poems by such aristocratic
authors as Constance, who married James II of Mallorca,
or by Pedro el Ceremonioso, owe their preservation as much
to the social position of their authors as to their inherent
merits, and are doubtless typical of a mass of occasional
verse that has perished. The fourteenth century also saw
the growth of a taste for the didactic moralizing of the
literature known as *ensenyaments*, and for narrative poetry,
in which the borrowings from the Arthurian cycle show the
workings of French influence. The *Faula d'en Torrella* by
Guillem Torella, who wrote before 1380, carries the reader
to the country :

> On repaira Morgan la fea
> E missire lo reys Artus.

The growing taste for foreign literature is also shown by the
Catalan translations of Matfre Ermengau's *Breviari d'Amor*
and of the *Roman des Sept Savis*.

Mention has been made of the foundation of the Consistori
de la Gaya Sciensa in Barcelona by Juan I in 1393. His

successor, Martin, supported the institution, but the political disturbances which broke out after his death obliged the Consistori to move from Barcelona to Tortosa, and its activities were not renewed until 1412, when Ferdinand I came to the throne. Arrangements were then made that poetical contests should be held annually at Easter or Whitsuntide, and four judges or *mantenedors* were provided. This work of revival was largely fostered by Enrique de Villena, more properly called Enrique de Aragon, whose fragmentary *Arte de Trobar* gives an account of the work and ceremonial of the Consistori.

" On the appointed day the mantenedors and the troubadours assembled in the royal palace where I was staying, whence we proceeded in order, with the apparitors at the head, bearing the books of art and the minute book in front of the mantenedors to the main hall, which was already prepared for the occasion, the walls being hung with tapestry. Don Enrique sat upon a seat raised upon steps with the mantenedors on either side of him. The secretaries of the Consistori stood at our feet, and the apparitors beyond them. The floor was carpeted, and the troubadours sat upon two rows of seats in a semicircle, while upon a platform in the middle, as high as an altar and covered with cloth of gold, lay the books of art and the prizes. To the right of this was a seat for the king who often attended the meetings, together with a numerous audience. When silence had been proclaimed the Doctor of Theology, who was one of the mantenedors, arose and made an introductory speech, with quotations and eulogies upon the gay science, explaining the purposes for which the Consistori had met, after which he sat down again. One of the apparitors then proclaimed that the troubadours there present might present and publish the works which they had composed upon the subject assigned to them. Each poet then rose and read in a clear voice, his composition, which was written upon Damascus paper in different colours in gold and silver letters, with such illumination as each could provide. After all the works had thus been published, each composition was handed in to the Clerk of the Consistori.

Two sessions were then held, one in secret and one public. At the secret session all the members swore to judge impartially and in accordance with the laws of the art, in deciding which of the works thus published was the best. Every one pointed out the mistakes that he had observed, which were noted in the margin, after which all the compositions were compared, and the one which was without mistakes, or had the fewest of them, was awarded the prize by the decision of the Consistori. For the public meeting the mantenedors and the troubadours assembled in the palace. Don Enrique then proceeded with them to the chapter-house of the preaching monks. When all had taken their places, and silence had been secured, I made a speech and praised the works that had been produced, with special reference to that which had gained a prize. The Clerk of the Consistori then brought this composition forward upon finely illuminated parchment. Upon the top was painted the golden crown, and beneath were the signatures of Don Enrique and of the mantenedors, while the Clerk sealed it with the appended seal of the Consistori. The composer was summoned, and received the prize and his composition, which was then included in the register of the Consistori, permission being thus granted for its public performance. After this, we returned in procession to the palace, the prize-winner walking between the mantenedors, while a page, accompanied by minstrels and trumpeters, carried the prize before him. Sweets and wine were then served in the palace, after which the mantenedors and troubadours, with the minstrels, withdrew and escorted the prize-winner to his house. By this means was made clear the distinction which God and nature has set between the talented and the ordinary members of mankind, and thus ignorance learned to respect the accomplishments of genius."

Poetry produced under these conditions was inevitably artificial in character. Form was of more importance than thought, and ingenuity took the place of inspiration, but the movement was not without its importance. The Provençal-Catalan poetry found favour with Juan II of Castile (1407–1455), whose conjunction of literary aspirations and political incompetence reminds us of Juan I of Aragon. Poetry came to be regarded as a *ciencia*, a business of rules and technicalities which could be mastered with due diligence, and the typical poet was a learned man to whom these rules were familiar and not that rare and favoured person upon whom some divine inspiration had descended. Hence poets looked continually to Provençal models, and found their own admirable vernacular unsuited to the conceits of troubadour style. Even men like Muntaner, while writing their chronicles in good *Catalanesc*, declared that those who wished to write poetry should use Provençal. While Catalan poets

18

thus preferred Southern French language and form, their
outlook upon life was not that of the Provençal troubadour.
Catalan poetry is informed with moral seriousness, and
religion or patriotism are its leading motives. The *Leys
d'Amors*, the treatise upon grammar and poetical form drawn
up by Guilhem Molinier for the Consistori of Toulouse
(of which two versions are extant), was well-known to the
Barcelona Consistori. Molinier's résumé in verse of this
treatise, *Las Flors del Gay Saber*, has been preserved in
a Catalan manuscript, and a Catalan version of the prose
treatise is also in existence. With the *Leys d'Amors* are
connected the treatises produced by the first founders of the
Barcelona Consistori. Jacme March brought out a *Diccionari*,
a work which the Toulouse Academy never undertook, and
Luis Aversó compiled a so-called *Torcimany*, a work which
included a dictionary and an *Ars poetica*. The doctrines of
the Barcelona school spread into Spain, and the Marquis
of Santillana was informed of them by his tutor, Enrique
de Villena.

The fifteenth century may be regarded as the golden age
of Catalan literature and, in particular, of its lyric poetry.
Of the numerous poets who then flourished two obtained a
reputation which gave them a definite place in the history
of European literature. Ausias March was the most distinguished representative of a family of poets ; he was the
nephew of the Jacme above mentioned, his father, Père
March, was the author of a didactic work, the *Arnes del
Cavaller*, and his cousin, Arnau, was held in esteem for his
Cançò d'Amor. Ausias was a Valencian, born in 1393 at
Gandía ; he took part in the Sardinian expedition of 1420,
in company with two other poets of renown, Jordi de Sant
Jordi and Andreu Febrer. Like most literary men of his
time, he was well known to Carlos of Viana. After his
service in Sardinia, he lived upon his Valencian estate,
taking some part in local affairs, and died in 1459. He was
a typical product of the humanism of his age, learned in the
classics and in scholastic philosophy, and well acquainted
with the troubadours, whose influence upon his work is
obvious, though he was an eminently original writer and
thinker. Ausias is not easy reading ; he was a psychologist
and a philosopher and the difficulty of his poems is due

rather to subtlety of thought than to preciosity of expression. The greater part of his work consists of love poetry, but his religious and moral verse is not inferior to the rest of his compositions. His poems were translated into Spanish and Latin, and the Marquis of Santillana in his letter to the Constable of Portugal speaks of him as " *grand trobador e hombre de assaz elevado espíritu.*" In the same paragraph of his letter the Marquis refers to Mossen Jordi de Sant Jordi, " *cavallero prudente,*" in whose work Italian influence is more clearly marked. He also was a Valencian and held a Court post under Alfonso V in 1416. Eighteen of his poems have come down to us, a small number in comparison with the one hundred and twenty of Ausias March. He is remembered for his *Cançò d'Opposits,*

> Tots jorns aprench e desaprench ensemps,
> E visch e muyr, e fau d'enuig plaser,
> Axi mateix fau de l'avol bon temps,
> E veig sens ulls, e say menys de saber.
> E no strench res e tot lo mon abraç ;
> Vol sobre.l cel e sol no.m moch de terra . . .

which is an adaptation of Petrarch's sonnet XC, though for some time various critics insisted that Petrarch was the imitator. The third of the trio who went to Sardinia, Andreu Febrer, the chief *alguacil* of Alfonso V, translated Dante's *Divina Commedia* into Catalan in 1428. The translation is literal, but Catalan cannot reproduce the terza-rima, as Boscán realized at a later date, and as even the first three tercets will show.

> En lo mig del cami de nostra vida
> me retrobé per una selva escura,
> que la dreta via era fallida.
> Ay ! quant a dir qual era, es cosa dura,
> esta selva selvatge, aspera e fort,
> quel pensament nova por me procura.
> Tant amargant que poch es plus la mort !
> Mes per tractar del be qu'eu hi trobé
> diré l'als que hi descobrí si.n record.

Among the Valencian poets mention should also be made of Jaume Roig, whose fame is based upon his *Spill o Libre de les dones*, a work of 12,000 verses, which contains the elements of a picaresque novel and satirizes not only women, but other aspects of life as he knew it. Critics have compared him with Petronius and Boccaccio. His laconic mode of expression is full of vigour and energy, and his work is valuable for the side-light which it throws upon the civilization of his age.

Foreign influence from other quarters was also strong. Fra Rocaberti's allegory, the *Comedia de la Gloria d'Amor*, which was finished shortly after 1461, certainly refers to Dante and to the classical troubadours, but is also inspired by the allegorical methods of the Roman de la Rose. Alain Chartier's *La Dame sans Merci* found a competent translator in Francesch Oliver, and at the close of the century Miguel Carbonell's *Dança de la Mort* reproduces the character of the Danse Macabre, even if it was not directly derived from a French original. In prose, Martorell's famous romance, *Tirant lo Blanch*, owes much to the English *Guy of Warwick*, if it also borrows from Bernard Metge and Muntaner; *Curial y Guelfa*, the other romance of the period which is much inferior to *Tirant*, is a product of Italian influence.

Catalan literature during this period produced no dramatic writing worthy of mention and the theatre remained in a wholly rudimentary state. In other respects, as has been seen, intellectual energy and interest was abundant and fertile in results, and foreign influences notwithstanding, the literature of the country has an originality of its own, apparent in capacity for thought, directness and clarity of statement and a profound and genuine sense of patriotism. After 1500 a period of decadence began, due, in the first instance, to the steady inroads of Castilian; in 1474 was held the famous poetical contest in Valencia, when forty people sent in songs in honour of the Virgin; these were published under the title, *Obres e trobes, les quals tracten de lahors de la sacratissima Verge Maria*, and formed the book generally supposed to have been the first book printed in Spain. It is significant that four of these poems were composed in Castilian. It was inevitable that the political union of Spain, and the discovery of America which diverted commerce from the Mediterranean to the Atlantic and transferred the glories of Barcelona to Seville, apart from such measures as the decree of 1714 and 1716 which displaced Catalan as the official language, should have made Castilian paramount in Eastern Spain. Such

collections as the *Cancionero, llamado Flor de Enamorados*
(por Juan de Linares, Barcelona, 1608), print Castilian and
Catalan romances on successive pages in a fashion which
suggests bilingualism ; but by the end of the eighteenth
century Catalan was in the same condition as Provençal, a
spoken patois with a great history behind it, awaiting the
renaissance of 1833.

EPILOGUE

" **C**ATALŨNA se constituye en región autónoma dentro Estado español. Su organismo representativo es la Generalidad, y su territorio es el que forman las provincias de Barcelona, Gerona, Lérida y Tarragona en el momento de aprobarse este Estatuto." Such is the first article of the much-debated Catalan statute of 1932. Valencia has declined to join in the movement for autonomy, and Catalonia thus reverts to the territorial position which she enjoyed, so far as the Spanish peninsula is concerned, at the time when James the Conqueror became king. The champions of autonomy have not failed to appeal to the evidence of history, and the preceding chapters of this book have shown that there is material for a plausible case. Catalonia and Aragon were never really united. The one bond of union was the royal house of Barcelona. The two provinces preserved separate administrations ; they spoke different languages ; they cherished different laws and privileges, and the outlook upon social and political life of an Aragonese noble and a leading merchant of Barcelona cannot have had much in common. The association of the two provinces was at no time more than federal, and it is not surprising that in the troubled times which followed the Compromise of Caspe in 1412, Catalonia should more than once have desired to return to the status of 1131. The preservation of union for so long a time was due in part to the stress of political and commercial forces and ideals ; much of the credit for its maintenance must also be given to the energy and competence of such kings as James I and his great successors.

The conquest of Constantinople by the Turks and the discovery of America were blows to Catalan commerce, the effects of which were felt with increasing severity. The Catholic kings curtailed such local privileges as they could, Madrid became the final centre of power under Philip II, and the process of centralization and unification which was apparent elsewhere in Europe induced Olivares to make the clumsy attempts in that direction which lost Portugal to Spain and drove Catalonia into revolt in 1640. Her support of Austria in the War of the Spanish Succession ended in the catastrophic defeat of 1714, when Barcelona was devastated by Berwick's troops and the remaining privileges of the province were finally abolished. In the very last Cortes held in Barcelona in 1702, the Catalans secured the right to trade with America and obtain some share in the stream of commerce which had shifted to the Atlantic from the Mediterranean, as the American settlements developed ; much of their Mediterranean trade had passed into other hands. The Catalan language had been forgotten or was despised by the upper classes and was current only in the country districts, after the decrees of Philip V in 1714 and 1716—the so-called Nueva Planta—had made Castilian the official language of the country for all legal, administrative and educational purposes. France had applied similar measures in Roussillon in 1700.

The renaissance of Catalan literature is regarded as beginning exactly a century ago with the publication of Bonaventura Carles Aribau's *Oda a la Pàtria* in which, among other calls to patriotic feeling, he dwells upon the associations of his own language :

> En llemosí sonà lo meu primer vagit
> Quan del mugró matern la dolça llet bevia.
> En llemosí al Senyor pregava cada dia,
> I càntics llemosins somiava cada nit.

Aribau wrote for his own solace or amusement, and would have been surprised to know that his work was to become a literary landmark. He was followed by Rubió i Ors in 1839 with his collection of poems, *Lo Gaiter del Llobregat*. There were writers of reputation at this time, such as Cabanyes, Piferrer, Balmes and others who might be regarded as a school, but their native Catalan was not yet a language of culture, and they were forced to write in Castilian. This state of affairs speedily changed ; the Romantic movement in Spain as well as the Renaixensa in Catalonia inspired an interest in the past and political considerations turned men's eyes to the future. Years of misgovernment by a race which had deprived Catalonia

of her liberties and had given her nothing in return aroused
the old spirit of independence and the linguistic and literary
revival went hand in hand with political aspirations. A free
Catalonia was the general ideal, but proposals for the attain-
ment of it were as varied as they were many. Some form of
federalism was the most popular proposal of the regionalist
movement and was preached by Pi y Margall in 1873 ; the
several regions of Spain were to be autonomous, but to be
members of a central government which would deal only
with matters of common interest. Vicente Almirall continued
to urge this solution and founded the society known as *Jove
Catalunya* in 1887 ; a number of similar societies were formed
in the next few years, most of which combined in 1892 to
form the *Unió Catalanista*. The literary movement was in
close alliance with the political ; celebrations of the *Jochs
Florals*, which were restored in 1857, became the occasion
for the expression of regionalist sentiments ; students'
associations supported the doctrine and periodicals, such as
the *Revista Catalana* or the *Renaixensa*, worked steadily
for the cause. Regionalism or separatism was not peculiar
to Catalonia ; similar movements were in progress in the
Basque provinces and in Galicia and may be regarded as a
reaction against the unifying and centralizing legislation
passed during the early part of the nineteenth century.
This legislation did not supersede many legal customs and
modes of procedure peculiar to individual districts, and desire
to preserve these variations led to demands for " juridical
autonomy," which were nowhere so pronounced nor outspoken
as in Catalonia. From 1887 autonomy and liberation were
the continual themes of every Catalan orator and publicist ;
Prat de la Riba was one of the most vehement supporters
of the movement, to which a further stimulus was given
by the scandals of the American War in 1898. Some Catalan
appointments to local government posts were made in order
to satisfy the discontented ; but the central government
alternated between repressive and conciliatory measures, and
in 1905 an uproar in Barcelona led to the passing of the law
of Jurisdiction, which practically ended all freedom of speech
or of journalism ; to criticize the government or the army
was to be guilty of high treason. The conflicting views of
Catalan regionalists were solidified under this pressure and

in 1906 all parties were united as a *Solaridad* which won 41 out of 44 seats in the parliamentary elections of the following year. In 1909, serious riots broke out in Barcelona as a protest against Maura's proposed campaign in Morocco, and the execution of Francisco Ferrer, who was accused as a ringleader of the movement, stirred public opinion far beyond the frontiers of Catalonia. In 1911 a bill was presented to Congress outlining a constitution for an autonomous Catalonia ; the bill was thrown out, but in 1913 an Order in Council allowed the formation of *mancomunidades* or local councils, which were merged in the Mancomunidad Catalana of 1914, by which time the general question of regional autonomy had become a permanent element in Spanish politics.

Meanwhile the question had been complicated for a considerable time by other local problems. Barcelona had become an industrial as well as a commercial centre and the associations and movements incidental to industrialism or parasitic upon it were operating energetically in Catalonia. At least six groups can be enumerated in a colour scheme ranging from pale pink to congested purple ; the U.G.T. or *Unión General de Trabajadores* is the official Socialist workmen's union, has the support of the Socialist party in Parliament and professes entire opposition to the extravagances of groups modelled upon Russian principles ; the C.N.T. or *Confederación Nacional de Trabajadores*, also known as the *Sindicato Único*, is similar and apparently affiliated to the syndicalist groups in France and other countries ; the *Sindicato Libre* was started in opposition to the *Sindicato Único* with the countenance of the governments before the Dictatorship period, and appears to be out of favour with the Republican Government ; the F.A.I. or *Federación Anarquista Ibérica* has a sufficiently descriptive title, and the *Partido Comunista Español* with the *Bloque Obrero y Campesino* are both openly connected with Moscow and demand the full Russian programme. The disturbances and the propaganda created by these organizations have confused issues and distracted attention both in Spain and abroad from the problem of regionalism : foreign opinion is more impressed by the Bolshevist and Communist gunmen of Barcelona than by the reasoned arguments of Catalan Home Rulers.

Moderate men in Catalonia, as in other countries, ask for a stable and competent government which will enable them to live and conduct their affairs undisturbed by interference from cranks and visionaries who wish to reform society in a hurry, or from incompetent office-seekers who regard politics as a means of livelihood. The average autonomist is convinced that Catalans can govern their own country better than a centralized government can do, for the reason that they understand local conditions which have little in common with those of other provinces, and because they have more than adequate evidence of the incompetence and corruption of centralized governments and of the exiguous benefits received from them in comparison with the taxes paid to them. The Catalan is a type as different from the Castilian or the Andalusian as is the Basque. The fact that Catalonia in the Great War supported the allies, while the rest of Spain was either pro-German or neutral, is evidence of a difference in mental outlook almost racial.

Thus the agitation for autonomy has been the outcome of racial sentiment as well as of discontent with the general misconduct of affairs. The central government had made little or no effort to deal with the social problem in Catalonia or elsewhere. Spanish industry had developed considerably during the Great War, but the condition of the workers did not reflect the prosperity of the manufacturers and no attempt was made to deal with agricultural problems of Central and Southern Spain. The old governmental parties were divided by faction and the newer republican and Socialist organisations were too busy quarrelling among themselves to form a coherent opposition or to gain public respect and prestige. To these standing causes of discontent was added the disaster in Morocco in 1921 and the incompetency of successive ministries to deal with the situation. Barcelona was the chief centre of ferment and it was there that Primo de Rivera, then military governor of the province, planned the *coup d'état* of September 13, 1923, which was accepted by the country on the theory that a military directorate might do better and could hardly do worse than the governments which had immediately preceded it. The reforms introduced by the Directorate included a decree repressing Catalanism, aimed rather at the turbulent elements in Barcelona than at the aspirations of Catalan patriots as such, but none the less offensive to Catalan sentiment, which naturally supported the republican revolution ; nor would this revolution have been successful without the help of the large following contributed by Catalonia.

The Catalan statute was debated in the Spanish Cortes during the summer months of 1932. During that period a vigorous campaign against the statute was prosecuted in every part of Spain. Newspapers, clubs, societies and delegations loudly asserted that Catalonia is not a racial entity, that its inhabitants did not want the statute, that regional autonomy is a mistaken principle and will be the ruin of the country and that any form of separatism will be the ruin of Catalonia. The principle was, however, recognized in the Constitution of 1931 and the statute became an accepted fact. As has been said, Valencia stood out of the proposal, and the territory concerned is composed of the provinces of Barcelona, Gerona, Lérida and Tarragona. Catalan and Castilian are both recognized as the official languages of the country and public documents and notices are to be published in both languages ; the general principle is that while Catalan is to be the official language in Catalonia, in relations with the central republican government the official language shall be Castilian. The rights of individuals are settled by the republican constitution and no difference is to be made between Catalans and other Spaniards ; Catalan citizenship is acquired by birth or by residence. The central government reserves a right of supervision, to see that the laws are carried out and that equality of treatment is given to all. The question of education gave rise to hot debates ; the Catalan Government is authorized to create and maintain such centres of instruction as it may think fit, subject to the relevant article of the republican constitution ; whether Castilian and Catalan culture are to march hand in hand, whether the University of Barcelona is to be bilingual or whether separate universities should be formed, is a question as yet unsettled. Catalonia receives administrative and judicial powers to be exercised in accordance with the republican constitution ; she is to pay an annual contribution to the central government, the amount of which may be reconsidered from time to time, while other sources of revenue are reserved to her for purposes of local administration.

The country thus has full local autonomy, with its own government and executive body, elected by its own people and responsible to them, its own courts of law and full liberty to use its own language. The ties connecting it with the Spanish Republic are of a federal nature ; there has been no " clean cut " nor " break away," and it is improbable that the moderate party of autonomists desire anything of the kind. It is doubtful if Catalonia could afford to lose its trade with Spain. The country is now confronted with the general task of beginning life again under a new régime and the no less important and difficult problem of dealing with the various Socialist and Communist influences which desire to control the kind of life to be led. Nothing is to be learnt by drawing misleading analogies from the position of Ireland, Belgium or other small countries, a line pursued by more than one speaker in the Cortes during the debates upon the statute. Catalonia's problems are her own, and only her own experience will solve them. The outstanding feature of Catalan political movements is the manner in which they have been accompanied and, indeed, created by literary developments. Catalan nationalism owes everything to the Catalan language and literature.

CHRONOLOGICAL TABLE

THE chronology and order of counts and kings earlier than 950 is extremely uncertain. For Barcelona, see the *Gesta Comitum Barcinonensium* (Redacció Primitiva), ed. L. Barrau Dihigo i J. Massó Torrents (Barcelona, 1925). The *Historia de los Victoriosíssimos antiguos Condes de Barcelona*, by Francisco Diago (Barcelona, 1603), is based upon original documents, but must be used with caution.

Counts of Sobrarbe.	*Counts of Aragon.*	*Frankish Counts of Barcelona.*
Garcí Ximenez, 724–758	Aznar, ?–795	Bera, 801–820
Garci Iñiguez, 758–802	Galindo	Bernardo, 820–832
Fortún Garcés, 802–815	Ximeno Aznar	Berenguer, 832–844
Sancho Garcés, 815–843	Ximeno García	Seniofredo, 844–848
	García Aznar, †843	Aledran, 848–852
	Fortún Ximenez	Alarico (Udalric), 852–857
Garcí Iñiguez———=———Urraca		Wifred I (Humfrido), 857–864
|		Salomon, 864–873
Fortún Garcés II		
Sancho Garcés Abarca		*Independent Counts*
Interregnum.		
Iñigo Arista		Wifred II, El Velloso, 873–898
García Iñiguez, 870–885		Wifred Borrell I, 898–912
Fortún Garcés III, 885–901		Suñer, 912–954
Interregnum.		Borrell II and Miron, 954–992
Sancho Garcés I, Abarca, 905–933		Ramón Borrell, 992–1018
García Sanchez I, Abarca, 933–969		Berenguer Ramón I, 1018–1035
Sancho Garcés II, Abarca, 969–990		Ramón Berenguer I, 1035–1076
García Sanchez II, Abarca, 990–1005		Ramón Berenguer II, 1076–1082
Sancho Garcés III, El Mayor, 1005–1035		Berenguer Ramón II, 1082–1096
Ramiro I, 1035–1065		Ramón Berenguer III, 1096–1131
Sancho IV, 1065–1094		
Pedro I, 1094–1104		Ramón Berenguer IV, 1131–1137
Alfonso I, 1104–1134		
Ramiro II, 1134–1137		
Petronilla		

to 1162

Aragon.	*Leon and Castile.*
Alfonso II, El Casto, 1162	
Pedro II, El Católico, 1196	
Jaimè I, El Conquistador, 1213	Fernando III, El Santo, 1217
Pedro III, El Grande, 1276	Alfonso X, El Sabio, 1252
Alfonso III, El Liberal, 1285	Sancho IV, El Bravo, 1284
Jaimè II, El Justo, 1291	Fernando IV, El Emplazado, 1295
Alfonso IV, El Benigno, 1327	Alfonso XI, El Juez, 1312
Pedro IV, El Ceremonioso, 1336	Pedro I, El Cruel, 1350
Juan I, El Cazador, 1387	Enrique II, El Bastardo, 1369
Martin, El Humano, 1395–1410	Juan I, 1379
Fernando I, El de Antequera, 1412	Enrique III, El Doliente, 1391
Alfonso V, El Magnánimo, 1416	Juan II, 1407
Juan II, 1458	Enrique IV, El Impotente, 1454
Fernando II, El Católico, 1479 =	Isabel, La Católica, 1474

BIBLIOGRAPHY

GENERAL

J. Zurita. *Anales de la Corona de Aragón.* Zaragoza, 1610.

J. Zurita. *Indices Rerum ab Aragoniae Regibus Gestarum.* Zaragoza, 1576.
(The work of a great historian and indispensable to any student of early Spanish history.)

J. Blancas. *Aragonensium Rerum Commentarii.* Zaragoza, 1588.

Blasco de Lanuza. *Historias eclesiásticas y seculares de Aragon.* Zaragoza, 1622.

P. de Abarca. *Los Reyes de Aragón en Anales Históricos.* Madrid, 1682–4.

A. de Bofarull. *Historia General de Cataluña.* Barcelona, 1876–8.

V. de Lafuente. *Estudios críticos sobre la historia y el derecho de Aragón.* Madrid, 1884–6

Schmidt. *Geschichte Aragoniens im Mittelalter.* Leipzig, 1828.

Bofarull y Mascaro. *Condes de Barcelona.* Barcelona, 1836.

V. Balaguer. *Historia de Cataluña y de la Corona de Aragón.* Barcelona, 1861.

Colección de Documentos para el estudio de la historia de Aragón. Ibarra y Rodriguez. Zaragoza, 1904–1920.

R. Altamira y Crevea. *Historia de España.* Barcelona, 1909.

Luis Parral y Cristóbal. *Aragón y sus Fueros.* Madrid, 1907.

F. Valls-Taberner i Ferran Soldevila. *Historia de Catalunya.* Barcelona, 1922–3.
(Contains useful bibliographies.)

E. L. Miron. *The Queens of Aragón.* London, 1913.

A. G. Soler. *La Edad Media en la Corona de Aragón.* Barcelona, 1930.
(Colección Labor ; contains a bibliography.)

R. B. Merriman. *The Rise of the Spanish Empire.* New York and London, 1918.
(Contains excellent annotated bibliography.)

CHAPTER I

J. B. BURY. *A History of the Later Roman Empire.* London, 1889.

J. BOTET Y SISO. *Noticia histórica y arqueológica de la antigua ciudad de Emporium.* Madrid, 1879.

A. K. ZIEGLER. *Church and State in Visigothic Spain.* Washington, 1931.

Historia General de España : *Los Pueblos Germánicos.* Madrid, 1890.

T. HODGKIN. *Visigothic Spain,* English Historical Review, ii, p. 209.

MARTIN DE BRACARA. *De Correctione Rusticorum,* ed. C. P, Caspari. Christiania, 1883 (on pagan beliefs in Christian Spain).

E. DE SAAVEDRA. *Estudio sobre la Invasión de los Árabes en España.* Madrid, 1892.

CHAPTER II

E. LÉVI-PROVENÇAL. *L'Espagne Musulmane au Xème Siècle.* Paris, 1932.

R. DOZY. *Spanish Islam.* London, 1913.

P. BOFARULL. *Los Condes de Barcelona vindicados.* Barcelona, 1836.

(William, Count of Toulouse, was a leading figure in events from the year 790. See Bédier, *Les Légendes Epiques.* Paris, 1914, vol. 1, p. 154 ff.)

CHAPTER III

DOMINGO DE LA RIPA. *Defensa histórica por la antiguedad del Reino de Sobrarbe.* Zaragoza, 1675.

BARTOLOMÉ MARTÍNEZ Y HERRERO. *Sobrarbe y Aragón : estudios históricos sobre la fundación y progreso de estos reinos.* Zaragoza, 1866.

(Provides an account of the legendary history of the provinces.)

P. BOISSONADE. *Du nouveau sur le Chanson de Roland.* Paris, 1923.

R. MENÉNDEZ PIDAL. *Cantar de Mio Cid.* Madrid, 1908.

R. MENÉNDEZ PIDAL. *La España del Cid.* Madrid, 1929.

(Indispensable to any student of the Cid and his times.)

CHAPTER IV

J. RIBERA Y TARRAGÓ. *Orígenes del Justicia Mayor de Aragón.* Zaragoza, 1897.

E. HOEPFFNER. *La Chanson de Sainte Foy.* Strasbourg, 1926.

J. M. L. DEJEANNE. *Le Troubadour Marcabru.* Toulouse, 1909.

On linguistic questions :

J. BORAO. *Diccionario de Voces Aragonesas.* Zaragoza, 1908.
(Has an introduction upon the dialect which is interesting, if not strictly scientific.)

R. MENÉNDEZ PIDAL. *El Idioma Español en sus primeros Tiempos* (Colección de Manuales Hispania). Madrid, 1927. *Orígenes del Español.* Madrid, 1926.

W. MEYER-LÜBKE. *Das Katalanische* (Sammlung Romanischer Elementar- und Handbücher). Heidelberg, 1925.

CHAPTER V

Forum Turolii, vol. ii of the *Colección de Documentos para el estudio de la Historia de Aragon.* Introduction and transcription by F. Azuar y Navarro. Zaragoza, 1905.

The following works give useful summaries of the Albigeois Crusade and provide adequate bibliographical references :

H. C. LEA. *History of the Inquisition*, Book II, chaps. i and ii.
(French edition, Paris, 1901, is preferable to the English edition.)

E. CAMAU. *La Provence à travers les Siècles.* Paris, 1924, pp. 121–239.

CHAPTER VI

Chronicle of James I of Aragon. Translated by Forster, with introduction and notes by P. de Gayangos. London, 1883.

F. DARWIN SWIFT. *The Life and Times of James the First, the Conqueror.* Oxford, 1894.
(An excellent work, which gives full bibliographical information.)

FERRAN SOLDEVILA. *Jaume I.* Barcelona, 1926.
For the Troubadours in Aragon, Milá y Fontanals, *De los Trovadores en España*, Barcelona, 1861, is still an indispensable book. See also R. Menéndez Pidal, *Poesía Juglaresca y Juglares.* Madrid, 1924.

CHAPTER VII

O. CARTELLIERI. *Peter von Aragon und die Sizilianischen Vesper.* Heidelberg, 1904.

BERNAT DESCLOT. *Crónica del Rey en Pere.* English translation by F. L. Critchlow, Princeton, 1928.

CHAPTER VIII

AMADOR DE LOS RÍOS. *Estudios históricos, políticos y literarios sobre los Judíos de España.* Madrid, 1848.

F. BAER. *Studien zur Geschichte der Juden im Königreich Aragonien während des 13 und 14 Jahrhunderten.* Historische Studien, No. 106. Berlin, 1913.

A. DE CAPMANY. *Memorias históricas sobre la Marina, Comercio y Artes de la antigua ciudad de Barcelona.* Madrid, 1779–92. (A mine of information upon Catalan naval and commercial affairs.)

E. DE HINOJOSA. *El Régimen señorial y la cuestión agraria en Cataluña durante la Edad Media.* Madrid, 1905.

CHAPTER IX

G. LA MANTIA. *Documenti su le relazioni del re Alfonso III di Aragona con la Sicilia* (1285–91). Anuari de l'Institut d'Estudis Catalans, ii. 357–363 (year 1908–9).

J. JORDÁN DE URRIES. *La Lucha por Sicilia en los años de 1291 a 1302.* Boletín de la Real Academia de Buenas Letras de Barcelona, vii. 73–86 (year 1913–14). *La política exterior de Alfonso III de Aragón,* ibid., 441–58, 472–85.

L. KLUEPFEL. *Die äussere Politik Alfonso III von Aragonien* 1285–91. Berlin, 1912.

H. E. ROHDE. *Der Kampf um Sicilien,* 1291–1302. Berlin, 1913. For the attack upon the Templars, see H. C. Lea, *History of the Inquisition,* vol. III, p. 238 ff. (French edition, Paris, 1902.)

CHAPTER X

Muntaner's account of the Catalan expedition is edited separately by Lluis Nicolau d'Olwer, *L'Expedició dels Catalans a Orient,* with introduction, notes and glossary. (Els Nostres Clàssics. Barcelona, 1926.) It has also been translated by Lady Goodenough, Hakluyt Society, London, 1920.

Francisco de Moncada. *Expedición de los Catalanes y Aragoneses contra Griegos y Turcos*, which is based on the narratives of Muntaner, Desclot and Zurita, has been several times reprinted. The best edition is that by R. Foulché-Delbosc, New York and Paris, 1919.

F. G. Schlumberger. *Expédition des "Almugavares" ou Routiers catalans en Orient*. Paris, 1925.

C. Banus y Comas. *Expedición de Catalanes y Aragoneses a Oriente*. Madrid, 1929.

A. Rubio y Lluch. *Estudios sobre los historiadores griegos acerca de las expediciones catalanes a Oriente*. Revista de Ciencias históricas, III, 57–70 (year 1881). *Los Catalanes en Grecia*, Madrid, 1927. See also his articles in *La Grecia Catalana* in Anuari de l'Inst. d'Estudis catalans, IV, 3–58, V, 393–485, VI, 127–200.

For the later history of the Catalan duchies in Greece, see *Libro de los Fechos y Conquistas del Principado de la Morea*, ed. A. Morel-Fatio. Geneva, 1885.

W. Miller. *The Latins in the Levant*. London, 1908.

CHAPTER XII

Bernat Dezcoll. *Crónica del Rey de Aragon, D. Pedro IV*. Ed. A. de Bofarull, Barcelona, 1850.

J. B. Siges. *La Muerte de D. Bernardo de Cabrera*. Madrid, 1911.

Interesting correspondence concerning the combined action against the Genoese in 1351–2 is printed in the *Memorial Histórico Español*. Madrid, 1851, vol. II, p. 249 ff.

CHAPTER XVI

The chief source for writers on the early years of Ferdinand and Isabella is the *Decadas* of Alfonso Fernando de Palencia, translated by A. Paz y Mélia as the *Crónica de Enrique IV*, Madrid, 1904–12. See also, *El Cronista Alonso de Palencia; su vida y sus obras*, by A. Paz y Mélia, Madrid, 1904. (Hispanic Society of America.)

CHAPTER XVIII

Einführung in die Geschichte der altcatalanischen Literatur, Otto Denk (München, 1893), is still a useful book, though naturally out of date in some respects. *Història de la Literatura Catalana*, by Josep Comerma Vilanova (Barcelona, 1923), summarises the main points and contains useful bibliographical information.

L. Nicolau d'Oliver. *Resum de Literatura Catalana.* Barcelona, 1928.

Ramon Lull, a Biography, E. Allison Peers (London, 1929), refers the reader to most of the relevant literature upon Lullian questions.

Ramon Llull, *Poesies,* in Els Nostres Clàssics, Barcelona, 1925, is a handy collection. His *Obras Rimadas,* by G. Rosselló, Palma, 1859, is now difficult to obtain.

For the chroniclers, a translation of *Muntaner* by Lady Goodenough is published by the Hakluyt Society. Desclot's chronicle has been translated by F. L. Critchlow (Milford, London, 1928). Dezcoll's chronicle has been edited by Ant. de Bofarull (Barcelona, 1850) ; on the question of the chronicler's relations with Pedro IV, see *Revista Histórica,* Barcelona, IV, p. 39, *La España Regional,* August, 1887, p. 531, and an article by A. Pages in *Romania,* XVIII, p. 237.

L'antiga Escola poètica de Barcelona, J. Massó Torrents, Barcelona, 1922, gives an excellent account of the history of Catalan lyric poetry and a full bibliography of the relevant literature.

H. Finke. *Die Beziehungen der aragonischen Könige zur Literatur, Wissenschaft und Kunst, im XIII Jahrhundert.* (Archiv für Kulturgeschichte, viii, 20–42, year 1910.) A Catalan translation by R. Balaguer in *Estudis Universitaris Catalans,* 1910.

Manuel de Montolius. *Manual d'Història Crítica de la Literatura Catalana Moderna,* Barcelona, 1922 (valuable guide to modern literature).

EPILOGUE

Rovira i Virgili. *Història dels Moviments Nacionalistes.* Barcelona, 1912–14.

Catalunya e la República, Barcelona, 1931 (well documented). The text of the constitution and comments upon it are given in the *Bulletin of Spanish Studies,* July, 1932, and following issues.

E. Prat de la Riba. *Nacionalisme.* Barcelona, 1918.

A. Royo Villanova. *El Problema Catalan.* Barcelona, 1908.

Francisco Curet. *La Mancomunidad de Cataluña.* Barcelona, 1922.

J. B. Trend. *A Picture of Modern Spain.* London, 1921.

APPENDICES

I

CHAPTER III

GENEALOGY OF THE KINGS OF ARAGON

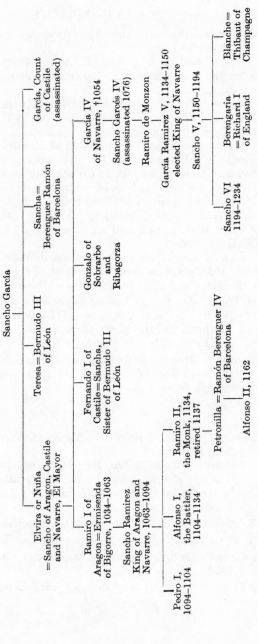

Sancho García

Elvira or Nuña
= Sancho of Aragon, Castile
and Navarre, El Mayor

Teresa = Bermudo III
of León

Sancha =
Berenguer Ramón
of Barcelona

García, Count
of Castile
(assassinated)

Ramiro I of
Aragon = Ermisenda
of Bigorre, 1034–1063

Fernando I of
Castile = Sancha,
Sister of Bermudo III
of León

Gonzalo of
Sobrarbe
and
Ribagorza

García IV
of Navarre, †1054

Sancho Ramirez
King of Aragon and
Navarre, 1063–1094

Sancho Garcés IV
(assassinated 1076)

Ramiro de Monzon

Pedro I,
1094–1104

Alfonso I,
the Battler,
1104–1134

Ramiro II,
the Monk, 1134,
retired 1137

García Ramirez V, 1134–1150
elected King of Navarre

Petronilla = Ramón Berenguer IV
of Barcelona

Sancho V, 1150–1194

Alfonso II, 1162

Sancho VI
1194–1234

Berengaria
= Richard I
of England

Blanche =
Thibaut of
Champagne

GENEALOGY OF THE KINGS OF ARAGON—(continued)

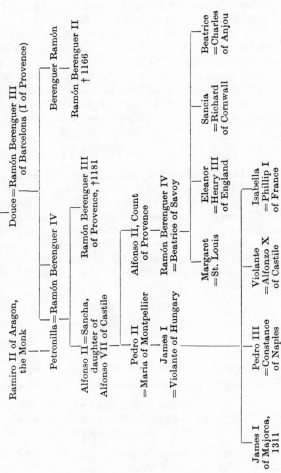

Gerberge, Countess of Provence = Gilbert, Viscount of Millau and Gavaudan

Ramiro II of Aragon, the Monk

Douce = Ramón Berenguer III of Barcelona (I of Provence)

Berenguer Ramón

Ramón Berenguer II † 1166

Petronilla = Ramón Berenguer IV

Ramón Berenguer III of Provence, †1181

Alfonso II = Sancha, daughter of Alfonso VII of Castile

Alfonso II, Count of Provence

Pedro II = Maria of Montpellier

Ramón Berenguer IV = Beatrice of Savoy

James I = Violante of Hungary

Margaret = St. Louis

Eleanor = Henry III of England

Sancia = Richard of Cornwall

Beatrice = Charles of Anjou

Pedro III = Constance of Naples

Violante = Alfonzo X of Castile

Isabella = Phillip I of France

James I of Majorca, 1311

III

CHAPTER IV

The term " Catalan " was used to include Southern France, as appears in a *tenso* between Albert and Monge (Appel Provenzalische Chrestomathie, Leipzig, 1920, No. 92).

" Monges, cauzetz, segon vostra sciensa, qual valon mais : Catalan o Frances ? e met de sai Guascuenia e Proensa e Limozin, Alvernh' e Vianes." The question is whether " Catalans " or French are the better, and the name Catalan is explained as including Gascony, Provence, Limousin, Auvergne and Vienne or Dauphiné. If this was a common use of the term, the passage in Dante is more easily explained ; but I have no other instance.

CHAPTER VI

For heresy and the Iniquisition in Aragon, see H. C. Lea, *History of the Inquisition*, vol. II, p. 162 ff. (French edition, Paris, 1901.)

The first articles in the *Constitutions de Cathaluna* (Barcelona, 1588) show the readiness of James to avoid trouble on the question of heresy ; he forbids " que nunca de alguna persona layca sie licit publicament o privada disputar de la fe catholica," and likewise the possession of the Old or New Testament " en romanç," and anyone who has a copy is ordered to take it " al Bisbe del loc cremadors."

IV

CHAPTER VII

1

An anonymous Provençal *planh* on the death of Manfred in 1266 is given by Bertoni, *Trovatori d'Italia*, Modena, 1915, p. 480.

Lo valen rei Manfred, que capdelaire
Fon de valor, de gaug, de totz los bes,
Non sai cossi mortz aucir lo pogues.

The lengthy passage in Dante, *Purgatorio III*, 102 ff., is well known ; in the *De Vulgari Eloquentia*, I, 12, Dante eulogises Manfred's interest in literature.

2

Pedro III and the " crusade " of 1285.

Pedro III, like other kings of Aragon, was a patron of letters and able himself to turn a stanza, as is shown by an interchange of stanzas or " coblas " between himself and other poets of Aragonese or French sympathies on the eve of the crusade. The first exchange is with a troubadour or joglar of his own court, one Peire Salvage, who is known from other sources to have been trusted by him (see Miret y Sans, *Viatges del Infant en Pere, fill de Jaume I en els anys* 1268 y 1269, Barcelona, 1908). The circulation of such poems was still a valuable means of propaganda and Pedro, no doubt, hoped to rouse some sympathy for himself in the courts North of the Pyrenees. For this reason he began the correspondence with his own court poet, the sense of whose reply was doubtless settled beforehand by the king. Replies were provoked from one Bernat d'Auriac of Béziers, who loudly proclaimed his loyalty to Philip III, and from the Count of Foix who, as we have seen, had joined in revolt against Pedro and had spent two years in imprisonment.

Peace had been made under an agreement by which the Count's daughter, Constance, was to be betrothed to James, Pedro's second son, and his castle of Castelbon was to be held in trust by the king. This agreement was made on May 27, 1284 ; the Count's stanza suggests that he was still in possession of his castle ; his daughter had been taken to Aragon and remained there until 1287 (see Baudon de Mony, *Les relations politiques des comtes de Foix avec la Catalogne jusqu'au commencement du XIVe siècle*, Paris, 1896) ; he was therefore obliged to remain neutral. The whole " correspondence " is too lengthy for quotation here, but a stanza by the King and the count's reply are of particular interest. The incident has been fully explained and the texts edited by A. Jeanroy, Les " coblas " provençales relatives à la " croisade " aragonaise de 1235 in *Homenaje a Menéndez Pidal*, Tomo III, p. 77, Madrid, 1925, from which article these extracts are taken.

Lo Reis d'Arago.

Peire Salvagg, en greu pessar
    Me fan estar
    Dins ma maizo
Las flors que say volon passar,
    Senes gardar
    Dreg ni razo,
Don prec asselhs de Carcasses
    E d'Ajanes
Et als Guascos prec que lor pes
Si flors mi fan mermar de ma tenensa,
Mas tals cuja sai gazanhar perdo
Que.l perdos l'er de gran perdecio.

" Peire Salvatge, in grievous anxiety within my house the flowers cause me to be, which desire to pass to this side of the mountains without considering right nor reason ; therefore I beg those of the Carcassés, of the Agenais and the Gascons that it may be painful to them if (i.e. not to allow) the flowers diminish my possessions ; but such a one thinks to gain pardon here whose pardon will be for him perdition."

Pedro calls for help against the invasion of the fleurs-de-lis, who are coming to gain the papal indulgence (*perdo ;* note the play upon words with *perdicio*) promised to those who join in the crusade against him, and appeals for help to the King of England, who was then ruler of the districts mentioned. In the next stanza he refers to the fact that his nephew, Charles of Valois, the son of Philip III and Isabella, his own sister, had been invested with the crown of Aragon.

Lo Coms de Foix.

Salvatge, e tuit qu' ausem cantar
E'namorar
Rei d'Aragon
Digatz me se poira tant far,
C'a mi no par,
Qu'el e.l leon
Sian ensems en totas res
Contra.l Frances,
Si qu'el sieu afar sia ges ;
E car el dis qu'el plus dreituriers vensa,
De faillir tost a cascun ai raison :
Pero sapchatz qu'eu deteing Castelbon.

" Salvatge and all who can sing, as a lover, of the King of Aragon, tell me if he will be able to do so much, for it seems not so to me, that he and the lion may be united in all things against the French so that there may be some good in his affair (that he may have some chance of success) ; and as he desires that the more righteous may conquer, I am right in standing aloof from either party : but know that I am in possession of Castelbon."

v

CHAPTER VIII

1

A summary of the Fuero of Jaca, granted by Sancho Ramirez in 1064, will give an idea of the matters with which these documents dealt. (*Parral y Cristobal,* vol. I, p. 368. *Martinez y Herrero,* vol. II, p. 448.)

The Fuero begins by abrogating all previous *malos fueros* and constituting Jaca a *cuidad*. Citizens are to enclose their own houses and to live in peace with one another; anyone guilty of wounding another in a quarrel when the King was in residence was to pay a fine of a thousand *solidos* or lose a hand; if a robber were killed, no fine was to be exacted. If citizens were called out for war, they were to be provided with bread for three days and could be summoned only for a regular campaign; householders who could not go, might send a foot soldier as substitute. Rights of property were secured and possession might not be disturbed after a year and a day. Rights of pasturage and forestry were granted over a space within a day's journey from the township. A scale of fines for adultery, assault, falsifying weights and other offences was laid down; he who struck another with his fist or seized him by the hair, was to pay 25 *solidos*; if he threw him to the ground, 250 *solidos*. The *merino* or magistrate was to levy fines with the consent of six principal citizens. Citizens could grind corn where they pleased, but for Jews and bakers, mills were assigned. Citizens were not to give land away nor to sell it to the Church nor to *infanzones*. If a man were imprisoned for debt, the creditor must feed him; if a slave were pledged, his master must provide him with food, " as he is a man and should not starve like a beast."

2

The Almogávar or Almugávar was a light armed soldier, extremely mobile, capable of finding a living anywhere and accustomed to any kind of fatigue and hardship. Desclot's chronicle (chap. CIII) gives an account of one who was captured by the French in the course of the war in Sicily under Pedro III. " It happened one day that a company of Almogávares met a company of French horse and foot; the almogávares were few in number and fled to the mountains, so that the French captured only one who was unable to escape. For a wonder they did not kill him, but took him to the Prince and told him that there was an almogávar whom they had captured. The Prince saw that he was dressed only in a surcoat with no shirt, was thin and burnt black by the sun, with long black hair and beard; he wore a leather cap, leather breeches and sandals. The Prince marvelled much at the sight of him and asked him who he was. He replied that he was one of the almogávares of the King of Aragon. ' Of a truth,' said the Prince, ' I know not what excellence or bravery there can be in such as you; for you seem to me to be poor, wretched and savage folk, if you are all like this.' ' Indeed,' said the almogávar, ' I am one of the meanest of them; none the less, if one of your knights, the best that there is, will come forward, I will readily fight with him, and he shall be in full harness and mounted ; only give me back my lance, my spear and my knife ; and if it should be that I can conquer him, you shall let me go safe and sound ; and if he conquer me, do with me as you will.' ' Truly, a fair wager,' said the Prince. Thereupon, a French knight, young, tall and proud, rose and said that he would fight. ' Certainly,' said the Prince, ' if you will. Go and arm yourself and we will see what this man can do.' Then the Knight went to arm himself and his horse ; and the Prince returned to the almogávar his lance, his spear, his knife and his belt and he was led outside the camp. And all the army went out there and the Prince with his knights. And the Knight rode up in full armour on his horse, and rode upon the almogávar with his lance in rest to smite him ; and the almogávar, when he was close upon him, avoided him and drove his spear into the chest of the horse two handsbreadth between the chest and the shoulder, and therewith leapt aside, so that the Knight missed his blow. The horse fell to the ground forthwith. And at once the almogávar drew his knife, ran to the Knight who was lying on the ground and began to unlace his helmet with intent to cut his throat. But the Prince ran to him and forbade him and said that he had won his wager and should let be. And the almogávar left the Knight and the Prince took him to his tent and gave him one of his garments and told him to go forth safe and sound. And the almogávar rejoicing at his fortune, went off to Messina and came before the King and told how he had been captured and what had happened and how the Prince had set him free. When the King had learned this, he was pleased and sent for two of the French prisoners whom they had taken, clothed them well and sent them to the Prince with a message, that whenever the Prince should send him one of his own men, he would return two of his." Estébanez Calderón wrote a prologue to *La Campana de Huesca*, the novel by Cánovas del Castillo, and there drew a detailed picture of the Almogávares which combines most of the facts known concerning them.

CHAPTER IX

FREDERIC III OF SICILY AND THE COUNT OF AMPURIAS

Fadrique of Sicily appears as one of the last of the troubadours in his poetical correspondence with the Count of Ampurias, Hugo or Uc, who was one of the first Spanish nobles to throw in his lot with Fadrique and who saved his life in the battle of Cabo Orlando in 1299. Of Eble, the messenger of Fadrique, nothing is known ; Pedro, the Count's messenger, has been identified with Pietro Lancia, who became Count of Caltanissetta. The text is given by V. de Bartholomaeis, *Poesie Provenzali Storiche relative all' Italia*, Roma, 1931, II, p. 298 ff. ; he refers to M. Amari, *La guerra del Vespro Siciliano*, II, p. 287 ; III, p. 438, p. 529, and agrees with him that the poems were written in the spring of 1296 ; the general tone of hopefulness and of confidence in the Sicilians is characteristic of Fadrique, and while he complains of his brother's action, he does not mention him by name.

Dompn Frederic de Cicilia.

I. Ges per guerra no.m chal aver consir
Ne non es dreiz de mos amis mi plangna,
Ch'a mon secors vei mos parens venir
E de m'onor chascuns s'esforza e.s langna
Perche.l meu nom major cors pel mon aja ;
E, se neguns par che de mi s'estraja,
No l'en blasmi, ch'enmental faiz apert,
Ch'onor e prez mos lignages non pert.

II. Pero el reson dels Catelans auzir
E d'Aragon puig far part Alamagna,
E so ch' enpres mon paire gent fenir ;
Del Regn' aver crei che per dreiz me tangna ;
E, se per so de mal faire m'asaja
Niguns parens, car li crescha onor gaja,
Be.m porra far dampnage a deschubert,
Ch'en altre vol no dormi ni.m despert.

III. N'Ebble, va dir a chui chausir so plaja
Che dels Latins lor singnoriu m'apaja,
Per q'eu aurai lor e il me per sert ;
Mas mei parenz mi van un pauc cubert.

Responsiva del Con d'Enpuria.

I. A l'onrat rei Frederic Terz vai dir
Q'a noble cors no.s taing poder sofragna,
Peire qomte ; e pusc li ben plevir
Che dels parenz ch'aten de vas Espagna
Secors, ogan non creja ch'a lui vaja,
Mas a l'estiu fasa cont che.ls aja
E dels amics, e tegna li oll ubert
Che.ls acoilla pales e non cubert.

II. Ne no.s cug ges che.l seus parenz desir
Ch'el perda tan che.l Regne no.ill remagna
Ne.l bais d'onor, per Franzeis enrechir ;
Ch'en laiseran lo plan e la montagna ;
Confunda.ls Deus e lor gorgoil dezaja !
Pero lo Rei e Cicilia.n traja
Onrat del faitz, che.l publat e.l desert
Defendon ben ; d'acho sion apert.

III. Del gioven Rei me plaz car non s'esmaja
Per paraulas, sol q'a bona fin traja
So che.l paire chonquis, a lei de sert,
E, si.l reten, tenrem l'en per espert.

DON FEDERICO DE SICILIA

I. I care not to be anxious for the war, nor is it right that I
should complain of my friends, for I see my relatives coming to my
help ; and each one of my vassals striving and toiling that my
name may spread more widely through the world ; and if any one
appears to stand aloof from me, I blame him not for it, for he
makes open amends, since my lineage does not lose honour or
worth.

II. But I can make the reputation of the Catalans and of
Aragon heard as far as Germany, and bring to a fair conclusion
that which my father undertook ; as regards the possession of the
kingdom, I think that it belongs to me of right ; and if any relative
of mine tries to do me wrong on that account, for increase of his
own honour thereby, he will be able to harm me openly, for I
neither sleep nor wake in any other desire.

III. Sir Eble, go and tell him who cares to hear it, that the
lordship of the Latins pleases me, so that I shall have them and
they me assuredly ; but my relatives give me some cause for
misgiving.

REPLY OF THE COUNT OF AMPURIAS

I. Go, Count Pedro, and say to the honourable King
Frederic III that it is not fitting for a noble heart to yield ; and I
can assure him that the help which he expects from his relatives
in Spain will not, I think, come to him this year (i.e. immediately),
but in the summer let him rely upon their help and that of his
friends, and let him keep his eyes open, receiving them openly
and not in secret.

II. It is not to be supposed that his parent desires that he
should lose so much that the kingdom no more abide with him nor
that his honour should be brought low to enrich the French ;

they will abandon both plain and mountain (i.e. the whole country). May God confound them and overthrow their pride ! But may the King and Sicily draw honour from the exploit, for they well defend both town and country ; therein may they be ready.

III.   I am pleased with the young king, for he is not dismayed by words and desires to bring to a good end the conquest of his father, which was lawfully made, and if he keeps it, we shall in consequence regard him as a proven man.

INDEX

A

Abarca, Sancho, 31, *and see* Sancho
Abassids, the, 21
Abd er-Rahman, 21, 22, 23, 24
Abd er-Rahman III, 25
Abdal-Aziz, 44
Abdelaziz, 19
Abdurrahman, Zeid, 83, 85
Abenmerdanix, 58
Abiatir, Crexcas, 240
Abifilel, 54
Abruzzi, the, 134
Abu 'l-Aswad, 22
Abu-l-Hassan, 168, 169
Abu-Thaur, 23
Acciajuoli, Nerio, Lord of Corinth, 197
Acre, 91
Acropolis of Athens, the, 159
Adolfo, Vellido, 39
Adoptionism, 61, 70
Adrianopolis, 148, 149, 150, 151
Affonso, King of Portugal, 243
Africa, 18, 33, 44, 51, 84, 101, 102, 112, 123, 168, 169, 244, 246; relations with Damascus and Spain under the Muslims
Agramont, family of, 231
Agriculture in the Middle Ages, 122
Ahones, Pedro, 82
Aimerich, Viscount of Narbonne, 202 ; submission to Ferdinand I, 207–208
Alagon, Blasco de, 85
Alagon, Count Artal de, 191
Alans, the, 8, 10, 143, 144, 145, 146, 149 ; massacred by the Almogávares, 152–153
Al-Arabi, 22, 23
Alarcos, 68, 75
Albarracín, 105, 164, 167, 186
Albertus Magnus, 93
Albi, centre of the heresy, 71
Albigeois heresy, 62, 70–72, 94 ; War, 87, 112
Al-Cadir, 39, 43, 44, 45, 46, 47, 48
Alcalá, Peace of, 82
Alcalá, University of, 266
Alcañiz, 206
Alcoraz, 48

Alcoy'l, 102
Aledo, 45
Alet, Corberan de, 146
Alexander II, Pope, 36
Alexander V, Pope, 209
Alfonso I of Aragon, 113 ; marriage with Urraca, 52–53 ; wars and death, 54–55
Alfonso II of Aragon, 58, 66, 67, 68, 94
Alfonso III of Aragon, son of Pedro III, 97, 104, 107, 108, 109, 115, 120, 124, 178; quarrels with the nobility, 124–127 ; relations with Edward I of England, 128 ; breach with Castile on the question of succession, 128–129 ; the Sicilian question, 130 ; the Peace of Tarascon, 131–132 ; death and character, 132 ; treatment of the *mudéjares*, 247 ; and the nobles, 248
Alfonso III of Leon, 25
Alfonso IV of Aragon, 140, 166, 170, 204, 266, 270 ; accession, 161 ; Castilian policy, 161–162 ; Moorish invasion, 162 ; war with Sardinia and Genoa, 162–163 ; domestic troubles, 164 ; death and character, 165
Alfonso V of Aragon, 256, 275 ; accession, 212 ; his methods with the Great Schism, 212–213 ; campaigns in Sardinia, 213 ; in Corsica, 213–214 ; in Naples, 216 ; relations with Juana II, 216–217, 221–223 ; relations with Castile, 218–220 ; alliance with Duke of Milan, 222 ; in Italy, 223–225 ; Pope Eugenius IV, 225 ; the kingdoms of Navarre, Aragon and Castile, 226–228, 230–231 ; his operations in Italy as King of Naples, 228–230 ; his devotion to literature, 232–233 ; Pope Martin V, 250
Alfonso V of Leon, 31
Alfonso VI of Leon, 38, 39, 40, 41, 46–52 ; policy, 43–46
Alfonso VII of Castile, 56
Alfonso VIII of Castile, 66, 75
Alfonso X of Castile, 99

T

Tagliacozzo, battle of, 101, 102, 143
Tagus, the, 53
Taillebourg, battle of, 87
Talmud, the, 246
Tarascon, terms of the Peace of, 131–132
Tarazona, 54, 83, 178, 182, 185
Tarazona, Archbishop of, 107, 111, 112
Tarazona, bishop of, 11
Tarentum, Prince of, 222, 223
Tarif, 18
Tarifa, 18 ; siege of, 169
Tarik, 18, 19, 20
Tarraconensis, 6, 8, 11 ; situation at beginning of Muslim conquest, 21
Tarragona, xiii, 2, 5, 8, 11, 24, 49, 67, 84, 104, 127, 131, 196, 278 ; under Roman administration, 6 ; foundation of Spanish Church by Saint Paul, 7 ; surrender of, 237
Tarragona, Archbishop of, 97, 230, 236
Tarragona, bishop of, 11
Tarragona, Council of, 250
Tarragona, University of, 261
Tarrasa, bishop of, 11
Tárrega, 237
Taurus, 16
Taurus, Mount, 159 ; Turks defeated, 146
Templars, the, 55, 66, 82, 114, 121, 122 ; suppressed by James II, 140
Tennebello, Sforza de, 214, 215, 216, 217, 221
Teresa, 53
Terouenne, Cardinal de, 190
Teruel, 54, 67, 85, 126, 177, 179, 185
Tesoro, the, 266
Teter, usurper on Bulgarian throne, 146
Thasos, island of, 156
Thebes, 157, 158
Thekla, 7
Theobald of Champagne, 84, 85
Theodore, son of Andronicus II, 153
Theodored, 10
Thessalonica, 158
Thessaly, 156, 158
Thrace, 143, 146 ; and the Almogávares, 149, 151, 154, 155, 158
Tirant lo Blanch, 149, 276
Tiresias, 199
Toledo, 16, 18, 20, 25, 39, 43, 44, 45, 48, 52, 54, 64, 136
Toledo, Archbishopric of, 43, 49, 238, 240, 251
Toledo, Fourth General Council of, 11
Toledo, King of, 38, 40

21

Torcimany of Luis Aversó, 274
Tordesillas, 218
Torella, Guillem, 271
Torellas, 233
Toro, battle of, 243
Tortosa, xvi, 2, 24, 33, 34, 42, 57, 58, 85, 114, 123, 164, 186, 206, 239, 246, 257, 272
Tortosa, bishop of, 11
Tortosa, University of, 261
Toulouse, 10, 24, 59, 71, 76, 77, 79, 87, 94, 198 ; attacked, 19
Toulouse, Academy of, 274
Toulouse, Counts of, 31, 54, 56, 68, 87, 88
Toulouse, University of, 201
Trajan, 6
Trapani, 103, 197
Tremecen, 168 ; King of, 162
Trencavel of Béziers, 87
Tudela, 25, 34, 105, 184, 241
Tunis, 102, 168, 222 ; King of, 90
Turdetani, the, 3, 4
Turks, the, 197, 225, 229, 278 ; and the Byzantine Empire, 143, 146, 148, 155, 156
Tuscany, 140, 229
Tuy, Lucas de, 53
Tyrranim, battle of, 145–146

U

Uclés, battle of, 52
Union, the, extorted from Alfonso III by the nobles, 120 ; its fight with Alfonso, 126–127 ; its privileges, 127 ; hostility to Pedro IV, 173–176 ; victory over Pedro IV, 177 ; defeat by Pedro IV, 178–179 ; summary of its development, 248–249
Union, the Act of, 141
Urban II, Pope, 49, 53
Urban IV, Pope, and Pedro III, 100
Urban VI, Pope, opposition to Sicilian claim of Pedro IV, 191
Urgel, bishop of, 11, 112
Urgel, count of, 56, 57, 82, 97
Urgel, county of, 29, 41, 57, 82, 86, 98
Urraca, sister of Sancho II, defends Zamora, 39
Urraca, d. Alfonso VI of Castile, m. Alfonso I of Aragon, 52–53, 56
Urrea, Pedro Ximenes de, family quarrels in Aragon, 201, 204, 206
Usatges, formulation of the, 41

V

Val de Junquera, battle of, 31